Frank Zappa, Captain Beefheart and the Secret History of Maximalism

MICHEL DELVILLE is a writer and musician living in Liège, Belgium. He is the author of several books including *J.G. Ballard* and *The American Prose Poem*, which won the 1998 SAMLA Studies Book Award. He teaches English and American literatures, as well as comparative literatures, at the University of Liège, where he directs the Interdisciplinary Center for Applied Poetics. He has been playing and composing music since the mid-eighties. His most recently formed rock-jazz band, the Wrong Object, plays the music of Frank Zappa and a few tunes of their own (http://www.wrongobject.be.tf).

ANDREW NORRIS is a writer and musician resident in Brussels. He has worked with a number of groups as vocalist and guitarist and has a special weakness for the interface between avant garde poetry and the blues. He teaches English and translation studies in Brussels and is currently writing a book on post-epiphanic style in James Joyce.

Frank Zappa,
Captain Beefheart
and the Secret History
of Maximalism

MICHEL DELVILLE

and

ANDREW NORRIS

SALT

CAMBRIDGE

PUBLISHED BY SALT PUBLISHING
PO Box 937, Great Wilbraham PDO, Cambridge CB1 5JX United Kingdom

© Michel Delville and Andrew Norris, 2005

The right of Michel Delville and Andrew Norris to be identified as the
authors of this work has been asserted by them in accordance
with Section 77 of the Copyright, Designs and Patents Act 1988.

First published 2005

Printed and bound in the United Kingdom by Lightning Source

Typeset in Swift 9.5 / 13

ISBN-10 1 84471 099 8 hardback
ISBN-13 978 84471 099 7 hardback

ISBN-10 1 84471 059 9 paperback
ISBN-13 978 1 84471 059 1 paperback

SP

1 3 5 7 9 8 6 4 2

Contents

Acknowledgments

We would like to thank Chris Emery, Louis Armand, Simon Warner, Ed Mann, Gilbert Delville, The Wrong Object, Gérald Purnelle, Jimmy Carl Black, John Havelda, Ben Watson, Marco Maurizi and the CIPA research team at the University of Liège for their contributions, whether direct or indirect, to the writing of this book.

Introduction

Exploring the Maximalist Body

There's no single ideal listener out there who likes my orchestral music, my guitar albums and songs like "Dyna-Moe-Humm." It's all one big note. Ladies and gentlemen . . .

—Frank Zappa

Like Mozart's "Marriage of Figaro," Zappa's music has often been accused of being far too noisy and of containing too many notes. Because of their density and complexity, his sound sculptures have alternately enthused and alienated several generations of critics and listeners. With more than sixty albums (including no less than twenty-one double albums and two triple albums) released over a period of twenty-eight years, and fifteen "official bootlegs", Zappa is one of the most prolific artists of the 20th century, a composer whose sheer output could stand accused of maximalist excess. His attempts to embrace different genres and creative practices (rock, jazz, blues, orchestral music, film, opera, . . .) have been interpreted as a bulimic desire to explore the totality of past and present modes and styles in order to create strongly contrasting musical collages and establish his reputation as an outsider in both the rock and the art music communities. As James Grier writes:

> Zappa clearly relished the conflicting images he projected as rock musician and knowledgeable observer or practitioner of art music. This posture allowed him to remain an outsider in both fields (rock musician who employed the language of art music; practitioner of art music who

played rock) while capitalizing on the cultural hegemony of art music to create an ironic distance between himself and other rock musicians, and assert the superiority of his cultural sophistication and musicianship.

(unpag.)

As we will see, however, Zappa's maximalist poetics, as well as his more general disdain for genre boundaries, goes well beyond the fashionable levelling out of high vs low dichotomies that has become associated with postmodern art. Zappa has repeatedly alluded to the fact that all the diverse aspects of his musical output were to be perceived as part of a single "Project/Object," a formulation meant to describe "the overall concept of [his] work in various mediums":

> Each project (in whatever realm), or interview connected with it, is part of a larger object, for which there is no "technical name."

(*Real* 139)

The art of connecting apparently antithetical styles and items usually seen or experienced in radically different contexts has long been a feature associated with the international avant-garde, and Zappa's aural collages have been compared with the equally democratic and undogmatic aesthetics of Kurt Schwitters's *merzbau*.[1] But Zappa's extension of collage aesthetics to the non-musical and even the non-artistic materials and phenomena that gravitate around his published works and performances (Zappa repeatedly insists on the importance of interviews, audience participation and cover art) reflects above all his commitment to compositional methods that consider musical works as having an existence that exceeds the sum of their parts. Zappa's holistic poetics is also indicative of his desire to experience the whole world as a material extension of a single, prime-moving vibration which he calls the "BIG NOTE" ("Everything in the universe is, is, is made of one element, which is a note, a single note. Atoms are really vibrations, you know. Which are extensions of the BIG NOTE, everything's one note").[2] The suggestion that the universe began with one primal sound can be related to the theories of the astronomers and Nobel-Prize winners Arno Penzias and Robert Wilson who, in 1965, accidentally discovered the existence of Cosmic Background Radiation, a residual vibration from the Big Bang which comes to us from all directions with the same intensity and a tone a little flatter than B, as defined by standard tuning. Once translated into aesthetic terms, Penzias's and Wilson's primordial hiss from the beginning of time can be seen as the cosmological justification of various forms of (intentional and nonintentional) "conceptual continuities" that incorporate Zappa's works into a constantly evolving "event-structure", poised between careful calculation and chance operations:

> The *project/object* contains *plans* and *non-plans*, also precisely calculated *event-structures* designed to accommodate the mechanics of fate and all the bonus statistical improbabilities attendant hereto . . . [It] incorporates any available visual medium, consciousness of all participants (including audience), all perceptual deficiencies, God (as energy), THE BIG NOTE (as universal basic building material), and other things.
>
> (quoted in WALLEY 122)

Zappa's conception of his work as an organic-event-structure-in-expansion is indicative of his decision to let the material itself suggest ways of connecting apparently unrelated musical objects and live idiosyncracies which are liable to be fitted together and synchronized into further studio constructions. Whole tracks from *Sheik Yerbouti, Joe's Garage* and *Shut Up 'N Play Yer Guitar* were developed around live guitar solos extracted from other pieces. This process of gradual musical and conceptual recycling, which Zappa termed "xenochrony" (or "strange synchronization"), evokes the aesthetics of James Joyce, another maximalist artist, whose "epiphanies" were recycled into his longer and more ambitious works of fiction, of which more will be said later. As for Zappa's "Big Note" itself, it amounts to what David Walley calls "a painting of time in time, the purposeful working with coincidence," a structure over which the composer sometimes has only limited control, as Zappa explains:

> I can say that I control the structure of it perhaps acting as an agent for some other contractor . . . I'm a sub-contractor, from time to time I'm a master of ceremonies in the larger sense, if I bring to the attention of a certain audience an event or situation which is not of my own manufacture.
>
> (Walley 147)

Of "Rubber Shirt," a piece entirely composed of a bass track and a drum sequence performed independently from one another, Zappa writes:

> The drummer was instructed to play along with this one particular thing in a certain time signature, eleven-four, and that drum set part was extracted . . . The bass part which was designed to play along with another song at another speed, another rate in another time signature,

four-four, that was removed from the master tape. . . . Then the two were sandwiched together. . . . The musical result is of two musicians who were never in the same room at the same time, playing at two different rates in two different modes for two different purposes, when blended together, yielding a third result which is musical and synchronizes in a strange way. That's xenochrony, and I've done that on a number of tracks.

(Marshall, unpag.)

In the years that followed the release of "Rubber Shirt," the possibilities afforded by multitrack recording and remastering enabled Zappa to manipulate time and disrupt the linear sequentiality of his own career by mixing materials from many different periods into composites that do justice to the multidimensional dynamics of the "Project/Object". From the mid-1980s onwards, the Synclavier provided Zappa with even more ways of exploring the wonders of electronically-transmitted signals turned into musical notes. The complicated, kaleidoscopic geometries of *Jazz from Hell* (1986)—an album consisting almost exclusively of tracks electronically composed and recorded on the Synclavier—were eventually performed live by the Ensemble Modern in 1991. Ironically enough, the gestural interpretation of the German musicians, who turned out to be Zappa's last band, restored the Benjaminian "aura" of the original compositions whose digitally produced sounds had until then been completely divorced from the primal gesture of the composer or musician. Zappa's well-documented delight in conducting and composing for the Ensemble would seem to confirm the fact that his interest in electronic music had been first and foremost prompted by practical rather than aesthetic reasons. (The problem of having to deal with the ego problems of real musicians and the costs of having his scores performed by classical orchestras such as the London Symphony Orchestra in the late 1970s had proved too discouraging for him to proceed with his orchestral projects).[3]

Air Sculptures and Other Musical Objects

As suggested by the "Big Note" theory discussed above, Zappa regarded music as a material construction, a kind of synaesthetic "air sculpture" (or "molecule-sculpture-over-time" [Walley 188]) that is "'looked at' by the ears of the listeners—or a microphone" and creates "perturbations [that] modify (or sculpt) the raw material (the 'static air' in the room—the way it was 'at rest' before the musicians started fucking around with it)" (*Real* 161). In his interview with Bob Marshall, Zappa makes another interesting remark connecting his musical theories to the realm of modern physics. Here, Zappa's awareness of the physicality of sound (see also our discussion of Zappa and Satie's "musique d'ameublement" in Chapter One)—an awareness gained from Edgar Varèse and other composers interested in timbre and noise rather than traditional notions of harmony and rhythm—leads him to posit the existence of musical *matter*, namely the transformation of sound waves into solid objects:

> If you buy the idea that the vibrational rates translate into matter, and then if you understand the concept of vibrational rates above perception and below perception combining to create a reality, that opens up the door to some pretty science fiction possibilities. If you can create an audible reality by a sine wave above the range of what your ear can hear and another one from below, and you put them together and suddenly it creates something that your ear can detect, is it not possible that solid matter of an unknown origin could manifest periodically because of the frequencies of some unknown nature above and below which, for short duration, manifest solid objects? It could explain a lot of strange things that people see.
>
> (Marshall; unpag.)

In the mid-1980s, Zappa discovered that the Synclavier's G page (which contains the machine's inaudible inner codes and numbers) could be used to generate "G numbers" that never surface at the level of the "user-friendly" part of the machine. "The Girl in the Magnesium Dress," from the *Jazz from Hell* album, was based on the rhythms indicated by the "dust particles" resulting from guitar notes recorded by the Synclavier and which Zappa subsequently converted into pitched sounds:

> So we found a way to convert bunches of G numbers into note blanks. And G numbers occupy points in time. They indicate that something happened on the guitar string at a certain point in time. It takes a little piece of eternity and slices it up, and if your finger moved, there's a G number that says what your finger did besides just playing the note. So we converted this dust into something that I could then edit for pitch, and the dust indicated a rhythm. So what I did was take the rhythm of the dust and impose pitch data on the dust and thereby move the inaudible G number into the world of audibility with a pitch name on it. That's how "The Girl in the Magnesium Dress" was built.
>
> (Menn 60)

As we will see, Zappa's commitment to the materiality of sound and the physicality of performance is inextricably linked with an aesthetic geared towards the creation, appropriation and (mis-)consumption of everyday objects, a tendency most apparent in the radical fetishism of such songs as "Montana", "Evelyn, A Modified Dog" and "Sofa." The most everyday object of them all is the human body, and in what follows we will explore how maximalist art projects and exploits a pluralisation of the body's material means. In Chapter Two we will argue that so-called degenerate art reflects and enacts a re-materialisation of the body which detonates conservative mythologies of perfection, leaving the body radically potentialised, subject to a new maximalisation of forms. This hybrid condition has affinities with theories of abjection, and in Chapter Three we pursue these connections in the context of the gothic, which has traditionally exploited the in-betweenness of the body as a source of trauma; where the relation of the subject to the object is fraught with the anxiety of becoming other. In Chapter Four the liminal maximalist body is associated with an eroticisation of the edge between self and world, and a notion of style emerges as an expression of the body beyond objects.

Like the human body, criticism is pervious to its objects, and just as maximalist art develops out of and contributes to a sense of the body as a point at which subject and object interpenetrate and reconfigure each other, so any bid to write about maximalism can only accept a similar suspension of its traditional limits and certitudes. The degenerate critical method we develop in the course of our readings culminates in Chapter Five in a discussion of the problem of maximalist pleasure. The cross-contamination of subject and object reveals itself at this point as an unavoidable condition of our writing as well as one of its guiding thematics. The maximalist body-in-progress, like any attempt to define it, is located at a point of double contingency, where it is impossible to decide whether pleasure is a concomitant of meaning or vice versa; and where it is all but impossible to decide what criticism is for.

Maximalism vs Minimalism?

There are the minimalist pleasures of Emily Dickinson—"Zero at the Bone"—and the maximalist ones of Walt Whitman.

—John Barth

Was the maximalist potential of the Big Note for Zappa a way of defying generic categories in order to avoid being pigeonholed as either a classical or a rock musician? Of defeating the expectations of both rock and classical listeners by breaking down the barriers separating low and high art forms? Of creating a multidimensional art project that is no longer subject to such distinctions? Of filling the empty space of the Mojave desert of his youth with "imaginary guitar notes that would irritate an executive kind of a guy"?[4] Of composing an œuvre which seems *as big as* his century? Of doing justice to a world in which "time is a constant, a spherical constant" and "EVERYTHING IS HAPPENING *ALL THE TIME*" (*Them* 62)? Or of cheating closure and death through a creative application of Stephen Hawking's "no-boundary proposal", the notion that the universe has neither singular beginning nor ultimate end (Zappa dedicated *The Real Frank Zappa Book* to the author of *A Brief History of Time*)?

Certainly one of the difficulties in dealing with Zappa's (or anybody elses's) maximalist art arises from the lack of serious attention to the development of maximalist aesthetics itself. That the history of maximalism in the arts is the *parent pauvre* of contemporary criticism is already indicated by the fact that the term is systematically absent from all lexicons of literary terms and, indeed, most discussions of contemporary music except when it refers to Milton Babbitt's "maximal" extension of Schoenberg's ideas of serial composition or, more rarely and even more loosely, to the "New Complexity" school of Brian Ferneyhough and Michael Finnissy. One of the rare exceptions to the rule comes from the American novelist John Barth, who in an article first published in the *New York Times Book Review* in 1986, offers the following definition of literary maximalism:

> The medieval Roman Catholic Church recognized two opposite roads to grace: the via negativa of the monk's cell and the hermit's cave, and the *via affirmativa* of immersion in human affairs, of being in the world whether or not one is of it. Critics have aptly borrowed those terms to characterize the difference between Mr. Beckett, for example, and his erstwhile master James Joyce, himself a maximalist except in his early works. Other than bone—deep disposition, which is no doubt the great determinant, what inclines a writer—sometimes almost a cultural generation of writers—to the Negational Path?
>
> (1)

For Barth, the distance that separates Joyce from Beckett (or Whitman from Dickinson, or Faulkner from Hemingway), cannot be reduced to an aesthetic option (the desire to embrace richness and completeness, on the one hand, or aim for precision and brevity, on the other), but is immediately translated into social terms. Barth opposes maximalist fiction to the so-called "New American Short Story" of the early 1980s, a tendency represented by Ann Beattie, Raymond Carver, Bobbie Ann Mason and others who are "both praised and damned under such labels as 'K-Mart realism,' 'hick chic,' 'Diet-Pepsi minimalism' and 'post-Vietnam, post-literary, postmodernist blue-collar neo-early-Hemingwayism'". The collusion of style and politics in minimalist fiction echoes a number of similar accusations made against postmodern art in general, whose success story has been linked with the expansion of capitalist hegemony. For Fredric Jameson, for example, this tendency reaches a climax in Andy Warhol's work which, far from parodying commercial culture in a "modernist" (e.g. Joycean) fashion, incorporates it into its very substance, thereby abolishing the critical distance that separates artists from their socio-economic environment.[5] The total interpenetration of aesthetic and commodity production is indeed the logical result of the gradual process of "immersion in human affairs" brought about by Barth's *via affirmativa*. Another critic of postmodernism, Takayoshi Ishiwari, believes that the "style which is broadly called maximalism" is characterized not only by a tendency to embrace the time's modes and conventions but also by a typically pomo attitude to the notion of the "authentic":

> Under this label come such writers as, among others, Thomas Pynchon and Barth himself, whose bulky books are in marked contrast with Barthelme's relatively thin novels and collections of short stories. These maximalists are called by such an epithet because they, situated in the age of epistemological uncertainty and therefore knowing that they can never know what is authentic and inauthentic, attempt to include in their fiction everything belonging to that age, to take these authentic and inauthentic things as they are with all their uncertainty and inauthenticity included; their work intends to contain the maximum of the age, in other words, to be the age itself, and because of this their novels are often encyclopedic. As Tom LeClair argues in *The Art of Excess*, the authors of these "masterworks" even "gather, represent, and reform the time's excesses into fictions that exceed the time's literary conventions and thereby master the time, the methods of fiction, and the reader."

(1)

Zappa's ambition "to be the age itself" clearly manifests itself in his penchant for works that seek to incorporate—albeit in a frequently ironical fashion—nearly all existing musical genres and modes, from blues-rock and doo-wop to *musique concrète*, free jazz and symphonic orchestral works. And Tom LeClair's definition of maximalism as an art that exceeds its own historical context and represents more than the sum of all past and present compositional styles would seem perfectly suited to the development of Zappa's aesthetics. But we will see that the impact of maximalism on contemporary art cannot be reduced to the decision of what to include or exclude in a literary text or musical score or even to the rather dubious notion that such a decision should be dictated by a Baudrillardian sense of "epistemological uncertainty." Zappa's disdain for accepted distinctions between the "authentic" and the "inauthentic," high and low art, as well as other aesthetic and generic hierarchies, is in fact only one aspect of his commitment to the *via affirmativa* of contemporary music, one which allies him with other musical eccentrics such as Charles Ives—who was among the first to integrate elements of "low" music (gospel hymns, jazz, fanfare) into classical/orchestral music—and Zappa's self-confessed master Edgar Varèse, with whom he shares not only an interest in bruitism, tape music and percussion-based orchestral pieces but also a penchant for gigantic compositional structures that exceed traditional performance formats (Varèse used 400 speakers to perform his "Poème électronique" at the 1958 Brussels World's Fair).

Does the Body Belong in Music?

According to David Jaffe, one of the very few composers to address the development of a "maximalist" *musical* style, the maximalist approach in contemporary music "embraces heterogeneity and allows for complex systems of juxtapositions and collisions, in which all outside influences are viewed as potential raw material." The example of Charles Ives once again comes to mind and Zappa's tribute to Ives in the fifth box set of the *You Can't Do That On Stage Anymore* series confirms his early interest in his predecessor's use of "multiple colliding themes" (*Real* 167) and fragments of (sometimes distorted) melodies, a technique emulated in Zappa's "Call Any Vegetable" which, like many of Ives' compositions, seeks to convey "the musical illusion of several marching bands marching through each other":

In our low-rent version, the band splits into three parts, playing "The Star-

Spangled Banner," "God Bless America" and "America the Beautiful" all at the same time, yielding an amateur version of an Ives collision.

(*Real* 167)

Ben Watson rightly underlines the historical significance of Ives's "simultaneous musics" as probably one of the first instances of pre-digital "xenochrony" and points out that "while a boy [Ives] would sing one hymn while his father played the accompaniment to a different one" (358). For readers familiar with the aural collages of Zappa's *Freak Out* and *Absolutely Free*, Zappa's delight in merging fundamentally incompatible materials and rhythms cannot be considered as a simple manifestation of the modernist cult of irony or its hypothetical extension into postmodern eclecticism, quotation and pastiche. Rather, the satirical spirit of Zappa's xenochronic experiments originates in what Amiri Baraka describes as Coltrane's decision to "murder the popular song" and "do away with weak Western forms" (quoted in Harris 174). Nowhere is this more apparent than in the doo-wop sendups collected in *Cruising with Ruben and the Jets* (1968), which Zappa claimed to have conceived "along the same lines as Stravinsky's neoclassical period" ("If he could take the forms and clichés of the classical era and pervert them, why not do the same thing with the rules and regulations that applied to doowop in the fifties?" [*Real* 88]).[6]

As indicated by both Baraka's comments on Coltrane and Barth's description of the K-Mart aesthetics of the New American Short Story, the maximalist vs. minimalist axis inevitably invites a political reading. In another chapter of his *Negative Dialectics of Poodle Play*, Ben Watson discusses the work of the feminist critic Susan McClary, for whom Schoenberg's twelve-tone technique is the expression of an "asexual" musical language that puts an end to the binarisms (major/minor, masculine/feminine) around which sexism articulates itself. McClary claims that minimalist music, being based on repetition-with-variation and therefore deprived of the sexual climaxes of, say, Beethoven's Ninth or Bizet's *Carmen*, simultaneously undermines the supremacy of the male models of phallic telos and verticality that characterizes a sexist culture. Compared with the soothing sounds of Brian Eno's *Music for Airports*, Zappa's "The Torture Never Stops" would no doubt be condemned by McClary as too sensual and orgasmic to qualify as anything other than an expression of the male libidinal self. Whatever one makes of McClary's suggestion that female sexuality is fundamentally anti-climactic, it would be pointless to try and defend Zappa from accusations of sexism or even deny that his music and lyrics derive much of their energy from the representation (or shameless endorsement) of popular archetypes of masculine domination, rawness and obscenity. But Zappa's own remarks about minimalism indicate his desire to shift the debate from the domain of sexual politics to more largely political and economic matters. Reflecting on the popularity of minimalist music with established critics and foundations, Zappa suggests that minimalism arose out of the necessity of being cost-effective (in the same way as, for instance, the success story of the "theater of the absurd" format is at least in part due to the fact that it lends itself to low-budget productions requiring only two or three actors and very few additional staging costs):

> ... it used to be that they would fund only *boob-beep* stuff (serial and/or electronic composition). Now they're funding only *minimalism* (simplistic, repetitive composition, easy to rehearse and, therefore, *cost-effective*). So what gets taught in school? *Minimalism*. Why? Because it can be FUNDED. Net cultural result? Monochromonotony.
>
> *(Real* 189)

Ironically enough, the only work by Zappa which could conceivably be described as possessing certain minimalist features is his last masterpiece, *Civilization Phaze III*, a Synclavier-based opera derived from "a vague plot regarding pigs and ponies, threatening the lives of characters who inhabit a large piano" and incorporating various fragments of spoken material, some of which dates back to the recording sessions of *Lumpy Gravy* in 1967. Here, Zappa's attention to the physicality of sound once again manifests itself in the music performed by the "ponies" who make music "with a very dense light" ("How the Pigs' Music Works"). Zappa's use of space and silences in such pieces as "N-Lite" or "Beat the Reaper" represents a break from his earlier works and even led Ben Watson to suggest some connection with New Age music in his last interview with the composer:

> OTL: I noticed certain "new age" sounds in the music that preceded "Beat the Reaper" on disc two of *Civilization Phaze III*—surely you're joking?
> FZ: What's a "new age" sound?
> OTL: Sounds I associate with new-age music—shakuhachi or some kind of flute ...
> FZ: Mmm. [Affirmative grunt]
> OTL: ... and the throat-singing—quite atmospheric sounds. I was quite surprised to hear you use them. Normally ...
> FZ: Normally in new-age material there is no hint of dissonnance, so no

matter what you're orchestrating it with, the fact that you're not dealing with lush triads would set it apart anyway. The only thing it has in
common with new age music is that the chords are held a very long
time, but you couldn't go out and get a new age record contract with
that tune, because there's too much going on in it.

(548)

Characteristically, Zappa uses a pro-maximalist argument ("there is
too much going on in it") to defend himself from allegations of deriva-
tiveness and distance himself from a musical tradition which capitalizes
on the soothing effects of repetition and endless atmospheric chords.
The New Age sounds of *Civilization Phaze III* are only the tip of the iceberg
of Zappa's preoccupation with the relationship between matter and
sound, as well as a number of other questions related to those which
have occupied the mind of Stephen Hawking and other contemporary
physicists. Among these, the notion of infiniteness and finitude in both
extent and content figures prominently. Where does a sound-wave or a
movement begin and where does it end? Was it determined by chance or
by a set of rules and equations designed by the composer? What is the
relationship between time and space and how does a sound exist in
space as well as time?

In this sense, *Civilization Phaze III* (1994) is perhaps the ultimate example of Zappa's maximalist-objectist aesthetics as well as a climax in the
development of his materialist-objectist musicosm(icomic)ology. It can
also be seen as the last of Zappa's xenochronic experiments in that it
alternates Synclavier pieces with spoken word fragments recorded over
a period of more than 25 years. Whereas the short bits of conversation
sandwiched between the instrumental pieces returns us to the collage
techniques of *Uncle Meat* and *Lumpy Gravy* (Zappa had originally meant
the album to be titled "*Lumpy Gravy* Part II"), the compositions themselves create a space in which the sound environment becomes a living
structure that expands along the lines of an (anti-)method best
described by the composer himself as "AAAFNRAA"—an acronym for
"Anything, Anytime, Anyplace For No Reason At All". The "plot continuity" of the work, Zappa argues, is derived from a serial rotation of
randomly chosen words, phrases and concepts, including (but not
limited to) *motors, pigs, ponies, dark water, nationalism, smoke, music, beer*,
and various forms of *personal isolation*" (sleeve notes 3), a description
which evokes the aesthetics of *Uncle Meat* (1969), where "the words to the
songs on this album were scientifically prepared from a random series
of syllables, dreams, neuroses & private jokes that nobody except the

members of the band ever laugh at, and other irrelevant material. They are all very serious and loaded with secret underground candy-rock psychedelic profundities."

The liner notes estimate that 30% of the music of *Civilization Phaze III* was played by the Ensemble Modern who, Zappa claimed, was meant to beat what Stockhausen called "the lazy dogma of impossibility" by performing the most complex, "unplayable" music he ever produced (Menn 44). Whereas "Dio Fa" incorporates sounds created by Tuvan Throat Singers, and "N-Lite" contains piano parts which were played by Zappa himself, the bruitist "Waffenspiel" features the sounds produced by construction workers as Zappa's kitchen was being remodeled, the sound of barking dogs, automobile noises as well as sounds of semi-automatic weapon fire reportedly sampled from CNN newsreels. With its emphasis on the dialectics of the gestural and the mechanical, *Civilization Phaze III* confirms Zappa's attraction to Hawking's no-boundary proposal. Listeners, who are deprived of the irrevocable illusion of "real time"—which gives us the sense that we can grasp the singular reality of sounds and objects, that they can be traced to their sources— find themselves in the position of the post-quantum physicist confronted with the impossibility of determining both the velocity and the position of any given particle. They are forced to resist the illusion that turns the musical object into an objective fact liable to be enjoyed and consumed passively and uncritically. The enjoyment of Zappa's *Civilization Phaze III* is subject to a similar principle of radical uncertainty, one which is further emphasized in the second CD, where it is often hard to distinguish between the sounds that are computer-generated and those which are performed by the Ensemble Modern. Such a radical blurring of the boundaries between different states of the physicality of sound creates a space for the creative transformation of musical matter into a physical experience which resists analytical thought, accentuating its flight into abstraction and the void. The general body of the piece will only materialize for those who allow themselves to explore the most improbable reaches of sonic physicality.

This is not to suggest that Zappa's *Civilization Phaze III* is the only example of such a radical use of musical materiality. A maximalist alternative to Eno's "Music for Airports", Anthony Braxton's *Composition No-173* (1996), a "one act play" for "4 actors, 14 instrumentalists, constructed environment and video projections", is a structuralist speculative opera based on a series of dialogues taking place in an airport, "a kind of orange-like luminous state area-space" containing four giant video screens that give off "'image motion' projections and moving shadows", a circular table and four white chairs around which four people are seated, examining various maps including a large one that "almost covers the whole table but doesn't". Like Zappa's, Braxton's sounds "have a sense of humour":

> One can make you jiggle over to the left side of the room-space like a spinning top or something, or one can send out a smoke-trail of sonic imprint flashes that dart up and down the ceiling of the event-space. It's a kind of action-experience thing.
>
> (liner notes; unpag.)

Like Zappa's "Black Page" or Satie's fruit-shaped *divertissements*, Braxton's composition not only incorporates visual signs into his musical performance but also builds upon the visual potential of the material signs to create "different imaginary sound occurrences" (one also thinks of the "imaginary guitar notes" and air sculptures of *Joe's Garage*) liable to effect psychological changes in the actors and their audience. Braxton attempts to create an "animate-experience" born out of a synaesthetic awareness of the interaction of space, sound and image. His characters spend most of their time trying to "map" their environement and make sense of the strange sounds that swoop around them, bouncing on and off the stage and occasionally trying to come into their bodies causing them to check their "body-areas" for signs of physical alteration. They also try to create or represent new sounds by tracing their "physical" trajectories with their hands. The patterns of recognition vary according to the reactions of the four characters–one of them thus points at a sound which has just "landed" at his feet and speaks of a "'sponge-like' sonic garden" while another one immediately proceeds to formulate a "kind of sound that sinks in under the fireplace (light)". A third actor, using a typically Zappaian vocabulary, is more interested in the material texture of sound and seeks to identify a "kind of sound that sneaks up behind the lumpy area in the 'shade area'". A little earlier in the play, the "air sculpture" postulated the existence of a "creamy sound texture that blended into a ray of pulsing light–flashes (like at the Vegas floor show spectacles)". Braxton's synaesthetic *art total* reminds one of *Lumpy Gravy*, of course, but also of the "hot and putrid" sound and the pigs making music "with a very dense light" on *Civilization Phaze III*, which was originally envisioned as a theatrical production which was to be adapted and produced by Matt Groening and choreographer Jamey Hampton (of the ISO dance troupe). Zappa's description of the work, in the liner notes to the album, as "an opera-pantomime, with choreographed physical activity (manifested as dance or other forms of inexplicable sociophysical communication)" (3) confirms both his growing interest in making the body an integral part of his compositions and his attraction to the idea of a maximalist *Gesamtkunstwerk* that would trascend traditional genre boundaries and constitute an alliance of music, poetry, the visual arts and dance.

The closing chapter of *The Real Frank Zappa Book* establishes Zappa's status as the Mark Twain of American music, a man whose variety of occupation—as a composer, producer, businessman, social satirist, politician, writer, publisher, and inventor—is perhaps best illustrated by what he calls his "own personal collection of crumbled dreams" (*Real* 333), a series of extra-musical projects he sought to develop in the early 1980s and which range from a late-night adult program called "Night School" (340) to a cable network broadcasting 3-D movies (334) and a proposal to replace traditional record merchandising with a system allowing music consumers to access digital files by phone or via cable TV.

It is hard to imagine what kind of turn Zappa's career would have taken had it not been brought to an end by his untimely death. But one is tempted to believe that he would have given up on touring altogether and devoted himself to his orchestral and Synclavier-generated compositions. The notion of a maximalist *spectacle total* was becoming dear to his heart in the last years of his life, as attested to not only by the projected performances of *Civilization Phaze III* in various European theaters, but also by the "Proposal for a World Cup Football Opera" entitled *Dio Fa*, which Zappa claims to have presented to the Socialist Mayor of Milan in 1988 in advance of the World Cup Football Finals in the Summer of 1990 (*Real* 343).

Baby Take Your Teeth Out

the swollen lips from where
she munched them down
to the strawberry roots
when the bottles ran out
stupid voice tries to sing

stupid feeling for everything
irritation: pond—leg—pond—leg—pond—leg
>   —Andrew Norris. Recorded by
>   The Wrong Object as "Cunnimingus"

Like marron-glaced fish bones
Oh lady hit the road!
>   —King Crimson, "Ladies of the Road"

Baby take your teeth out
Try it one time
Baby take your teeth out
Try it one time
Leave 'em on the kitchen table
>   —Frank Zappa, "Baby take Your Teeth Out"

The synaesthetic dynamics of *Civilization Phaze III* are only one example of how Zappa's relationship with the perceiving/thinking/functioning body reflects the true essence of his maximalism. More generally, the examples discussed in the following chapters indicate that the body imposes itself as the essential receiver and be-all-and-end-all transformer of maximalist art. This, incidentally, is by no means a contemporary, or even a modern, phenomenon. The best-known maximalist artist of the Renaissance, François Rabelais, had already understood that only an aesthetics of corpo-reality is liable to multiply the vectors of perception while allowing the body to become its own food for conceptual thought and artistic experimentation. For Rabelais, maximalism allies itself with the grotesque through the essential component of bodily excesses. As Mikhail Bakhtin reminds us, the carnivalesque insistence on bodily functions and the liberation of instinct, far from being degrading, is meant to express the vital energies of mankind. Indeed, Rabelais's "grotesque realism" has a regenerative effect as the reduction of all aspects of human life to primary bodily functions "digs a bodily grave for a new birth," conceiving of new possibilities arising from the body's nether regions.

The profusion of grotesque and abstract(ed) bodies and body parts in the works of Frank Zappa and his old friend and occasional collaborator Don Van Vliet (aka Captain Beefheart)—from the latter's *Trout Mask Replica* to the exaggerated, phallic noses that appear on the cover of *Ruben and the Jets*[7]—represents "the epitome of incompleteness" (Bakhtin

26), an unfinished unit transgressing its own limits through eating, excretion and sexuality. The stress, therefore, is on the excesses and potentialities of its orifices, "on the apertures or the convexities, or on various ramifications and offshoots: the open mouth, the genital organs, the breasts, the phallus, the potbelly, the nose." This "unfinished and open body (dying, bringing forth and being born)," Bakhtin adds, "is not separated from the world by clearly defined boundaries; it is blended with the world, with animals, with objects" (26–27). Zappa's and Beefheart's lyrics are full of similar images of bodies coming out of themselves to meet the world of animal and objectist reality. The point where body and things enter each other (literally or figuratively) is where the unfinished chain of growth, proliferation and metamorphosis comes to represent the whole potential of the integrated body, the body emptying itself to become like nothing and preparing itself to go out and m-eat the world again, devouring the universe and being devoured by it.

Rabelais' poetics of degradation, with its focus on food, drink, digestion and sexual life, clearly anticipates Zappa's own "carnivalesque" compositions. These also enact the peculiar logic of the inside-out explored in Chapter Four, shifting accepted models from top to bottom, front to rear and delighting in imagining a new musical space in which inside and outside are one. According to such a totalizing/maximalist notion of art production (and consumption), scatological jokes become one of the prime movers of artistic creation itself. When Gargantua almost gets expelled from his mother's loins during a fit of diarrhoea, Rabelais establishes a symbolic link between the digestive cycle and the act of giving birth to a new human being, or a work of art—artistic fertility and peristaltics go hand in hand, so to speak. The following chapters will show that Zappa, like Rabelais (and Swift), does not shy away from describing fantasies of infantile regression (see our readings of "Lost in a Whirlpool" and "Let's Make the Water Turn Black" in Chapter Three) and puts them to the service of a popular art that delights in imagining how the most banal situations can degenerate into absurdist extremes. In "For Calvin (And His Next Two Hitch-Hikers)" (*The Grand Wazoo*), a song about back-seat fucking and eating, punning on the various meanings of the word "leakage", this absurdist logic typically takes us in the direction of abstract connections between sex and food:

Where did they go?
When did they come from?

What has become of them now?
How much was the leakage
From the drain in the night
And who are those dudes in the
Back seat of Calvin's car?
Where did they go?
When they got off the car?
Did they go get a sandwich
And eat in the dark?

The examples discussed below suggest that Zappa's irreverent humor revels in all things related to the body, from eating, farting and belching to defecation, laughing, dancing and masturbation. Scatology imposes itself as an important strategy, one of the most common manifestations of the conjunction of diet and discourse (one thinks, for example, of the Chaucerian farting devil of "Titties and Beer" or the poo-poo jokes of the "Illinois Enema Bandit") at the same time as it invigorates Zappa's satirical spirit. ("Satire is traditionally associated with filth, and the satirist is described as throwing turds and urine on those whom he ridicules. [Ehrenpreis 691]")

More generally, Zappa's treatment of the body confirms Bakhtin's dictum that "all that is bodily becomes grandiose, exaggerated, immeasurable" (19). This principle extends of course to the representation of sexuality in both literature and music. The alliance of the grotesque and the obscene in Zappa's explicit lyrics (in 200 *Motels* and other socio-documentary materials of life-on-the-road, the word "ob-scene" can often be taken in its literal sense, of that which happens "behind the scenes") has often been seen as the expression of Zappa's radical politics. Still, it would be a mistake to reduce it to, say, Wilhelm Reich's famous assertion that fascism is an expression of man's "orgastic yearning, restricted by mystic distortion and inhibition of natural sexuality" (24). There are similarities between Reich's sex economy and Zappa's warnings against the dangers of an authoritarian and sexually repressed society (see our discussion of Zappa's and Anthony Braxton's "Enema Bandits" in Chapter One). But more often than not Zappa's explicit lyrics do not take us in the direction of social-psychological emancipation. Rather, they seek to develop abstract forms of sexual behavior that enact the gradual decontextualization and abstraction of body parts from their traditional functional uses.[8] In such songs as "Charlie's Enormous Mouth," "Cocaine Decisions" or "Your Mouth,"[9] the mouth and the teeth (to which a whole section of Chapter Two is devoted) as organs of both speaking, eating and sexual intercourse, are often subjected to such a process of a physical decontextualization:

> Your mouth is your religion.
> You put your faith in a hole like that?
> You put your trust and your belief
> Above your jaw, and no relief
> Have I found.[10]

As the rest of this book will make clear, such a radical use of the grotesque indicates a tendency to move away from social and political satire per se. This tendency for the grotesque to drown or obscure the point of satire is well-attested:

> The grotesque artist exaggerates at first only for satirical purposes. But it is in the nature of this kind of powerful, extreme satire that its exaggerates burst through all limits. The grotesque satirist becomes intoxicated with its own creation. Gradually he loses sight of the satire. The exagerrations which he had at first unleashed in full awareness of their purpose become more and more wild, until they get out of hand, obliterating like a turbulent stream everything around them.
>
> (Thomson 42–43)

The opening section of this book will show that Zappa's and Don Van Vliet's use of the grotesque, the abject and the repellent (the fundamentals of post-Dada anti-totalitarian art) nonetheless lends itself to a political reading, one which is not geared towards practical changes (if one excepts, of course, Zappa's crusade against the PMRC campaign to label obscene lyrics) but seeks instead to create mediations between imaginary objects "liberated from the curse of being useful"[11] and abstract forms of behavior that put degenerate art to the service of an aesthetics that follows Kundera's recognition that beauty and harmony are first and foremost a political lie.

At this point, one is led to consider the ways in which Zappa used his own body as a stage on which to perform further practical eccentricities. The liner notes to the first album of the Mothers of Invention, *Freak Out*, set the tone for the first few years of his career, a period characterized by his satire of teenage America and in which the group tended to present themselves as disgusting and revolting "freaks". At the time, the phrasal verb "to *Freak Out*" was itself described as "a process whereby an individual casts off outmoded and restricing standards of thinking, dress, and social etiquette in order to express CREATIVELY his relationship to his immediate environment":

> These Mothers are crazy. You can tell by their clothes. One guy wears beads and they all smell bad. We were gonna get them for a dance after the basketball game but my best pal warned me you can never tell how many will show up . . . sometimes the guy in the fur coat doesn't show up and sometimes he does show up only he brings a big bunch of crazy people with him and they dance all over the place. None of the kids at my school like these Mothers . . . specially since my teacher told us what the words to their songs meant.
>
> Frank Zappa is the leader and musical director of THE MOTHERS of invention. His performances in person with the group are rare. His personality is so repellent that it's best he stay away . . . for the sake of impressionable young minds who might not be prepared to cope with him. When he does show up he performs on the guitar. Sometimes he sings. Sometimes he talks to the audience. Sometimes there is trouble.
>
> (liner notes; unpag.)

From the 1960s to the mid-1970s, Zappa systematically opted for an aesthetics of abjection, forcing his audience to contemplate (or imagine) the most degenerate parts of the human body ("Stink Foot", "What's the Ugliest Part of Your Body"). Zappa's use of the abject, in this respect, clearly allies him with the spirit of Dada. His 1967 revue entitled "Pigs and Repugnant", to cite but one example, deliberately used the shock tactics of the avant-garde. In the years that followed, Zappa acquired a reputation for obscenity and the rumor spread that he went as far as defecating on stage and eating the turd. Zappa later denied these rumours, but he nonetheless posed for the now famous "Phi Beta Krappa" poster.

In his later works, Zappa's relationship with his own body became more and more ambiguous. The mid-1970s, in particular, saw the construction of a more explicitly sexual persona. In those days, Zappa frequently appeared on stage with straggly hair, wearing tight trousers and an open shirt revealing the hairy chest of a glamorous demon-lover, a public image reinforced by his growing reputation as a guitar hero. An extreme example of this change can be found in the bold, phallic exhibitionism of *Zoot Allures*, whose cover, conceptualized by Cal Schenkel, features Zappa with his long untidy mane of thick dark hair and his skintight narrow hipped white jeans revealing a bulging crotch, perhaps intended as an ironic response to the rather feeble penis joke perpetrated a few years earlier by Andy Warhol on the cover of the Rolling Stones' *Sticky Fingers*.

This sexualized period, during which Zappa even appeared on the cover of *Vogue*, came to an end in the early eighties. At this time he began to adopt a more sober style which culminated in the classical, posh-looking cover portrait of *Jazz from Hell* and his numerous appearances on TV, not as a musician but as a defender of the 1st Amendment of the US Constitution and an opponent of the PMRC campaign. The last major modification in Zappa's appearance was brought on by his last illness which eventually conferred to him, on the front cover of *The Yellow Shark* (1993), the timeless, mortified solemnity of David's dying Seneca.[12]

That Blues Thing: Enter Captain Beefheart

When Frank Zappa and Don Van Vliet sat around after school eating pineapple buns (from the remains of Mr Vliet senior's bread round) and listening to rhythm and blues records, they were indulging in an early form of maximalist synaesthesia, performing the basic tenets of an aesthetic philosophy and way of life which was, at various points throughout the next thirty years, to unite and divide their parallel careers as American maverick artists: buns and blues, the listening body eating, this was an auspicious beginning.

Van Vliet was one of Zappa's earliest and most significant collaborators who eagerly assisted in the forging of links between discourses of bodily experience and music-making; along with Motorhead Sherwood and Ray Collins, he was a key figure in the conversion of teenage gross-out humour into an expanding aesthetic of the body's parts and processes. Zappa's account of the origin of the name "Captain Beefheart" captures the atmosphere of those formative years and illustrates how so much of what we analyse below can be traced back to the lewd anecdote or obscene gesture:

> Captain Beefheart was a character I invented for the film ["Captain Beefheart Versus the Grunt People"]. His name derives from one of Don Vliet's relatives who looked like Harry Truman. He used to piss with the door open when Don's girlfriend walked by and make comments about how his whizzer looked just like a beef heart.[13]

The vortex of Zappa's maximalism is a toilet, and here we see him seizing on a creative *détournement* of the human body: the penis becomes a heart, a conflation of two organs of love—the literal and the symbolic are fused together in an anthropomorphic leap of imagination curiously prophetic of Van Vliet's later pictorial style with its Wellsian miscegenations. Artistic experiment is already inseparable from research into what the body can do physically, how it behaves socially, and how it can be manipulated aesthetically.

Van Vliet finally abandoned music for painting in 1982, and Captain Beefheart was no more. His recording career was characterised by an intermittent striving for an innovative rock-blues-jazz-avant-gardist *mélange* which would sing back to us in crazy voices from beyond the beat. In his assault on the "moma heartbeat" and the sedimentation of form and response it imposes, Van Vliet seemed to be working towards a maximalist enhancement of possibilities; and his efforts in this direction have proved very useful to us in our attempts to show how musical maximalism incorporates its opposite, and how the meeting of extremes more generally is one of the vital blowholes of maximalist art.

As a musician, Van Vliet lacked both the formal know-how of technique, and an interest in advanced musical technologies, and this may explain his unwillingness to extend the experiments he was making at the level of the group to the broader plane of conceptual and materialist manipulation, his failure to objectify his moments of transcendent insight into a Project/Object with a life of its own. Regularly, also, the Captain tried to conform to the norms of popular music, writing songs which seem to labour under a load of assumed sincerity while lending themselves to a perversely melancholic listening experience. Much of the *Unconditionally Guaranteed* album falls into this category (especially "Magic Bee" and "This is the Day"), together with the notorious "Too Much Time" from *Clear Spot* and the *Bluejeans and Moonbeams* album, where the Magic Band was replaced with the critically lambasted "Tragic Band". This hesitation between modes of creativity, together with his eventual selection of a neo-primitive abstract-expressionist aesthetic for his painting contrasts interestingly with Zappa's self-consuming commitment to the Big Note and its cosmic ramifications. And it is significant that Zappa's own attempts to write songs that could be played on the radio always contain elements of social and/or formal satire ("Bobby Brown", "Dancing Fool", "Valley Girl").

After his musical researches, where questions of sound and form were complicated by the struggles of individual and group, Van Vliet settled into a painting *style* which has achieved a traditional coherence (and a degree of international recognition to go with it) through the accumulation of signature effects from work to work. This kind of artistic practice is diametrically opposed to the genre-leaping of Zappa, and its origins in the fraught abutments of collage.

In spite of these differences, many of Van Vliet's texts are thematically consistent with Zappa's concerns, and both hark back in various ways to the anti-art activities of Dada (perhaps the key maximalist movement of the modernist period):[14] Van Vliet drew on the paradox of ordered disorder exploited by Hugo Ball in his sound poetry, together with the "primitivism" of Tzara, rendered urgently audible in the free jazz of Ornette Coleman; while Zappa fell in love with the materiality of sound, and the theatrical extravagances of burlesque, key components in his self-recharging brand of social satire. While Van Vliet played with the paradox, evolving his own surrealist slant on those odd overdetermined objects so dear to Zappa, the latter branched out and out into parody, satire and beyond. Often, in Van Vliet's work, these objects are freakishly human, the Ant Man Bee, the Man With the Woman Head, Apes-Ma, The Human Totem Pole, and express his ludic approach to the lineaments of human being, a delight in monstrous combination and subtraction which has affinities with the gothic tradition and the uncanny stresses of the "is it or isn't it?" exploited in the art and literature of terror. Here again, Van Vliet seems to cross Zappa's maximalist trajectory, and we explore the double intersection of their work with the gothic tradition and some of its more recent avatars in Chapter Four.

Van Vliets's neo-primitivism proclaims itself through his interviews in the denial of all influence; a rhetorical move which is often coupled with an enthusiasm for the existential and ethical purity of animals. While Zappa could satirize the notion of natural being (and its racist overtones) in "You Are What You Is", Van Vliet seems to work within the tradition of the individual genius, whose every act is a work of art, the quality of which is directly related to the sincerity of the gesture. In this system, authenticity remains the final index of artistic value: If Picasso wanted to paint like a child, Van Vliet wants to paint like an animal. From the relativisng perspective of post-modernism, Van Vliet's stance might seem quaint or merely stubborn in its attachment to the mystique of essence, the "It" which the Beat generation venerated, that indefinable something which connects one to life and separates one from the mass of people who don't have or haven't found "It".[15] Whether or not Van Vliet had "it", he was at the very least capable of remarkable idiosyncrasy; and Zappa, who was equally disdainful of the cultish "it" and the dogma of cultural relativity which came to oppose it, regularly sought to tap this source.

Even if finally not a maximalist himself, Van Vliet participates in and engenders a series of maximalist moments through his lyrics and musical ideas, his physical presence and bodily projections, his ego statements, and his shifts between the verbal, visual and sonic media. By examining some of these moments below, we hope to shed more light on Zappa's developing art and the key ideas of maximalism, and our essay will culminate with a comparative discussion of the two artists and their relationship to that vexed and faintly illicit subject—aesthetic pleasure.

Electric Carnival

Chapter Three discusses Zappa's and Beefheart's relationship with the blues in a way that continues to emphasize their poetics of the carnivalesque body. In his study of the blues and the vernacular stratum of American culture, Houston A. Baker, building upon Barthes' "zero degree writing" and Kristeva's discussion of Bakhtin in *Desire in Language*, writes of the social and political protest enacted by the "ambivalent word". In the fiction of Richard Wright and other African-American novelists, the ambivalent word (which is defined by Kristeva not just as an ambiguous utterance but as a word that is given a new meaning "while retaining the meaning it already had" and is therefore "the result of a joining of two sign systems" [216]) is reflected in a wealth of "obscenities, parodic utterances, inversive or ironical phrases [that] function as reductive junctures." Wright's use of carnivalesque, Baker concludes, reduces conventional language to "dialogical (two discourses 'yoked,' sometimes 'violently,' together) symbolic occasions." The result is "language of starting misalliances, sacreligious punnings, scandalous repudiations" (150).

As we have seen, Zappa's own work is often associated with ferocious attacks on both mainstream compositional strategies and conventional pop lyrics. As in the case of blues, the parodic and inversive power of his best lyrics provides us with a symbolic mode of processing the real that promotes semantic shifts and displacements which are rarely encountered on the rock scene. What makes Zappa's work interesting in this respect is perhaps not the postmodern *pasticcio* which is observable in, for instance, his Ivesian use of "multiple colliding themes" (*Real* 167) in "The Duke of Prunes"—where Stravinsky's *Firebird Suite* floats into a theme from the *Rite of Spring*—or in his striking cover of Jimi Hendrix's "Purple Haze," in which the staccato lyricism of the original song is dismantled by the dry and cybernetic "Fake Devo texture" (166) of Zappa's impish arrangement. A similar, and arguably more powerful strategy, can be observed at the level of his use of language, as suggested by our reading of the song "Montana," discussed below in Chapter One, which confirms that the significance of fetishism, in Zappa's œuvre, lies in its capacity to de-code and redefine the parameters of language and the instrumental meanings of objects.

Houston Baker conceives of the blues as a "matrix," "a point of cease-less input and output, a web of intersecting, crisscrossing impulses always in productive transit" (3). For Baker, the blues is the equivalent to Hegelian "force," "a relational matrix where *difference* is the law" and which, like electricity, is a "simple force . . . indifferent to its law—to be positive and negative." Once the instrumental energy of the blues is envisioned as such a force, Baker adds, it becomes a mediational site where "familiar antinomies are resolved (or dissolved) in the office of adequate cultural understanding" (6). One of the most common avatars of blues mediation is its capacity to "contain both lack and commercial possibility":

> The performance that sings of abysmal poverty and deprivation may be recompensed by sumptuous food and stimulating beverage at a country picnic, amorous favors from an attentive listener, enhanced Afro-American communality, or Yankee dollars from representatives of record companies traveling the South in search of blues as commodifiable enter-tainment. The performance, therefore, mediates one of the most preva-lent of all antinomies in cultural investigation—creativity and commerce.
>
> (9)

The promise of material success and sexual gratification (humourously reduced by Zappa to "the blow job" effect in *The Real Frank Zappa Book*) has characterized the history of blues and rock music from their origins to the present. In the context of his relationship with the music industry, Zappa, who gradually worked his way from deep poverty to financial success, has always relied on the mediation of blues-rock performance and commodified entertainment to finance his most ambitious projects, resolving the familiar dualities of the music indus-try by mocking the absurd conventions of conventional rock while simultaneously thriving on the immediate impact of his parodic style on huge popular audiences.

On a superficial level, quoting a passage from "Petrushka" in the middle of a cheap, three-chord ballad ("Status Back Baby") or using a Varèsian siren as an introduction to the pounding jazz-rock riff on "Filthy Habits" certainly helps to efface the frontier between high art and so-called mass or commercial culture. But what redeems Zappa's eclecticism from, say, Fredric Jameson's postmodernism—with its insistence on the dissolution of subjective styles and the degeneration of parody into the "neutral" realm of pastiche—is his commitment to an aesthetics that refuses to limit itself to the anti-hierarchical dynamics of collage, hybridity and juxtaposition. By privileging the satiric impulse (the Latin word "satira" originally meant a "medley" or a kind of "mixed stew") and injecting the combining energies of rock, jazz and classical music into the very fabric of his compositions, Zappa refuses to indulge in the unironic "depthlessness" that, according to Jameson, characterizes much postmodernist art. Likewise, to reduce Zappa's genre-jumping and his continuous commitment to low art forms to a mere stylistic trick intended to help him court the popular-culture industry would be as naive as to suggest that musical dissonance and inacessibility are automatically concomitant with social and political emancipation. It would also be to ignore the importance of a work that finds its most powerful expression in the radical interplay of social, cultural and political influences that are held together by Zappa's use of various forms of "conceptual continuities," particularly as regards his use of the body as a key site of the uncontrollable and excessive in art production and consumption. Finally, Baker's understanding of the blues as a web of intersecting cultural impulses indifferent to familiar antinomies can help us make sense of the dynamics at work in a song like "Ship Arriving Too Late to Save a Drowning Witch", where Zappa's soaring guitar solo interrupts a simplistic reggae riff and plunges listeners into a maelstrom of raw, convulsive energy which is informed as much by Hendrix as by Coltrane or Varèse's "blocks of sound". Once again, the significance of Zappa's soloing practice is indeed to be found not in the so-called postmodern pastiche that, as we know, supposedly bridges the gap between high and low, past and present styles, but, rather, in its complete disregard for such dichotomies.

Hegel's notion of electricity as a pure activity and process, a unifying force of social desire that abolishes the separation of form and content, Notion and Being, positivity and negativity, is also relevant to a close reading of Captain Beefheart's "Electricity", in which the Magic Band's electric instruments are both the ground and the medium of the "truth" shouted "peacefully" by the thunderbolts described in the song. One of the lessons to be drawn from Hegel's definition is that the necessity of any existing fact or impulse is based on a force which is responsible for its immediate existence and manifest effects. In Beefheart's hymn to electricity, such a force is taken as a manifestation of social desire. Beefheart sings about love, friendship and mutual understanding, but the language of Van Vliet's "free-seeking electricity" is completely devoid of any sentimental content:

> Singin through you to me; thunderbolts caught easily
> Shouts the truth peacefully Eeeeeee-lec-tri-ci-teeeeeeee
> High voltage man kisses night to bring the light to those who need to
>   hide their shadow deed
> Go into bright find the light and know that friends don't mind just
>   how you grow
> midnight cowboy stains in black reads dark roads without a map
> To free-seeking electricity (repeat)
> Lighthouse beacon straight ahead straight ahead across black seas to
>   bring
> Seeking eeee-lec-tri-ci-teeeee
> High voltage man kisses night to bring the light to those who need to
>   hide their shadow-deed hide their shadow-deed (repeat)
> Seek electricity . . .

Van Vliet's refusal to treat emotion in terms of standard objects and relations is linked with a holistic vision of the real which posits the existence of a dynamic system of interrelationships that clearly exceeds the conventions of self-expressivity that govern the popular song. A song like "Electricity" helps explain why W. C. Bamberger has described Van Vliet as an Emersonian or "ecological" artist seeing his environment as "one network, or web, interdependent, with man no more important than any other element," a philosophy which becomes even more fully developed in Van Vliet's paintings of landscapes and animals (see the section on Van Vliet's environmentalism in Chapter Four).

As we will see, the ecological impulse that underlies Van Vliet's lyrics is inextricably linked with his gothic imagination. Like Big Joan, who pull[s] up her blouse and compare[s] her navel to the moon," the narrator of "Frownland" asserts his feeling of oneness with the natural world. His spirit is "made up of the ocean / and the sky 'n the sun 'n the moon", and cannot be contained by the world of "gloom", shadows and lies represented by "Frownland" (*Trout Mask Replica*). He aspires to a place "where uh man can stand by another man / Without an ego flying: With no man lyin' / 'n no one dying by an earthly hand". Many of Van Vliet's poetic personae seem to strive for such an unalienated setting which allows for disinterested cooperation, human solidarity and self-determination. In "When Big Joan Sets Up" (*Trout Mask Replica*), for example, the overweight couple's decision to retreat from the world because of their eccentric appearance recalls countless other stories of human freaks who, like Victor Frankenstein's monster (and, before that, Milton's Adam), are "promoted from darkness" to an existence of fear and pain; wretched creatures thrown into being, rejected by the community and condemned to a life of darkness and loneliness. In Beefheart's more optimistic reworking of the traditional gothic plot, Big Joan finds herself a mate and the tacit understanding that unites the two lovers brings the song to a happy conclusion. Later in the album, the seriousness of intent of Van Vliet's political gothic gives way to more visionary pieces such as "Dachau Blues" (discussed in Chapter Three) or "Bill's Corpse", whose quaint Poesque diction is nicely deflated by Beefheart's more habitual blues idiom:

> Quietly the rain played down on the last of the ashes
> Quietly the light played down on her lashes
> She smiled 'n twisted she smiled 'n twisted
> Hideously looking back at what once was beautiful
> Playing naturally magically
> O' her ragged hair was shinin' red white 'n blue
> All 'n the children screamin'
> Why surely madam you must be dreamin'
> You couldn't have done this if you knew what you were doin'

In a frozen tableau which evokes the aestheticized, cold-blooded violence of Browning's "Porphyria's Lover", the lady who has apparently just murdered her lover remains unimpressed by the children's screaming while the rain is "playing naturally magically" with her perception of the scene. Like the narrator describing the oriole singing "like an orange / His breast full of worms" in "Orange Claw Hammer" (*Trout Mask Replica*), she is confronted with the revelation that, to quote Hélène Cixous, "there is a bit too much death in life, a bit too much life in death" (Gelder 44)—in this respect, her tragic recognition of the dialectics of the hideous and the beautiful is perhaps the cause of her enigmatic, twisted smile. Her ragged hair "shinin' red and white 'n blue" recalls Beefheart's painting technique and his penchant for unaldulterated, primal colors. The song ends with an urgent plea that the fallen lady should "have us all" and "have us fall". We can only guess at the meaning of this final secular prayer but the implication seems to be that the Frownland people, who can only get together "not in love but shameful grief", will never build a true community of souls but that a relationship based on fear, grief, and mistrust may be better than no relationship at all.

Along similar lines, "The Thousandth and Tenth Day of the Human Pole" (*Ice Cream for Crow*) sounds like a warning against the lack of communal consciousness that prevents human beings from cooperating in the face of a hostile environment. A Tower of Babel made of flesh and bone, the human totem stands as a metaphor for a society defeated by its own aspirations to freedom and transcendence and relying too much on abstract and devalued ideals of autonomy and progress; the appearance of the "small child / with statue of liberty doll" at the end of the song will not keep the human pyramid from crumbling down. The reference to the "integrated pole" also makes Beefheart's song stand as an open-ended parable on US racial politics:

The thousandth and tenth day of the human totem pole.
The morning was distemper grey,
Of the thousandth and tenth day of the human totem pole.
The man at the bottom was smiling.
He had just finished his breakfast smiling.
It hadn't rained or manured for over two hours.
The man at the top was starving.
The pole was a horrible looking thing
With all of those eyes and ears
And waving hands for balance.
There was no way to get a copter in close
So everybody was starving together.
The man at the top had long ago given up
But didn't have nerve enough to climb down.
At night the pole would talk to itself and the chatter wasn't too good.
Obviously the pole didn't like itself, it wanted to walk!
It was the summer and it was hot
And balance wouldn't permit skinning to undergarments.
It was an integrated pole, it was taking on an reddish brown cast.
Exercise on the pole was isometric,
Kind of a flex and then balance
Then the highest would roll together,
The ears wiggle, hands balance.
There was a gurgling and googling heard

A tenth of the way up the pole.
Approaching was a small child
With Statue of Liberty doll.

Van Vliet's imaginary scenarios of spiritual emancipation often take the form of paroxysmal visions which are less a symptom of the psychic disintegration of the self than a consequence of the desire to lose one's attachment to oneself and reach for a higher plane of consciousness. For Beefheart, sex, violence and death are not merely agents of libidinal release but experiences which purport to transcend the boundaries of selfhood. Since such an escape from the self and the advent of a communal consciousness seem doomed to failure by the lack of honesty and stability of ordinary human relationships, it is only through the liminal experiences of (weird) sex ("White Jam" [*Spotlight Kid*], "Neon Meate Dream of a Octafish" [*Trout Mask Replica*]), death and rebirth ("Fallin' Ditch", "The Dust Blows Forward 'n the Dust Blows back" [*Trout Mask Replica*]) that they begin to realize their fantasies of wholeness. Among such fantasies of psychic integration, the dream of being one with nature figures prominently, as does that of approximating the mythic plenitude of the real or imaginary "homeland" of infancy. Repressed infantile complexes abound in Van Vliet's lyrics throughout the 1970s as, for instance, in "Doctor Dark" (*Lick my Decals Off*), where, in an interesting reversal of the bogeyman story, the naughty child is anxiously waiting to be carried off by a mysterious dark stranger:

Mama, mama, here come Doctor Dark
Horse clippin, clappin' 'n his ol' hooves makin' sparks
Gotta git me who I want to

The Freudian psychodrama of "When I see mommy, I feel like a mummy" (*Shiny Beast*) enacts the coincidence of incestuous, scopophiliac and necrophiliac urges. In a Poesque narrative of emotional dispossession, the desire for union and oneness symbolized by the mother gives way to a desire to preserve the physical integrity of the body. But the mother's body remains undescribed or invisible, it escapes into vapor and mirage. In a typically gothic fashion, the fear of death and decay leads to murder: the impossible object of desire has to be obliterated or wrapped away in order to be controlled and fully (re)possessed. The final stage of such radical, narcissistic fetishism is here represented as a symptom of the fear and loathing created by the specular realm of fantasies that infect the mind of the "Mirror Man":

oh woe—when I see mommy
I feel like a mummy
gonna wrap her up
every time I see her
I want to grab her
pull her up to me
till I look through her
but she moves so fast
that I can't even see her
her interest fades
like breath on a mirror
every time I see her
I try to grab her
and the wind from my hand
blows away like a feather
every time I grab her
oh—when I see mommy
I feel like a mummy
gonna wrap her up
next time I see her
I'm gonna seize her
then I'm gonna freeze her
it's the only way
that I might get to see her
gonna wrap her up—oh, mommy

In "When I see Mummy . . . ", as elsewhere, Van Vliet's gothic roman-
ticism has its origins in wonder and mystery, the essence of his poetry
lying in the sense of something hidden, of something about to be
revealed by the power of the poet's painterly imagination and its dedi-
cation to the dialectics of fear and attraction, pleasure and disgust. His
lyrics are peopled with otherworldly hybrids of meat, blood and hair,
fraught with unknown (perhaps best unexplained?) significances of
what the "dark" powers of the subconscious mind force us to do or
think. In many ways, Van Vliet's use of the conventional paraphernalia
of Romantic poetry (dark nights, moonlight, dreams, desolate and
dreary landscapes, madness, incest, . . .) is simultaneously regressive
and progressive as it seeks to bring back a mythic past at the same time
as it strives to correct the energies of a culture dominated by greed and
hypocrisy and stimulate psychological changes that would lead to the
emergence of a new sensibility based on a renewed attention to the
mystery of natural forces. Suspended between nothingness and infinity,
the unnamable and the formless, Beefheart's poetic personae enter a
sleepy region where their own troubled dreams take us to the source of

the sublime:

> My life ran through my veins
> Whistlin' hollow well
> I froze in solid motion well well
> I heard the ocean swarmin' body well well
> I heard the beetle clickin' well
> I sensed the thickest silence scream
> Then I begin t' dream

Your Mouth

> Ugly is bad
> And bad is wrong
> And wrong is sinful
> And sin leads to eternal damnation

–Frank Zappa, "I'm So Cute" (*Sheik Yerbouti*)

The first chapter of this essay concentrates on Zappa's use of foodstuffs as one of the foundational materials of his art. The convergence of food and performance is of course not new, and the Italian Futurists, to cite but one example, prefigured the creations of performance artists such as Alicia Rios and Janine Antoni[16] by subscribing to Marinetti's famous dictum, "the distinction of the senses is arbitrary," which signalled the advent of a new maximalist (syn-)aesthetic promoting the dissociation of food from eating and encouraging the transformation of the gastronomic into the theatrical. The Futurists' "Manifesto on Tactilism" (1921) introduced many synaesthetic experiments meant to maximalize the combination of sense experiences. These experiments included such idiosyncratic happenings as "Tactile Dinner Parties" and "Polyrhythmic salads" which were to be manipulated and consumed while listening to music and smelling natural essences. The Futurists' "extremist banquet" featured many such culinary events separating food from its use-value and turning it into an aesthetic fetish whose main purpose was to teach Marinetti's contemporaries how "to distinguish between things which serve to please the stomach and those destined to delight the eyes" (Marinetti 95).

Zappa's own oeuvre—which takes us from the Futurists' "Steel Chicken" (whose body was "mechanized by aluminium-coloured bonbons" [Marinetti 89]) to the rubber penis-measuring chicken of "Tengo Na Minchia Tanta" (*Uncle Meat*) — tends to externalize actions which are usually kept inside the body, or relegated to the margins of art history. His use of offensive and obscene materials, in particular, opens up a space where further dissociations (between food and eating, sex and sexuality, life and art, etc.) produce disorders and interferences that bypass or short-circuit traditional modes of art production and consumption.

By reconciling the mouth that sings with the mouth that eats, the experiments carried out in Zappa's Utility Muffin Research Kitchen also combat the compartimentalization of physical and mental pleasure which has characterized Western civilization. The power of laughter and satire in his music and lyrics creates a profusion of festive, farcical expressions that frees the body from its instrumental destiny. Like Rabelais's work—which mixed popular and learned idioms, classical and modern languages, lewd jokes and erudite Humanist talk—Zappa's music brings together not only different musical genres and subgenres, from the most refined to the most trivial, but also antipodal modes of apprehension of the real. His imaginary mediations between the subjective and the objective, the abstract and the concrete, are important because they create a pivotal space where opposites meet and where the interpenetration of low and high art, film, orchestral music, blues-rock and noise is part of a larger conceptual nexus where ideas, feelings and gestures are exchanged and where Zappa's carnivalesque aesthetics contributes to the creation of alternative art forms that encourage an integrated approach to life and art in general (his role as a "documenter" of life on the road is crucial in this respect).

Maximalism as a Critical Method

James Joyce's application of the peristaltic process to literary technique in *Ulysses* introduces us to another interpretive model with which to appraise the cultural value of maximalist aesthetics. By likening the movement of food down the esophagus and, by extension, the entire digestive process, to the workings of narrative fiction in the Lestrygonians chapter, Joyce sets the tone for all later attempts to pursue analogies between diet and discourse in order to illuminate the tensions between physical and mental pleasures. In conversation with Frank Budgen, the author declared of this chapter:

> "Among other things . . . my book is the epic of the human body. The only man I know who has attempted the same thing is Phineas Fletcher. But then his *Purple Island* is purely descriptive, a kind of coloured anatomical

chart of the human body. In my book the body lives in and moves through space and is the home of a full human personality. The words I write are adapted to express first one of its functions then another. In LESTRYGONIANS the stomach dominates and the rhythm of the episode is that of the peristaltic movement."

"But the minds, the thoughts of the characters," I began.

"If they had no body they would have no mind," said Joyce. "It's all one."

(Budgen 21)

Joyce sees the body as the surpreme maximalist receiver and generator of meaning, rhythm and being. While Bloom's insistence on the simultaneously enjoyable and disturbing pleasures of food and sex anticipates some of the issues explored in our first chapter, Joyce's peristaltic prose argues for a kind of interpretive reading that causes his writing to inflate with unexpected meanings that exceed the sum of its individual parts.[17] Since the very early years of Zappa's career as a musician, songwriter, composer and producer, his works have resisted the purgative/gastrokinetic properties of critical exegesis. And it seems that even the most creative fits of connectivitis and canine aesthetics of Ben Watson's Poodle Play, far from reducing Zappa's opus to an œuvre à *clef* liable to be elucidated in the light of buried narratives, have added to the non-absorptive nature of his works by multiplying the vectors of aesthetic/instrumental and social meaning produced by them while encouraging readers to extend them by drawing upon their own imagination and cultural background. Such a method, which calls on the reader's/listener's imaginative individual responses to the works, affords us many opportunities for the maximalist repossession of both high and low art forms, *including* minimalist music. For as Brian Ferneyhough notes, "one of the few possible justifications for minimalist music" is that "the maximalisation comes through the individual, rather than through the object" (Potter 15).

Readers looking for an exhaustive study of the music of Zappa and Van Vliet will be disappointed. For those who are already familiar with Zappa and Captain Beefheart, we hope that this book will appear as a welcome addition to the already existing literature on two of the best-known American mavericks of the last century; not another critical biography, but an interpretive essay investigating what we feel is the cultural and historical importance of both artists in the context of a wide-ranging network of references that run from Michelangelo and Arcimboldo to William Burroughs and Vaclav Havel. Readers who are only vaguely familiar with their music will be introduced to a projected pantheon of maximalist artists and "moments" which will in turn give rise to poetic–associational readings designed to encourage the exploration of the processes of art production, consumption and rejection in their expanding totality and to considerations of the body as the fluctuating constant against which all composition (addition and subtraction of parts) is attempted. In many ways, this book is also intended as a maximalist alternative to the cultural studies take on the study of popular music, which generally neglects aesthetics in favor of the merely semiotic and sociological and is reluctant to investigate the relationships and coincidences of mass, underground and "elitist" culture, while paying lip service to the postmodern fashion for works that purport to undermine the high vs. low art dichotomy. In what follows, we will propose an (anti-)method, a conspiracy theory of the mind that seeks to do justice to Jaffe's definition of musical maximalism while simultaneously proposing a promotional application of "paranoid" criticism risking its very credibility (and sanity) to abandon itself to the energizing virtues of connectivitis and coordinology.

CHAPTER ONE

Breaking You Down

Moving to Montana soon
Gonna be a dental floss tycoon.

—Frank Zappa, "Montana" (1973)

Now some folks loves ham hocks
And some folks loves pork chops
And some folks loves vegetable soup
And Roland the Roadie loves Gertrude the Groupie,
But Gertrude the Groupie loves groups.

—Dr Hook, "Roland the Roadie" (1976)

Zappa's song, "Montana" (*Overnite Sensation*), tells the story of an aspiring entrepreneur with a strong belief in the future potential of the dental floss market. He is about to move to Montana to raise "a crop of Dental Floss" ("raisin' it up / Waxen it down / In a little white box / I can sell uptown"). He is riding a "small tiny hoss"—also described as a "pigmy pony"—named "MIGHTY LITTLE" and is riding "him all along the border line / With a / Pair of heavy-duty / Zircon-encrusted tweezers in [his] hand." The zircon gem that adorns the dental floss cowboy's heavy-duty tweezers is clearly an outward sign of social superiority and material success that is meant to impress the other wranglers ("every wrangler would say I was mighty grand"). Surely, one of the lessons to be drawn from Zappa's "Montana" is that, to quote Gertrude Stein's "Glazed Glitter," "certainly glittering is handsome and convincing" (161). Here, Zappa's parodic treatment of the Western myth is remarkably similar to that of Ed Dorn's mock-epic, mock-allegorical poem, *Gunslinger*. Begun in the late 1960s but first published in full in 1989, *Gunslinger* relates the adventures and encounters of a man who embarks on a quest in search

[37]

of "an inscrutable Texan," a businessman whose ruthless capitalism is inspired by the figure of Howard Hughes. The cowboy fetishism of "Montana" recalls Dorn's opening description of the "Cautious Gunslinger / of impeccable smoothness / and slender leather encased hands" (3).[1] A brilliant blend of narrative, lyric, mythic and phenomenological material spiced up by countless comic-book types, Dorn's cycle contains many parodies of folk ballads and even what appears to be a direct reference to Zappa's "Montana". At the end of the poem, Dorn's hero is taking leave of one of his companions, The Poet, a "drifting singer," and asks him "what's in the cards" for him. The Poet answers: "Moving to Montana soon / going to be a nose spray tycoon" (199). Like Zappa's "Montana," whose narrator begins the song by declaring "By myself I wouldn't / have no boss, But I'd be raisin' my lonely / Dental Floss", Dorn's *Slinger* is about the perils and attractions of private entrepreneurship, a world Zappa was to play an increasingly active part in as a producer and owner of several record companies. The Poet's final decision to give up his itinerant art and enter the world of privately-owned business rings the knell of Slinger's quest at the same time as it confirms the ultimate victory of Howard Hughes over Shelley.

In songs such as "Montana" or, as we will see, "Evelyn, A Modified Dog", Zappa develops a kind of fetishism that functions as a foundation for both the apprehension and reinterpretation of instrumental objects and commodities. Here, as elsewhere, Zappa's interest in objects goes beyond the dynamics of projection and introjection—in a mode that hesitates between description and definition, fetishism becomes an act of interpretation of the real. In his best lyrics, it promotes radical semantic shifts and displacements rarely encountered on the rock scene.

Zappa's approach to food displays a similar desire to create a new ground on which our eating habits can be questioned and redefined. Culinary references abound in Zappa's lyrics—they range from the comic and the anecdotal (the doo-wop nostalgia of "White Port 'n Lemon Juice" and "Electric Aunt Jemima" or "Jelly Roll Gum Drop") to the sociological ("Cruising for Burgers"). Like Dalí, Zappa seems to have a special interest in vegetables and beans.[2] In "Mr. Green Genes", from the album *Uncle Meat*, the ingestion of beans and celery develops into a comic vision of the compulsive eater and consumer of commodities that degenerates into cannibalism, thereby unveiling the most disturbing and sinister implications of consumer capitalism (the song urges the listener to eat his own shoes, "the box he bought'em in," "the truck that brought'em in" and finally to "eat the truck and driver / And his gloves").

In "Call Any Vegetable", the suggestion that our lives can be improved by eating vegetables that "keep you regular" once again recalls the flatulent humor of Ed Dorn in *Gunslinger*: ("Youre in Beenville, is that a place / or THE FLATULENCE TENSE" [135]).[3] If "Montana" can be said to be indirectly about the American fixation on dental care, "Call Any Vegetable" touches upon what Paul Spinrad describes as the American obsession with "regularity of stool", an obsession which led John Harvey Kellogg to call constipation the "most common and most destructive disease of civilized people" (*Colon Hygiene* [1917]; quoted in Spinrad 25). More seriously, perhaps, one of the favorite targets of Zappa's scatological lyrics is the anal-retentive behavior of middle-class America, the "Po-Jama People" whose repressed desires Zappa frequently tries to awaken through the electrifying power of his blues-based repertoire and his most flamboyant guitar solos. As Henry Threadgill's and Zappa's respective salutes to the "Illinois Enema Bandit" in the mid-1970s indicate, the purgative power of jazz and blues is a possible remedy against the conformism and hypocrisy of a society which was "full of shit" and "going backwards after the increase in freedom and honesty in the 1960s" (Threadgill quoted in Watson 322). For Zappa—a musician and songwriter convinced of the power of the "ambivalent word"—the language of the blues, described above by Houston Baker as the "language of startling misalliances, sacreligious punnings, scandalous repudiations" (150) must have appeared as the perfect idiom through which to expose "a world of secret hungers" in which "every desire is hidden away / In a drawer, in a desk / By a naugahyde chair" ("Brown Shoes Don't Make It" [*Absolutely Free*]).

You Are What You Is

A dream of eggplant or zucchini may produce fresh desires. Some fruits are vegetables.

—Harryette Mullen, *S*PeRM**K*T*

The title song of Zappa's 1981 album, *You Are What You Is*, transposes his food-related concerns onto the domain of race and identity politics. It describes the behavior of two "foolish young men" who are confused about the racial stereotypes they should adopt in order to feel better about themselves. They both believe that they can become the other by changing their eating habits. One of them is a black guy who "devotes his life / to become a caucasian". He stops eating pork and greens—thereby reducing the risk of flatulence and opting for the low-fat diet promoted by mainstream white culture—and "trade[s] his dashiki / for some Jordache jeans". The other character, by contrast, is

> A foolish young man
> From a middle class fam'ly
> Started singin' the blues
> 'Cause he thought it was manly

The white musician's adoption of black mannerisms and fascination with the romanticized street credibility of the negro hipster has influenced the whole history of rock 'n roll and jazz. In "You Are What You Is", the young man's attempts to eat chitlins and talk the black talk in order to escape from the narrow, constipating confines of his white middleclass education are doomed to failure, and he only succeeds in making himself ridiculous by sounding like the Kingfish from the Amos 'n Andy show (who, as we know, provided the inspiration for the idiolect developed by Zappa in the Broadway operetta, *Thing Fish*). He thinks "he's got / de whole than down" but is completely devoid of any historical consciousness and does not understand the significance of chitlins as a cultural stereotype rooted in the history of slavery (slaves had to eat parts of animals that others did not want, such as pig intestines, fat back, and pigs' feet). Finally, the aspiring "White Negro's" conclusion that "chitlins taste like candy" takes us back to the deliberate confusion between the sweet and the salty discussed later in connection with Beefheart's "Neon Meate Dream of a Octafish".[4] Zappa's "Call Any Vegetable" also insists on the necessity of distinguishing between sugar and salt, the taste of sweet fruit and that of sour vegetables. Towards the end of the song, Zappa declares:

> A prune is not a vegetable
> Cabbage is a vegetable

To readers of American poetry unfamiliar with Zappa, these lines might well have been taken from the "Food" section of Gertrude Stein's *Tender Buttons*. In fact, Stein's prose poem, "A Substance in a Cushion," begins with the recognition that "sugar is not a vegetable". On a superficial level, Zappa's baroque maximalism appears to have little in common with the serial (cereal?) abstractionism of Stein's *Tender Buttons*. Still, Zappa, who was probably not familiar with Stein, would no doubt have enjoyed the sensuous and visceral humor that characterizes her "cubist" still-life. In the following excerpt from "Breakfast", the rhythms of Stein's prose convey the pleasures of ingestion at the same time as they attempt to pump all the jaded "wornout literary words" (168) out of the reader's stomach and rinse the poet's mouth of the unpleasant taste of stale poetic images and post-Romantic decorum:

> A breeze in a jar and even then silence, a special anticipation in a rack, a gurgle a whole gurgle and more cheese than almost anything, is this an astonishment, does this incline more than the original division between a tray and a talking arrangement and even then a calling into another room gently with some chicken in any way.

("Breakfast"; 183)

Uncannily enough, Stein's "Breakfast" contains a number of key ingredients encountered in Zappa's most bizarre lyrics: the Beckettian "unnamable" jar of "Living in a Jar", the gurgling "voice of cheese" of *Uncle Meat*, the inevitable measuring chicken of "Tengo na Minchia Tanta" and, above all, the "curious breeze" of "Evelyn, A Modified Dog" (*One Size Fits All*). "Evelyn" takes us to the subjects of flatulence, dyspepsia and bad/dog breath in Zappa:

Evelyn, a modified dog
Viewed the quivering fringe of a special doily
Draped across the piano, with some surprise

In the darkened room
Where the chairs dismayed
And the horrible curtains
Muffled the rain
She could hardly believe her eyes

A curious breeze
A garlic breath
Which sounded like a snore
Somewhere near the Steinway (or even from within)
Had caused the doily fringe to waft & tremble in the gloom

Evelyn, a dog, having undergone
Further modification
Pondered the significance of short-person behavior

In pedal-depressed panchromatic resonance
And other highly ambient domains . . .

"Evelyn, a Modified Dog" has something of the picturesque lyricism of a Gilbert and Sullivan operette. The classical solemnity and sentimental rubato stylings of the piano melody are gently parodied by Zappa's crooning vocals which, once they have reached the last stanza, shift to the mock-poetry reading style one encounters, for instance, in the introduction to "Muffin Man". The story of Evelyn is told by a neutral, cerebral narrator who remains unimpressed by the incursion of the irrational snoring and farting noises that emanate from the piano, disturbing an otherwise quiet and respectable setting in a way that is evocative of Edward Gorey's surreal descriptions of Victorian domestic interiors. Typically, Zappa's vision of bourgeois interiors in "Evelyn" gives birth to speculations that alternate between the farcical and the metaphysical—after all, "dog" is the anagram of "god". The title itself recalls the ludic "cynicism" and poodle play of Erik Satie's "Chanson Canine" in "Préludes flasques (Pour un chien)".[5] As for the synaesthetic "curious breeze" which "sound[s] like a snore", it may well have been influenced by the "bubbly, thick stagnant sound, a sound you could smell" (132) of William Burroughs' famous parable on the failed domestication of peristaltic ex-pression, "The Talking Asshole", a piece read by Zappa at the Nova Convention in New York in December 1978.[6]

The "panchromatic resonance" mentioned at the end of the piece would seem to refer to the absence of tonal hierarchy that characterizes some of Zappa's more experimental pieces (Schönberg preferred "pantonality" to "atonality"). More specifically, the "pedal-depressed panchromatic resonance" of "Evelyn, A Modified Dog" takes us back to an episode related in the *Civilization Phaze III* booklet:

> In 1967, we spent about four months recording various projects (*Uncle Meat, We're Only In It For The Money, Ruben and The Jets* and *Lumpy Gravy*) at APOSTOLIC STUDIOS, 53 E. 10th St. NYC. One day I decided to stuff a pair of U-87's in the piano, cover it with heavy drape, put a sand bag on the sustain pedal and invite anybody in the vicinity to stick their head inside and ramble incoherently about the various topics I would suggest to them via talk-back system.
>
> (liner notes; unpag.)

The dialogues later developed into "a vague plot regarding pigs and ponies, threatening the lives of characters who inhabit a large piano". Some of them found their way into the *Lumpy Gravy* album where they were laced with various sound effects, electronic noises and orchestral music. Others provided the basis for the plot of Zappa's posthumous Synclavier opera, *Civilization Phaze III*. This use of the prepared piano as a means of creating a "highly ambient domain" for the recording and transformation of semi-spontaneous dialogue (the heightened reso-nance results from the vibrations of the strings reacting to the sound waves created by the speakers) is only one example of the experimenta-tion with spoken material which has characterized Zappa's work from the orgasmic screaming of "Help I'm a Rock" to the remarkably success-ful close-miking performance on "Cucamonga" or the sophisticated collage of sampled and electronically-processed quotes from the PMRC Senate house hearing in "Porn Wars". More often than not, what these experiments have in common, besides the ever-favored cut-up method and technical treatment of sounds, is a desire to create a documentary narrative of life on the road that moves "beyond mere rock&roll into the dangerous realm of social anthropology" and offers listeners "the chance to participate vicariously in the touring world of the early 1970s" (sleeve notes to *Playground Psychotics*; unpag.). This is particularly true, of course, in such recordings as 200 *Motels*, *Uncle Meat* and *Playground Psychotics*, in which members of the Mothers are responsible for generat-ing their own dialogues around ideas provided by Zappa. The transfor-mation of dialogue into "vocal noises" (*Real* 58) in such tunes as "Help I'm a Rock" and "The Return of the Son of Monster Magnet"—with their revolutionary use of electronics, electric feedback, belching, animal noises, percussions and avant-garde vocals—blurs the institutional line that separates Zappa's freak music from the aesthetics of *musique concrète*, Schönbergian *Sprechgesang*, the sound poetry of Henri Chopin or the hybrid poetico-musical creations of Erik Satie.

Satie is particularly relevant to an analysis of Zappa's music and lyrics, not only because of the "poodle play" aesthetics that inform their respective oeuvres, but also because of the resemblance of Zappa's musi-cal still-lifes to Satie's "musique d'ameublement." Satie's "furniture music," incidentally, also originated in an attempt to transpose the tech-niques of visual arts onto a musical medium, a tendency which also characterizes his "visual scores" or, for that matter, Zappa's own "Black Page" which, like the "black dots" of Satie's "Sports et divertissements", also confers on musical signs a certain degree of autonomy by allowing them to acquire an existence which is independent from the musical codes they seek to materialize.

"Celui qui n'a pas entendu la 'musique d'ameublement'", Satie writes, "ignore le bonheur" ("He who has not heard 'furniture music' does not know happiness"). For Satie, "furniture music" lies outside the domain of art and is "foncièrement industrielle" ("fundamentally industrial")—its main purpose is to "create vibration" and "fulfil the same function as light, heat and comfort in all its forms" (Rey 117). According to Zappa's own recognition of the materiality of music and song, the aim of a musical performance is to "cause air molecules to wiggle" so the musical object can be "detected by the audience's ear" (Zappa, "Air Sculpture" BBC interview). Such are the more positive and creative aspects of the curious breeze that informs and deforms Zappa's musical objects, from the furnished interiors of "Evelyn" to the metaphysical couch of "Sofa".[7] When musical signs are turned into matter, the meanings and moods they express give way to the dream of a material object recharged with energy, a "living thing"—the "vibrations" created by the strings of Zappa's prepared piano in *Civilization Phaze III*, the creation of an "air sculpture" moulded by Zappa's polytonal guitar solos, an evocation of sounds and streams that cluster into an intangible structure liable to be objectised. The fascination with objects, the eroticisation of connections, the transformation of thought and signs into (virtual/fecal) matter: all these aspects of Zappa's poetics belong to an artistic tradition which privileges the need for imaginary constructions of body and mind and promote, in a Situationist fashion, the creative mis-use and mis-consumption of foodstuffs and commodities.

Zappa's "The Torture Never Stops" features one of his most extraordinary "air sculptures." The song takes us into a stinking dungeon of despair full of "flies all green and buzzin'" and prisoners "grumbl[ing] and piss[ing] their clothes". It also features "an Evil Prince" "eat[ing] a steaming pig / in the chamber, right near there":

> He eats the snouts and the trotters first
> The loins and the groins are soon dispersed
> His carving style is well-rehearsed

The proximity of food, torture, sex and death in "Torture" proves an ideal platform for Zappa's improvisational skills.[8] The seemingly endless, distorted convolutions and unfinished lines of Zappa's solo on "The Torture Never Stops" (here I am referring to the 1977 live version on *You Can't Do That On Stage Anymore* Vol.1) evoke the equally tortured visual fantasies of Piranesi's "Carceri d'Invenzione"—despite the impossible perspectives and convulsive patterns built by Terry Bozzio's heavy drumming, Zappa's guitaristic efforts are sufficiently charged with blues energy to prevent the edifice from collapsing. The solo creates a succession of spirals that reverberate up and down the complicated symmetries of the backbone of the piece, its rhythms alternately expanding and relaxing with the pulsive irregularity of a living being stretched out on the rack. Or are they supposed to convey the movements of the Evil Prince's bowels as they attempt to digest the pig snouts and trotters? Or do they respond (or cause) the exaggerated overdubbed orgasmic sounds in the background, which mockingly evoke some cheap S&M ritual? The hypnotic effects of the solo performance (whether Zappa wanted it or not, he had definitely entered the pantheon of rock's most popular guitar heroes by the mid-1970s) are constantly undermined by atonal passages and unpredictable changes of direction. Zappa's use of feedback is also consistently non-hypnotic and sounds as influenced by Varèse's use of sirens (see also the opening movement of "Filthy Habits") as by Hendrix (to whom Zappa once claimed to have introduced to the wah-wah pedal) or the tough blues sound of guitar shredders such as Guitar Slim and Johnny "Guitar" Watson. The guitar's drive and thrust, its promise of unlimited energy and freedom is abruptly brought to an end by a last eructation that leads into the piece's final reprise of the chorus.

Shit or Kitsch?

Does the torture solo close with a climactic *petite mort*? Or with the death of one of the prisoners from overstuffing with guitar notes? Or with another climactic bowel movement bringing the art of the Master Fartist to a logical conclusion? Ben Watson opts for the last possibility when he likens Zappa's solos to peristaltic ex-pression. Commenting on Zappa's "anal licks," he writes:

> Freud associated anal sadism with curiosity, and over the next decade Zappa's guitar frequently sounds as if it is excavating what Joyce—in a pun that links scatology to curiosity about origins and the mother— called "anmal matter".

(327)

Scatological curiosity plays a significant role in Zappa's music, from the sphincteral dark humor of "Charlie's Enormous Mouth," "I Don't Want to Get Drafted" and "Tiny Sick Tears" to the piss experiments

(*Real* 86) of "Let's Make the Water Turn Black", the sinister Freudian lyrics of "Living in a Jar," the incontinent Mammy Nuns of *Thing Fish*, the sodomitic version of "Black Napkins" in *FZ plays the Music of FZ*, the "DUO-DEENUM dribblin's" ingested by the Evil Prince in "The 'Torchum' Never Stops" or the unpalatable schoolboy toilet jokes of the early Zappa/Beefheart collaboration, "Lost in a Whirlpool" which, for all the crudeness and immaturity of the lyrics, serves to remind listeners that "the sexual channels are also the body's sewers" (Bataille 57). If we refer to Milan Kundera's metaphysical interpretation of shit in *The Unbearable Lightness of Being*, an artist's preoccupation with faeces can be seen as an attempt to understand the "abhorrence of excrement" (Dalí quoted in Pauwels 92) that characterizes our society. For Kundera, the Western world's non-acceptance of shit results in *kitsch*, which is itself grounded in a "categorical agreement with being". Not only does the language and iconography of kitsch "exclude everything from its purview which is essentially unacceptable in human existence"; it is also based on the uncritical acceptance and consumption of feelings that "multitudes can share":

> Kitsch may not, therefore, depend on an unusual situation; it must derive from the basic images people have engraved in their memories. The ungrateful daughter, the neglected father, children running on the grass, the motherland betrayed, first love.
>   Kitsch causes two tears to flow in quick succession. The first tear says: How nice to see children running on the grass!
>   The second tear says: How nice to be moved, together with all mankind, by children running on the grass!
>   It is the second tear that makes kitsch kitsch.
>   The brotherhood of man on earth will be possible only on a basis of kitsch.
>
> (251)

Zappa's own crusade against musical and political kitsch displays an awareness of the danger of such a "dictatorship of the heart": emotional kitsch inevitably degenerates into "totalitarian" kitsch, a political space where "a deviation of the collective is a spit in the eye of the smiling brotherhood" (252). To the "tiny sick tears" of Kundera's political kitsch Zappa opposes the aesthetic value of the "Sleep [Eye]Dirt" which provides the ground for one of his most bulimic (and also most melancholy) solos. His refusal of the maudlin and sentimental, of the "second tear that makes kitsch", ("I think one of the causes of bad mental health in the United States is that people have been raised on 'love lyrics'"

[*Real* 89]), his rejection of (white) middle class art as an art of anal repression, his denunciation of "cheese" as a way of life that enables a whole nation to "perpetuate the fiction that it is moral, sane and wholesome" (sleevenotes to *You Are What You Is*) and, finally, his friendship with Vaclav Havel and their common celebration of the end of "communist kitsch" in the Fall of 1991, testify to Zappa's commitment to an aesthetics that works as a response to kitsch's idealization of the quotidian and familiar as well as its promotion of automatized forms of experience and existence.

Later, in *Identity* (1996), Kundera seeks to prove the falseness and worthlessness of kitsch through a (Frank) recognition of the lack of integrity of the human I/eye:

> The eye, the window to the soul; the center of the face's beauty; the point where a person's identity is concentrated; but at the same time an optical instrument that requires constant washing, wetting, maintenance by a special liquid dosed with salt. So the gaze, the greatest marvel man possesses, is regularly interrupted by a mechanical washing action. Like a windscreen washed by a wiper.
>
> (42)

An oral equivalent of this offputting blink might be the licking of the lips as performed by Momma in Captain Beefheart's "Old Fart at Play" when the "fishhead broke the window", surprising her in the kitchen:

> An assortment of observations took place
> Momma licked her lips like uh cat
> Pecked the ground like uh rooster
> Pivoted like a duck

The eyes that we would die for harden into optical automatism and the mouth we have loved and lusted after lubricates its parts not to receive our kisses but to make its next meal easier to swallow. That wet centre of erotic attention, provocative complement of the gaze, becomes a shit factory as we watch, readying itself to render even us, the would-be lover, down into "Lumpy Gravy" (*Lumpy Gravy*). Momma is readying herself, like any cartoon cat, to eat the fishhead, which seems natural enough until we remember that inside the head is "the chatter of the old fart"—the gaseous effluent of a previous meal, excrement's aperitif. Disgusting, then: Momma is about to eat a fart, the end of the process has caught up with the beginning and we are on the verge of coprophilia. With their constant references to food and eating Zappa and Van Vliet turn the tables on kitsch, forcing it to *include* the "unacceptable in human existence", and forcing us to swallow a good dose of what is best for us, culturally and politically. If you are still licking your lips in anticipation of more, then think of the Old Fart whose "excited eyes from within the dark interior glazed, watered in appreciation of his thoughtful preparation".

We are the Mothers and This is What We Sound Like: On the Uses and Abuses of Degenerate Art

What's the Ugliest Part of Your Body?

The centrality of orality and, in particular, dental (and canine) aesthetics to Zappa's work reaches a climax in the cover of the double album *Uncle Meat* (1969), a Cal Schenkel collage comprising, among other things, two juxtaposed sets of teeth. The first belongs to an old man wearing a salt and pepper moustache and whose lips are pulled up by the dentist's forefinger during a check-up. The man appears to possess at least one gold tooth. Next to it, there is a black and white photograph of a set of false teeth. The lower part of the front cover features another series of apparently broken or damaged teeth glued to some mixture of paint, bread crumbs (which may or may not be the "dried muffin remnants"[1] of the artist's breakfast) and other unidentifiable organic material. The back cover features polarized photographs of the members of the Mothers of Invention as well as three x-ray slides of teeth and a skull bearing the inscription "1348", the year of the first outbreak of bubonic Plague in Europe. The gatefold sleeve features a girl lying (and apparently posing) in an early 20th century dentist's chair on which Schenkel has glued a photograph of a dentist's x-ray machine.

In his illuminating sub-chapter on *Uncle Meat*, Ben Watson discusses the political significance of dental continuity in Zappa, a concern that traverses his oeuvre from the menacing overtones of "Hungry Freaks Daddy" on *Freak Out* to the blown-up rotten teeth on the cover of the posthumous *Everything Is Healing Nicely* (1999). Drawing upon an anecdote told by Lowell George, who was a member of the Mothers of Invention before he left to form Little Feat in 1970, Watson traces the roots of Zappa's "dental continuity" to the reification of the body by the Nazi regime:

> Lowell George enters dental continuity because of his part in a semi-improvised pantomime.
> "The albums I'm featured on most prominently haven't been released yet. There was a ten-album set in the works—one side had me as a German border-guard interviewing each of the band members, asking them about the condition of their gold fillings and things like that."
> This points to the reduction of the human body to an object by the Nazis, the notorious piles of gold teeth removed from victims' mouths before they were sent to the gas chambers. That this is not merely an historical outrage is shown by the fact that the banks that handled such loot are still in operation today. That human beings are not composed of pure spirit is of course emphasized by using *Meat* as a name. . . . The grubby fingers that pull away the lips of the old Jew in order to see if there is gold worth preserving before he is exterminated, extracting the element of exchange value before the subject is disposed of, finds an analogy in the X-ray machine, which also sees past lips and cheek to the teeth.
>
> (137)

The industrialization of death. The rationalization of mass extermination into the banality of an economic transaction. The baring of the teeth that permits the extraction of the gold performed in a grotesque caricature of the technical gesture of the dentist. The threatening quality of the record cover is reinforced by the Gothic letters in which the title of the album is inscribed. The reference to 1348 reemerges in the song "Dog Breath, In the Year of the Plague," which suggests that the illustrations were, at least to some extent, the result of a collaboration between Zappa and Schenkel. In addition to evoking the commodification of bodies in Nazi Germany, the themes of death and dentistry that pervade the cover of *Uncle Meat* also alert us to the huge symbolic potential of teeth extraction in Western culture. The stealing of the golden teeth of the Jewish victims evokes other forms of physical exploitation of the human body, such as that of the lower classes who, like Fantine in Victor Hugo's *Les Misérables*, were encouraged to sell their teeth to the rich in the 18th and 19th centuries, at a time when "live transplants" were in vogue (Feher Vol. 3 56).

The equation of dental with moral corruption in the popular and artistic imagination is also widely documented. In precontemporary iconography, the extraction of teeth often amounts to the extraction of evil and sin from the conscience of man. The consumption of sugar in 19th century Holland was repeatedly denounced by preachers and one of them, Abraham a Sancta Clara, went as far as retracing the root of rotten teeth to original sin: "We unfortunate humans! We all have tootache and suffer ever and always from the teeth with which Adam bit the forbidden apple" (31). In a similar register, the quack dentist and his patient who feature in the central panel of Bosch's Haywain triptych confers to the dental symbolism a religious dimension by associating bad teeth with a battery of deadly sins. As David Kunzle suggests, the association of toothache and guilt has survived into our own century: "in the past, tootache was regarded as a punishment for sexual guilt; and today, medical science warns us that tooth decay is the result of our excessive indulgence in the sweet things of life" (Feher Vol. 1 29).

For some XXth century artists, the visual representation of teeth becomes a means of articulating a politics of the body. Pablo Picasso's "Weeping Woman" (1937) lays the foundation of a radical poetics of the face, one which emphasizes the edges and lines of force of a being stretched between representation and abstraction. A couple of decades after the explosions of the battlefield, an exploded mosaic of forms acts out the centrifugal disappearance of the corporeal envelope dismembered by the painter's analytical gaze. In Karl Hubbuch's "Beim Arzt" (1930), the distortion of the mouth and the nose, the disruption of the natural rhythm of the eyebrows, lips and eyelids result in an involuntary grimace that defies the general principle of symmetrical organization of the face. As in the more recent enlarged pulled lips and pinched cheeks of Bruce Nauman or, for that matter, the carnivorous cover art of Zappa's *Everything Is Healing Nicely*—which presents a blown-up picture representing what appears to be Zappa's irregular teeth, darkened with coffee and tobacco deposits that the most powerful kind of dental floss could never remove—the distorted body becomes an alien landscape, its protuberances and cavities the site of countless visual divagations and speculations. Hubbuch's fascination with the structures of the face was shared by numerous other painters of the *Neue Sachlichkeit*, a movement which saw the light in the 1920s and was catalogued as "degenerate" art on the occasion of the first exhibition of *Entartete Kunst* organized in Karlsruhe (Hubbuch's home town) by the local Nazi party in 1933. For Hubbuch, as for many other German artists and writers of the same period, the patient's bad, uneven teeth are a metaphor for the more general feeling of psychological and moral decay that characterized the Weimar republic. Whereas Thomas Mann consistently treats carious teeth as a symbol of decadence and existential maladjustment,[2] the main character of Günter Grass's novel, *Local Anaesthetic* (1969), is a history teacher who is caught between two radically different attitudes to the "treatment" of the social and political decay brought about by capitalism. The first point of view is that of one of his radical Marxist students who advocates the use of violence as the only viable form of political action. The second is characterized by the dentist's distrust of radical politics and his preference for moderate reform and prophylactic medicine, a tendency manifested by his unrelenting attempts to remove his patient's tartar as so many layers of "petrified hate" (32).

Grass's novel returns Zappologists to a central dilemma surrounding Zappa's politics. In the late sixties, Zappa had acquired a strong reputation as a cultural agitator and naturally attracted the sympathy of the new left. A concert the Mothers played in Munich on September 9, 1968, was interrupted by a group of leftist students who wanted the band to make a statement against capitalism and urge their followers to burn down a nearby American Forces base. Zappa refused, and years after the incident—which inspired the song "Holiday in Berlin" included in *Burnt Weeny Sandwich*—continued to consider direct revolutionary action as useless and naive, thereby making himself unpopular with many post-1968 militants. According to Michael Gray's biography, in 1967 Zappa was even dumped by his then girlfriend, Pamela Zarubica, at the end of the Mothers of Invention's European tour because she felt that he could not really live up to the subversive potential of his music and satisfy all the people who looked to him for answers to the political problems of the age (Gray 86). When Zappa met President Vaclav Havel in Prague more than twenty years later, he had definitively opted for the prophylactic politics of Grass's dentist and was talking of putting the dynamics of capitalism and free entreprise to the service of the post-Communist Republic of Czechoslovakia. At the end of *The Real Frank Zappa Book*, Zappa goes as far as defining himself as a "practical conservative", a rather dubious term describing a "libertarian" attitude advocating "smaller, less intrusive government, and lower taxes" (315). As long as people keep confusing avant-garde art with revolutionary politics, Zappa's music will continue to be misunderstood by leftists and conservatives alike. As we have seen and will see, the specific contribution Zappa made to revolutionary aesthetics is not geared towards practical politics but, rather, towards the creation of imaginary objects and the depiction of abstract forms of behavior that seek to reveal and subsequently ridicule the hidden eccentricities, perversions and depravities of his contemporaries. Such manifestations of the repellent and the abject create a space where degenerate art meets slapstick comedy, where the self-consciously *entartet* spirit allies itself with the confectionery terrorism of the Belgian *entarteur*.

It is not by chance that Zappa, Schenkel, Mann and the New Objectivists privilege similar themes and techniques in their denunciation of the atrocities and hypocrisies of their times. For all of them, ugliness becomes an ideological tool against both aesthetic and political kitsch, whether it manifests itself in the idealized Germany of Hans Thoma or in the Norman Rockwellian vision of white middle class America. Like Georg Grosz and others before him, Zappa is determined to tell it like it is and tries to convince the whole world that it is, to quote Grosz, "sick, ugly and deceitful" (Michalski 27). The twisted and degenerate aesthetics of Grosz, Dix and Schlichter—with their sickly prostitutes, mutilated soldiers and cretinoid businessmen—stood as a rebuttal of the healthy, classical nudes of Arno Brecker and, more generally, the celebration of the athletic body in Nazi Germany. From the dirty, crazy Mothers of the *Freak Out* album to the Aunt Jemima checkered napkin-wearing Mammy Nuns of *Thing Fish*, Zappa's new version of degenerate art results in a Cabinet of Abnormalities peopled with fetishist maniacs, bubbleheaded groupies, sinister pimps, dysfunctional robots, corrupted politicians and sex-crazed televangelists.

The Air

In order to locate the origin of Zappa's interest in the aesthetics and politics of the body, we now turn to what Ben Watson describes as the composer's "horror and fascination for the structures beneath the face" (138), an obsession which can be accounted for by his childhood experiences of dentistry and experimental sinus treatment:

> Along with my earaches and asthma, I had sinus trouble. There was some "new treatment" for this ailment being discussed in the neighborhood. It involved stuffing *radium* into your sinus cavities. (Have you ever heard of this?) My parents took me to yet another Italian doctor, and, although I didn't know what they were going to do to me, it didn't sound like it was going to be too much fun. The doctor had a long wire thing—maybe a foot or more, and on the end was a pellet of radium. He stuffed it up my

nose and into my sinus cavities on both sides. (I should probably check if my handkerchief is glowing in the dark.)

(*Real* 20)

In the same passage from *The Real Frank Zappa Book*, Zappa also mentions the tanks of mustard gas that were located near his family home in Edgewood, Maryland, and comments that "mustard gas explodes the vessels in your lungs, causing you to *drown in your own blood*" (21). The fear of internal biological collapse caused by the irritating and poisonous properties of mustard gas return us to the atrocities of the First World War which fueled the spirit of outrage, subversion and negation of Dada, including the aesthetics of *Merzkunst* and sound poetry that prefigures the "noisy primitivism" (Tzara 4) of Schenkel's and Zappa's visual and phonic collages. But Zappa's anecdote, like Thomas Mann's description of "pleura-shock" discussed in Chapter Four of this book, also alerts us to the possibility of *witnessing* the changes taking place within the body, in this case the gradual transformation of one's insides into an amorphous puddle of putrefied organs and tissues. A modern equivalent of Marsyas contemplating the transformation of his body into a "large, continu'd wound".[3] Or Michelangelo's Saint Bartholomew holding the grotesque remnants of his skin-suit. The torture never stops.

In the domain of modern aesthetics, the exploration of the human body from the inside was greatly facilitated by radiography, an invention whose impact on the history of contemporary art is relatively undocumented. In a recent essay entitled "Impossible Anatomy," Jean Clair, explaining how the discovery of x-rays affected the history of painting, writes that the advent of x-ray technology divided contemporary artists into two categories according to their ways of representing the skull:

> . . . a clear-cut line was created between those who continued to portray the skull in the traditional way, as if x-rays had never been discovered, and those whose work takes account of the radical semantic and iconographical revolution they implied. The dividing line sometimes cuts unexpectedly, with "moderns" falling on the side they are not usually placed on. Thus Ensor and Cézanne emerge as traditionalist and outmoded, since they continue to use the *calvarium* as an accessory of Wordly Vanities. Munch and Duchamp, on the other hand, are modern. Looking forward to us, they explore the interiority of the body and its properties. The skeletal arm of the former, the jawbone of the latter, have

a harsh resonance. We are faced with a sort of clinical report, whereas
Ensor and Cézanne remain hostages to the romantic vignette.

(Brusatin xxvii)

By drawing attention to the power of abstraction of the x-ray machine
and the relationship between clinical and artistic practice, Clair's analysis recalls Benjamin's remark that the analytical vision of the body
afforded by the movies, which "promotes the mutual penetration of art
and science," also applies to radiography, which also proceeds by
abstraction and isolation and demonstrates "the identity of the artistic
and scientific uses of photography" by allowing objects and bodies to be
"analysed much more precisely and from more points of view than
those presented on paintings or on the stage" (Frascina 303). Clair's
reference to the *calvarium* returns us to the black and white skull on the
cover of *Uncle Meat* which is less a remnant of the ancestral tradition of
the memento mori than a proof of Zappa's and Schenkel's commitment
to a method that puts the grotesque and the macabre to the service of
an art that considers the body as the site of endless aesthetic and
psychological negotiations.[4]

Of course, the practice of dissection provided visual artists with other
ways of gaining access to the inner structures of living organisms long
before Röntgen's discovery of x-rays in 1895. Michelangelo himself reput-
edly sneaked into hospital rooms to perform dissections of the human
body, flaying cadavers in order to study the complexity of human
anatomy, defying the edicts of the Church in a gesture of frantic dese-
cration. His Saint Bartholomew is holding a stretched out human skin
to symbolize his martyrdom; he is also holding the knife used by his
torturers in flaying him alive. Michelangelo painted his own face into
the dead skin, probably in order to exhibit to everyone his growing
pessimism and fatigue after several years (1508–1512) spent on his back
seventy feet above the ground, painting over three hundred figures on
the curved ceiling of the Sistine Chapel. The art of dissection provided
Michelangelo with numerous anatomical models, and it probably also
influenced the philosophical and theological foundations of his work. In
an article entitled, "An interpretation of Michelangelo's Creation of
Adam Based on Neuroanatomy," Frank Meshberger directs our attention
to the striking similarities between Michelangelo's God and a mid-sagit-
tal view of the human brain. Was Michelangelo trying to represent God
as a huge brain bestowing intellect on man? Was he trying to reconcile
science and religion, matter and spirit, by evoking the return of the
human soul to its godly origin? Or did the artist simply mean to pay trib-

ute to the as yet unsung beauty of nerve tissue, pineal glands and corpora calosa?

Contemporary examples of such intersections between art and dissection abound, from the anatomical mannequin standing among the semi-human figures of Rudolf Schlichter's "Dada Dachatelier" (ca. 1920) to Frida Kahlo's esoteric self-portraits, stripping away the layers of flesh to reveal the wounds inflicted by illness and disillusionment ("The Two Fridas"; 1939). More recently, Professor Günter Van Hagens performed the first public autopsy in London. The procedure took place before a live audience and television cameras in the Atlantis Gallery with the Professor dressed in the garb of Josef Beuys. Still, the specific influence of radiography on contemporary art lies not merely in its capacity to violate the opacity of man and reveal the inside workings of the body—rather, what is at stake here is the promise it holds of capturing the invisible and giving birth to the "non-retinal" art dear to Duchamp and his followers, an art prefigured by Munch's "Self-Portrait with Elbow"(1895) and which paved the way for many later works such as Robert Rauschenberg's "Booster" (1967), which, like Schenkel's *Uncle Meat* collage, comprises a complete body reconstructed from a series of x-rays surrounded with washed-out magazine photographs and reproductions of technical instruments. Finally, it is a similar impulse that led Mona Hatoum to explore the body through endoscopic means, using the joint media of art and science to gain access to what Paul Valéry once called the Third Body, that which "has unity only in our thought" since "to know it is to have reduced it to parts and pieces . . . elements of varying sizes, fashioned so as to fit exactly in place: sponges, vessels, tubes, fibers, articulated rods . . . " (Feher Vol. 3 400).

Tight Butts and White Jazz

Before returning to Zappa's facial poetics, we now turn to his general treatment of the theme of ugliness as it expresses itself in his more "sociological" lyrics. In songs such as "Beauty Knows No Pain" and "I'm A Beautiful Guy" Zappa equates the cult of the body with the false pretenses of white upper-middle class culture and repeatedly opposes himself to the totalitarian claims of the fashion industry which, by diverting people's attention away from politics to the realms of sport and entertainment, contributes to a system that values form over content, surface over depth, passive consumption over creative action.

"I'm A Beautiful Guy" derides the efforts of joggers to lose weight and tighten their butts, a theme also developed by Zappa in his instrumental illustration of "youthening" trends on "Beat the Reaper" from the album *Civilization Phaze III*. The following lines are sung to a particularly banal and bloodless jazzy tune—probably the kind of watered-down jazz the white, water-drinking yuppie joggers listen to when they go back to their flats after indulging in their favorite sport:

They're drinking lighter
They're full of water
I hear them say:
"Let's jog . . ."
They're playing tennis
Their butts are tighter
What could be *whiter*?
Hey?

In a civilization where the dialectics of the sweet-sexy and the salt-sexy has been replaced by low-calorie sugar substitues and salt without sodium, in a world where politics, fashion and advertising are increasingly difficult to distinguish from one another—and where jogging in public has become one of the most powerful self-advertising gimmicks developed by prominent politicians to radiate an image of healthiness and reassuring normality—Zappa's lyrics acquire a special significance. Like Kundera, Zappa believes that beauty is first and foremost a political lie, and "Beauty Knows No Pain" logically leads into a sequence of songs dealing with what lies underneath that lie and analyzing the most unsavory aspects of life in modern America, including the adoption of lifestyles based on racial stereotypes ("You Are What You Is"), disco dancing as organized mass-entertainment (the Adornoite "Mudd Club",[5] not to mention the related songs "Dancing Fool" and "Disco Boy"), fast food diet habits ("Conehead"), televangelist crooks and religious fanatics ("The Meek Shall Inherit Nothing"; "Dumb All Over"; "Heavenly Bank Account"), and drug abuse ("Charlie's Enormous Mouth"; "Any Downers").

The near-moralistic "Cocaine Decisions," from the album *The Man from Utopia* (1983), is emblematic of Zappa's aesthetics of abjection in its ruthless analysis of his contemporaries' strategies of mis- or over-consumption. It is probably Zappa's most direct and bitter indictment of the drug culture, an aspect of his work which firmly separates him from the rest of the world of alternative music. Zappa's strict anti-drugs rules when working with the Mothers of Invention must be understood both as a rejection of the superficial mores and deadening habits of the "plastic" hippies ("Flower Punk" [*We're Only In It for the Money*]) and the realization that his most complex compositions could only be rehearsed and performed efficiently through the use of tightly disciplined working methods. By contrast, "Cocaine Decisions" presents the ingestion of cocaine as an activity that underlines the user's place in a logic of consumption geared towards material success (the success that results from a higher efficiency at work) and thereby reveals his absolute conformism and conservatism in a world dominated by the pressures of mercantilism and corporate interests.[6] In the Reaganite 1980s, the "plastic people" ridiculed in the early Mothers albums are indeed replaced by the "EXPENSIVE UGLINESS" of "high class" people who "fly to Acapulco / Where all their friends go" ("Cocaine Decisions"), "junior executives all in a row" ("Planet of the Barytone Women"), brainless yuppies and anorexic talk-show hostesses ("Any Kind of Pain").

"Charlie's Enormous Mouth," another song about drug abuse, conveys the absurdities of a life rendered meaningless by the pursuit of sex, money and the cheap ecstasies of the heavy drug user or compulsive dancer. Zappa's absurdist lyrics introduce us to various parts of Charlie's cocaine-wasted body which are reduced to the impersonal tasks and uses they serve to fulfill. His description of Charlie's body as a snorting, eating and sucking machine once more evokes Kundera and Burroughs and their recognition of the lack of wholeness of the human body and the mechanical "washing and wetting" that maintains the equilibrium of physiological functions.[7] Like Joyce in *Ulysses*, Zappa writes of the ungodly condition of man in terms that evoke the peristaltic doom of a creature whose life is controlled by chemical and mechanical processes over which it has very little control:

> Charlie's enormous mouth, well, it's awright
> The girl got a very large mouth, but it's awright
> She got lips all around the hole
> Where she puts her food in
> They call it THE MOUTH
> They call it THE MOUTH
> They call it THE MOUTH

and we stuffing food in one hole and out behind: food, chyle, blood dung, earth, food: have to feed it like stoking an engine.

(Ulysses 145)

The song ends with the girl's death after one last OD. As she enters her final hole, her body is gulped down into the earth, covered with the dirt that her friends have thrown into the grave. Charlie's death is a rather untragic one, and it can only arouse mockery or disgust. The friends who encouraged her to take "an extra hit" the night before and "were terribly excited while they / Watched her doin' it" complain that they need their "downers" and quickly leave the sphincteral ritual of the funeral to go back home and watch TV.

In an earlier piece such as "The Air", the anatomical inventiveness of Zappa's lyrics invites us to consider the futility of considering the body as the locus of integrity and individual freedom. Like the "airholes from which breath should come" described by Van Vliet before the Old Fart's wooden mask melts into an "intricate rainbow trout replica," the first part of "The Air"[8] stands as a cross between Tzara's vision of the body in *The Gas Heart* (where body parts such as a Mouth, an Eye, a Nose and a Neck acquire an independent existence and become actors in their own right) and the compulsive talking mouth of Beckett's *Not I*. Somehow, the sadness that emanates from Zappa's lyrics is increased by the imbecilic doo-wop melody of the song. What remains is a wheezing organism feeding on air, ex-pressing words that only signify the emptiness that lies behind a mask of flesh and bones. The theme of the body as an empty shell, also adumbrated in Michelangelo's Saint Bartholomew, gives way to a laughable (non-)self, an abstract body that is reduced to the impersonal, mechanical process that keeps it alive. Zappa's insane and compulsive rhyming suggests a mind which, like the body, is emptying itself and regressing, to some pre-human phase of existence characterized by rampant pilosity and phonetic idiocy:

The air
Escaping from your mouth
The hair
Escaping from your nose
My heart
Escaping from the craping
And the shaping
Of the draping
. . .

The air
Escaping from your pits
The hair
Escaping from my teeth

Grown So Ugly

We cannot close this sub-chapter on buccal aesthetics without discussing the most powerful facial icon associated with Zappa throughout his career: the now legendary mustache and goatee. Unlike Dalí, who saw his mustache as a protection against the outside world and a direct extension of his paranoid politics and aesthetics,[9] Zappa apparently never sought to consciously ascribe a particular function to his facial hair. The disfiguring of Mona Lisa by Zappa's moustache in a famous 1970 poster advertising a Mothers of Invention show in Boston may nonetheless provide us with a clue as to the way Zappa's pilosity has been received by his audience. Such a facile remake of Duchamp's "L.H.O.O.Q." (1919) may seem trivial at first, and yet, it is one of the first direct reference to the spirit of Dada in the context of Zappa's career, a tradition Zappa inevitably finds himself associated with despite his general indifference to genres, schools and movements, avant-gardist and otherwise.[10] Leonardo's painting has been done and redone by dozens of Dada-inspired artists from Dalí's "Self-Portrait as Mona Lisa" (1954) to Andy Warhol's serial prints. The Mona Lisa poster logically places Zappa in a line of artists that runs from Duchamp to Cornell and Jorn and beyond, one that celebrates the art of disfiguring the familiar in order to project the image of the artist's desires and neuroses onto the world of objects.[11] While Duchamp's "L.H.O.O.Q." was intended to ridicule the bourgeois idolatry of Renaissance art (rather than Leonardo's painting in itself), the disfiguring of classical art objects also has the effect of making them indigestible or unusable, thereby embodying Benjamin's interest in the "liberation of things from the curse of being useful" (Miklitsch 15). As we have seen and will see, one of the great merits of Zappa's art is precisely its capacity to interfere with the perception of the world as a single unified vision, enabling us to consider a given object, detail or composition in a way that does justice to the endless perceptual shifts of maximalist praxis. The creative misuse of traditional art forms in Zappa's music and lyrics is, as we have seen, apparent not only in his treatment of everyday objects but also in numberless acts of parody, satire and quotation, the sum of which tends to blur accepted boundaries between popular culture and the avant-garde.[12]

But the symbolic function of Zappa's mustache is not limited to its potential for maximalist defamiliarization. Responding to a journalist asking him when he decided to grow a mustache, Zappa evaded the question and declared: "I have to trim my mustache because if I don't, about every three or four days it grows into my mouth and I wind up eating my mustache along with my food."[13] Unsurprisingly, Zappa's idio-syncratic pilosity once again finds its place in the dialectics of organic growth and oral consumption explored in other parts of this book. The threat of autophagy is real since Zappa the Cannibal not only absorbs and satirizes past and current musical styles but also delights in a constant, self-parodic reworking and recycling of favorite themes from his own repertoire. His Project/Object seems to continually feed off itself, recycling, reproducing itself in an endless series of re-releases and alternate versions which are themselves, to a large extent, the result of Zappa's crusade against bootleggers and the anarchic consumption of his music.[14] (The appearance of posthumous releases of Zappa's music and the recent trademarking of the celebrated "moustache" by the Zappa Family Trust adds another, retrospective twist to the artist's life-long struggle with the dialectics of consumption and rejection.)[15] Zappa's autophagous methods are unconsciously captured by David B. McMacken's cover illustration for the album *Overnite-Sensation* (1973) which features a baroque whirl of mutually absorbing intestinal gargoyles creating a contemporary equivalent of the visceral energy of Bosch's paintings of Hell or the promiscuous gluttony of Pieter Breughel's "The Big Fish Eat the Little Fish" (discussed in more detail below). As always, the crucial factor in the creation of such grotesque imagery is the confusion of the comic and the repellent, the humorous and the terrifying—a method often encountered in Zappa's visual and musical imagination, from the Sadian blues of "The Torture Never Stops" to the squeaking trombone sounds and Synclavier-generated whining, gulping and grunting samples of "When Yuppies Go to Hell," on the live album *Make A Jazz Noise Here* (1991).

The Unpalatable Truth

Tout passera par sa bouche, Marin s'en fait le serment. Il devra d'abord
digérer le monde avec sa salive afin de le rendre visible et limpide.

—Eugène Savitzkaya, *Marin mon cœur*

Peter Greenaway's *The Cook, The Thief, His Wife and Her Lover* explores the
connections between political power[16] and the imperatives of food and
sex (and food sex).[17] For Greenaway's dictator-thief, food is a way of
asserting his authority over his wife and partners by stuffing them with
delicacies in order to prevent them from mouthing the unpalatable
truth. "A good cook puts unlikely things together", says the thief—like
duck meat and orange, or ham and pineapples. The oxymoronic potency
of bittersweet food is equated with the apex of good taste. But it also
signifies the ultimate form of violence that lurks beneath the varnish of
cultural refinement in a world in which every civilized gesture becomes
an act of barbarism. The multiplication of foodstuffs, the seemingly
endless banquets and the infinite refinement of the French chef's
cuisine is only the aestheticized background against which the most
atrocious crimes are perpetrated: "Eating is in the form of the Fall"
(Brown 167). A Wordsworthian parable on the loss of childhood innocence, Greenaway's film would seem to offer two possible remedies
against the political and moral corruption of the adult world. One can
be found in spirituality and a return to the innocence of childhood
through the power of religious ritual and song (the young apprentice, a
"growing Boy" who has not yet lost his capacity to "[behold] the light,
and whence it flows," sings: "purge me with Hyssop and I shall be
clean").[18] The other is a materialist recognition of the transiency of
human feelings which recommends "a bottle of gin to make you forget
what you ate for lunch". In Zappa's dirty blues rock idiom, this gets
translated into a narrative of regression, incontinence and animality:

> I went to the country,
> And while I was gone,
> I lost control of my body functions,
> On a roller-headed lady's front lawn.
> I'm so ashamed, but I'm a wino man and I can't help myself.
>
> I been drinkin' all night 'til my eyes got red.
> Stumbled on the gutter and busted my head.
> Bugs in my zoot suit have me scratchin' like a dog.
> Can't stand no water, and I stink like a hog.[19]

More often than not, the lives of Greenaway's characters are also reduced to the mechanical transit between the dining and drinking room and the bathroom, which, incidentally, is where most of the illicit sex takes place in the film. The association of food, sex, scatology and murder in *The Cook* . . . reaches an intensity unparalleled since Rimbaud's "Young Glutton," a little-known gem from the *Album zutique* which deserves to be quoted in full. The image of the ivory-pricked child sticking out his tongue at a pear like a chameleon trying to catch a fly creates a very strange atmosphere, to say the least:

> Silk cap,
> ivory prick,
> Clothes very black,
> Paul eyes the cupboard,
> Sticks his tongue out at a pear,
> prepares
> Wand & diarrhoea.[20]

Like the greedy child of Erik Satie's "Almond Chocolate Waltz,"[21] the chocolate syrup-coated girl in Zappa's "Brown Shoes Don't Make It," (*Absolutely Free*) or the little boys and little girls of Beefheart's "Sugar Bowl," (*Unconditionally Guaranteed*) Rimbaud's young glutton sums up the mysterious process that takes human beings into a realm of infinite *jouissance* where the use-value of food is divorced from the act of eating and transposed onto another, more abstract level. Greenaway's film is full of such symbolic displacements that convert food into an intellectual fetish. About halfway through the movie, we learn, for example, that one of the reasons why the French cook's cuisine is so popular is because it includes all kinds of black ingredients:

> "I charge a lot for anything black—grapes, olives, blackcurrants. People like to remind themselves of death—eating black food is like consuming death—like saying—ha, ha, Death!—I'm eating you."

Both within and outside the phantasmagorical universe of Greenaway's films, one way of exorcising death is of course through the pursuit of sex and the experience of the *petite mort* which both anticipates and symbolically postpones our final demise. But for the cook's clients, these "insatiable consumers of matter" (Valéry quoted in Feher Vol. 3 395), it is food that fulfils this essential life-affirming function. Black food also takes us in the direction of coprophilia, for the ingestion of caviar, black truffles, and olives provides one with the certainty that one can rehearse (and mock) not only the physical conditions of the inexorable putrescence and decay of the body but also the latter's ominous pre-mortem incarnation in the form of excrement. As the thief himself puts it, "how do I care—it all comes out as shit in the end." In Zappa's favorite movie, Terry Gilliam's *Brazil*, the plumber played by Robert De Niro drowns in his own excrement—his faeces become symbolical of the inevitable degradation of human cells which transforms dead body tissue into fertilizing matter. According to Bataille's notion of "heterology", excrement is the difference that must be expelled from the same in order for the same to remain the same. Shit becomes the condition for homogeneity which itself guarantees the illusion of wholeness of both the body and the body-politic (in which physical excretion is replaced by sacrificial rituals). The critic Clive Bloom offers a similar interpretation of the products of defecation as an ambivalent sign of presence and absence, identity and alterity. The scatological aesthetics of Rimbaud and Greenaway display a tendency to adress the issue of the emotional and ontological stability of the ego in a way that anticipates the dialectics of the inside-out as dramatized by Zappa's Didgeridoo Woman in *The Yellow Shark*, whom we discuss in Chapter Four:

> The products of defilement, products of our bodies, yet now unassimilable and alien, undermine our identity by their presence as both not-us and us. They take on a *ritualistic* and *totemic* symbolism determined by questions of what is clean/dirty, what is I/not-I, what is inside/outside. The jettisoned objects of the body map the collapse of the stable ego, clearly demonstrating its fragility.
>
> (Clive Bloom quoted in Punter 164)

There are a number of superficial similarities between Greenaway's *The Cook . . .* and Pasolini's *Salo, or the 120 Days of Sodom*, especially as regards their treatment of sadism, debauchery and gluttony as the gateway to power. Still, Greenaway's scenario does not lead into the coprophilic rituals of Pasolini's film,[22] which plunges the eater and the eaten into a tragical farce of self-consumption. For both Sade and Pasolini, the consumption of excrement was a way of encouraging the somatic internalization of oneself and of inscribing the body in a closed circuit of production and consumption. For Greenaway, it is above all through the maximalization of the senses, and the sense of taste in particular, that one seeks to conjure away the fear of death. In this, Greenaway's thief is very much like the protagonist of Marcel Moreau's *La vie de Jéju*,[23] which presents the following description of a man "observ[ing] his own meat" for the purpose of determining the conditions in which death can be deferred through a heightened awareness and appreciation of the life-affirming virtues of sensual experience.

> This man can be seen inspecting his own meat, looking for the first shivers, the first sign of agitation, the first itching sensations. As soon as he becomes hungry or thirsty, as soon as he gets an erection or begins to lick, chew, devour, he no longer wants to die. . . Death is what is no longer tactile, or tasty.
>
> (261)

Characteristically, the tingling, itching sensations afforded by physical nature and instinct are opposed to the literal and metaphorical tastelessness of the domesticated life. For Moreau, the question of death can only be exorcised and obliterated through the perpetuation of identity that results from a constant attention to one's own bodily functions.

Arcimboldo's Dream

Greenaway's film culminates in a failed cannibalistic ceremony which attempts to combine the forces of Eros and Thanatos through the catalytic virtues of French cuisine. The ritual is interrupted by the execution of the thief, who is shot by his wife after refusing to eat her dead lover's roasted genitals. The eater and the eaten are once again caught in a vicious circle, a perverted narrative equivalent to Arcimboldo's "Cook" (ca. 1570), a visual palindrome which can can be seen alternately as the cook's head and a plate full of roasted meat. Arcimboldo's collage of dead matter—a still-life ("nature morte") in the literal sense—embodies a more modern continuation of Breughel's infernal chain of ingestion and regurgitation, a pre-postmodern *trompe l'oeil* based on a playful recognition of the interdependency of figure and ground.[24]

But in the context of our exagmination of Zappa's visual imagination, it is to Arcimboldo's allegory of "Water" (1563–64) that we must now turn. In "Ship Arriving to Late to Save a Drowning Witch" Zappa describes an amphibious creature with "sardines in her eyebrows" and "lobsters up and down her forehead," an image which cannot but evoke Arcimboldo's painting, with its lobsters crawling up and down the figure's hair and breast, his crayfish eyebrows and his flying fish ears, lips like a dead shark. Arcimboldo's "Water" is full of monstrous excrescences, a disordered proliferation of asymmetrical discontinuous forms transgressing the boundaries that separate the human and the inhuman. In Zappa's composition, the organic orvergrowth of Arcimboldo's painting finds its musical expression in the polymorphous structure of the piece which is full of unexpected flurries and nervous complexities. A polyrhythmic fugue for the masses following the logic of a monster movie plot about industrial pollution, "Ship Arriving Too Late . . ." emerges as one of the most powerful representations of the amphibian mind since H.P. Lovecraft's "Shadow over Innsmouth" or Captain Beefheart's *Trout Mask Replica* (which was actually a carp's head bought by Cal Schenkel from a local fish shop [Barnes 108]).[25] Zappa's "drowning witch" captures the essence of the grotesque which, according to Wolfgang Kayser, creates:

> a world in which the realm of inanimate things is no longer separated from those of plants, animals, and human beings, and where the laws of statics, symmetry, and proportion are no longer valid . . . the sphere in which the dissolution of reality and the participation in a different kind of existence, as illustrated by the ornamental grotesques, form an experience about the nature and significance of which mankind has never ceased to ponder.
>
> (Thomson 24)

The deliberate distortion of symmetry and proportion, the fight between closed and open forms dramatized by Zappa's and Arcimboldo's compositions enact what Barthes has described as the "malaise of matter" (*Obvie* 137), a principle that transgresses the separation of the animal, the vegetable and the human, the living and the dead. The threat of formlessness that emanates from Arcimboldo's *trompe l'oeil* gets more acute as the viewer realizes there is nothing more terrifying than an object without form, a "thing" which defies definition and interpretation. Instead of a head, we are confronted with a protean flux of organic matter, a vast, literal-minded illusion teeming with autonomous creatures giving life and motion to an imaginary body whose shapes and contours are never fixed, but ever new and changing, a continuous alteration of the distinction between body and world. But what is at stake here is not just the horror of what has neither a clear form nor a definite name (the lack of integrity of the thing observed menaces the integrity and sanity of the observer) but, rather, the horror of the dissolution of the dead body-self into the realm of the undifferentiated and the amorphous.

This fear of the disintegration of the body accounts, at least in part, for Dalí's fascination with well-defined, well-rounded, edible forms (even the contorted contours of his limp watches and the stretched skins of his deformed elephant legs are always clearly defined). In the following fragment, from *The Secret Life of Salvador Dalí*, Dalí's hatred of the filandrous texture of spinach takes on a political dimension and is associated with his distrust of libertarian ideals and his adherence to strongly regimented political régimes:

> In reality I only like to eat things that have a clear and comprehensible form. I hate spinach because it is as formless as freedom. The very opposite of spinach is armor.
>
> (*Secret* 81)

In the world of modernist art, "clear and comprehensible" shapes ranging from squares, and circles to apples and eggs (the perfect, pristine shape that contains the viscous and amorphous goo) inspired Arp, Brancusi, Magritte and countless other painters who, for various reasons, sought to emulate the pristine elegance of "pure," "perfect" forms. Other artists, by contrast, have since directed their attention to the chaotic and the incongruous avatars of matter. The visceral, ecto-plastic, alternately glutinous and fibrous textures of Bernard Réquichot's *Reliquaires* would probably have horrified Dalí. And so, one imagines, would have the polymorphous, unedible, pun-ridden cephalo-pod of Beefheart's "Neon Meate Dream of a Octafish," which offers a different take on the theme of organic metamorphosis in a daring synthesis of the animal, the vegetal and the mechanical, an esemplastic creature held together by the amalgamating logic of dream and linguistic polysemy:

> Lucid tenacles test 'n sleeved
> 'n joined 'n jointed jade pointed
> Diamond black patterns
> Neon meate dream of a Octafish
> Artifact on rose petals
> 'n flesh petals 'n pots
> Fack 'n feast 'n tubes tubs bulbs

For Marcel Broodthaers, the undecipherable amorphism of the inver-tebrate, far from constituting a menace to the self, holds the promise of a material being that might resist the systematizing pressures of the conceptual clarity of the traditionally (re-)presented art object. The following poem, called "La Méduse," describes the freefloating jellyfish as a pure body without form. For Broodthaers, the medusa, which does not have any internal structure, skeleton or shell, becomes an even more perfect structure than, say, Manzoni's eggs or even the mussel and eggshell sculptures for which Broodthaers himself became famous:

> The Jellyfish
>   It's   perfect
>   No mold
>   Nothing but body

                    (28)

It is the absence of shape that turns the jellyfish into a perfect body, the dream of a protean being that exceeds the boundaries of internal or external structure. The last line of Broodthaers's piece runs as follows: "Crystal of scorn, of great price at last, gob of spit, wave, wavering" (29). The stinging, jelly-like creature becomes a symbol for the treacherousness of wavering, fluctuating forms. It also has the additional peculiarity of being already transparent and thereby precluding the possibility of internal exploration.[26] It is its very transparency that paradoxically guarantees its inviolability from the observer's gaze, for the jellyfish, by showing its lack of outer structure, interrupts the dialectics of inside and outside and ensures that nothing is left to be revealed.

CHAPTER THREE

Birth Trauma and the Blues-Gothic: The Body at the Crossroads

Sinking Down

Like most white musicians launching themselves into rock 'n' roll in the late fifties and sixties, Frank Zappa and Don Van Vliet had to run the gauntlet of the blues. Coming to terms with one's chosen instrument(s), manipulating musical structures, distilling a style from an inherited backlog of sounds, deciding on the relative importance of singing and lyrics, balancing the use of repetitive forms against improvisation, conceiving an attitude towards one's audience, adapting one's lifestyle to one's status as artist—for the vast majority of aspiring musicians, the blues functioned as *the* cultural nexus to be grappled with and assimilated during the making of these mental and physical moves. Creative activity in the sphere of rock 'n' roll was only possible after one had negotiated some kind of settlement with the blues. The motif of the crossroads, which originally emerged as a precise expression of the peculiar predicament of the African American, who found himself freed from slavery into a complex of open-ended oppressions, and was continually obliged to decide what he was going to do about it, suggests itself as a useful figure for the hesitant and self-doubting rock 'n' roller groping towards self-assertion and expression while grappling with a culture he knows is not his own. Admittedly, it is a very different kind of crossroads in each case, the dilemma of how best to survive has become the far less onerous conundrum of how to make good music; though for a figure like Robert Johnson these two sets of problems, one imagines, had always been inseparable. And indeed, if one teases out the implications of the crossroads and considers the various ways in which it may impinge on the consciousness of the artist, one can discover that the crux of blues anxiety can be traced back to the primal stresses of the species, to which our white bluesboomers are equally subject, and to which they testify through the invention of new forms of seriousness.

Unexceptionally, therefore, the juvenilia of Frank Zappa and Don Van Vliet conform to the patterns of blues experimentation, as we can hear on surviving recordings from the early Studio Z period of their association.[1] In an interview given in 1969, Zappa seems to reflect on the awkwardness he must have felt as a young musician serving out his blues apprenticeship:

> The blues thing in white rock is ridiculous and embarrassing. It's embarrassing to hear most white rock singers singing the blues. It's embarrassing that THEY aren't embarrassed. White blues players are deluding themselves—a Brooklyn accent singing 'Baaby!' Agh! B.B. King plays and then he invites all these white musicians in the audience on up to the stage and they play all his licks and he pats them on the head. White players using Negroid mannerisms on the guitar is the same as the Japanese synthesising miniature TV sets. (quoted in Kostalanetz 67)

Reading this assessment, it is easier to understand the motivation behind the series of subversive strategies which Zappa and Van Vliet applied to the problems of blues form: stylistic exaggeration, lyrical redundancy, repetition without dynamic development, and technical distortion of tempo and pitch all played a role in those early efforts to wrestle the conventions into more personal configurations. Linking all of these, and more important than any of them, however, was a derisive attitude to the body, a generalised interest in abjection as a curiously universal form of marginality which could be effectively employed as a deflective shield against charges of effeteness. The recourse to abjection in the Cucamonga period is perhaps best understood, then, as a reaction to this cultural embarrassment, an attempt to cauterise one's inauthenticity through the presentation of oneself as thoroughly repellent. The argument would run something like this: "I may not be poor and oppressed, this may not be my music, but look how revolting my body is, and see how ready I am to play with it in front of you". The humour of this is masochistic and guilty, totally self-conscious and unfunny in a particularly disturbing way, as if Zappa and Van Vliet were measuring themselves against a cultural stereotype (the big black man with a booming voice and an inexhaustible supply of virile authenticity)[2] and glorying in their queasy inadequacies. It is also possible that we can see here the first phase of Zappa's maximalist extrapolation of his art from the matrix of the human body and the ramifications of its social career. If Van Vliet quickly abandoned the repugnant as a vital aesthetic element, the key problematic of his musical career continued to revolve around his loathing for the soporific "moma heartbeat" of rock 'n' roll and his search for alternatives to the somatic rhythms imposed by the human body. This, as we shall see, relates directly to the blues dilemma of whether to break time or to stick to strict measure, which, in many ways is a social question, a matter of relating one body to another. Van Vliet's obsessive treatment of this blues crux raises questions about self-expression, the power of the individual to transcend his or her origins, the psycho-sexual power of the female imago, and the matricidal urge of the artist. For Zappa and Van Vliet, all roads off the blues crossroad seemed to lead back to the body.

"Lost in Whirlpool" (*Lost Episodes*) is a blues lament for a failed relationship, but instead of being put out or barred from the house, the speaker has been literally treated like shit. Embarrassment glides into punitive humiliation as the singer is "flushed" by his girlfriend and forced to cohabit with the "big brown fish". This scenario is a staging of the white kid's essential worthlessness in relation to the black blues artists whose work he is forced to copy. How many times have we heard the bluesman sing about leaving his baby, or being left? How many times have we heard him voice the experience of swirling around in the toilet pan, jostled by turds? The lyrical excesses and the predicament they commemorate are heightened ever further (how could it be otherwise?) by the fluidity of Zappa's single string lead playing, his over-adequate unpunctuated mastery of the reverberating sting of T-Bone Walker or Johnny "Guitar" Watson. Appropriation is possible, then, for the dedicated white guitarist with the right equipment; but blues is a vocal music, the guitar is supposed to sing a response to the words, capturing its inflections with a bend and a buzz, here a sustain, there a staccato stop, everywhere a melodic phrasing. In the "Whirlpool", Zappa's guitar sings to the shit in the pan, and Van Vliet forces out the self-lacerating text in a grating white falsetto which anticipates the heavy metal castrato of Robert Plant rather than the mature organ of Captain Beefheart. Even if the guitar, then, were serious in its blues aspirations, it would stand no chance against the wailing lamentations of this discarded lover, who, like Robert Johnson's "Crossroads" persona, is sinking down, but this time taking the music with him. Blues embarrassment has been effectively channelled into the theme of humiliation and this, it must be said, is finally much less abject than those early attempts to marry blues with emerging white styles, the grotesque blues-surf of "Diddy-Wah-Diddy" (*The Legendary A & M Sessions*) where the plantation cabin or the rent party in Harlem is exchanged for the hedonistic beach of the middle-class American dream, with frisky teenagers in their trunks hysterically dodging the sissy surf.

The toilet vortex is a fitting duct for the evacuation of such white trash, since as the shit goes down the pan through the eye of the whirlpool the rate of its revolutions increases, thus mirroring the tendency of rock 'n' roll to speed up and shy away from the more deliberate and determined tempi of the blues. When you play a blues too fast you loose the push, the groovy guts of the rhythm are stretched beyond their elastic limit, the darker more demanding pulses and retentions are sold out to a professional dog-walker who trips along the sunny surface with his fistful of clockwork poodles rushing them home as quickly as possible; everybody is too out of breath to reach into those organic gaps and twist, everything is coming too swiftly, too slickly-slackly with no friction and purchase. So let the punishment fit the crime.

In Samuel Beckett's *Happy Days*, the main character, like Johnson's crossroader, is also sinking down. When the play begins, Winnie is buried up to her waist in a mound of sand, by the beginning of the second act she is up to her neck. This agonising telos is, however, contradicted by the reappearance at the beginning of Act Two of the parasol, which has caught fire in Act One. A controlling force seems to be at work, restoring the environment at the end of each Act, re-setting the clock. Winnie, then, is caught at a junction between linear time (with its inherent threat of an end) and cyclical time, in which the notion of the end is a tantalising absurdity. Her personal history unravels within an unchanging timeless world of which she may be just one more cyclical element doomed to repeat its apparently unique fate *ad infinitum*. It is this hesitation between modes of being, this uncertainty as to where Winnie stands exactly in relation to the world, which accounts for the appalling stresses of the play. This in-betweenness goes far beyond the parallel torments of confinement and exposure, just as the in-betweeness of Johnson's crossroader exceeds the historical context of Jim Crow curfews and the cultural moment of the blues. The subject here is death, the existence or otherwise of an afterlife, the tensions this hesitation imposes on the individual consciousness, and the way these tensions play themselves out in social behaviour.

When economic opportunity presented itself elsewhere, in the neighbouring county or far away to the North, the bluesman would pack his bag and go; and so many songs capture this mood of imminent departure, the social amputation of "goodbye".³ To stagnate and sink down, or to roam and risk getting caught in between, this was the blues dilemma of the body in space. Fred McDowell equated the imperative of movement with the inevitability of death in "You Gotta Move": whatever you do, whoever you are, in the end there is only one way to go. Robert Johnson's sense of peril was too urgent for him to accept the consolations of McDowell's massive fatalism; his "Hellhound on My Trail" is an exhortation to "keep moving, keep moving". If we put these two moods together we get a sense of a life lived out in strained hesitation, a suffering mind incapable of deciding which way to go, which way salvation lies; a life lived at the crossroads. Johnson's self-motivation *in extremis* is, then, akin to Winnie in her mound telling herself to "Begin, Winnie. Begin your day, Winnie" (*Complete* 138) ; unable to move, unable to be still, she is caught in between, condemned to the diminishing returns of self-recognition in the social rituals she desperately accomplishes.

Something of this crossroads catch can be felt in Captain Beefheart's "Click-Clack" (*The Spotlight Kid*) , where the speaker's girlfriend is "always threatenin' to go down to N'Orleans/ Get herself lost and found". The repetition of this threat is indicative perhaps of an hysterical recycling of intention, or of a mutually destructive but structurally vital recycling of a situation which works for the couple. The vowel substitution of the title neatly captures this equivalence of the barely compatible, how a click is also a clack, and how neither can exist without its usurping double. We can sense the crossroads of indecision, and the social rituals which seem to perpetuate the hesitation by holding it at the limit of the bearable. The girl, finally, has no need to go down to N'Orleans since in the issuing and retracting of the familiar threat she has already got herself lost and found; there is no need to replace one crossroads with another, since she is living at the very crux of self-possession and self-loss. The abject joyous-misery of this line is that she doesn't have to go, there doesn't have to be a parting, while at the same time nothing has been done to alleviate her angst, her "all the time cryin'". This desperate need to behave according to type, to repeat moves which, even when accomplished, will be unavailing, reveals the force of that great question of social existence: for whom should I be? The superimposition of active and passive moods in "get herself lost and found" underlines this imperative doubt: the girl can provoke her loss, but, being lost, will have to rely on somebody else to find her. It is like a suicide attempt, where one hopes to be reborn though the timely intervention of a saviour. At the end of *Happy Days* Willie starts to crawl up the mound towards Winnie and the revolver, and she cheers him on, sensing a chance to get herself lost and found. At the same time, necessarily, Winnie wants things to continue as they are, and the future perfect of the last line alerts us to the twisted nostalgia which powers the process of denial: "this will have been another happy day" (*Complete* 168), as if happiness is all about the accomplishment of ritual. Through the compound tense, Winnie projects beyond the hesitation between love and death, murder and the caress; appropriating the final position from which the day's (life's) events can be assessed. She is in a hurry to lose herself to the past and repossess herself in reverence for what she has already been. The existential point of the question "for whom should I be?" is blunted by nostalgia, where one has the illusion of possessing oneself retrospectively. Instead of sinking down, one has the feeling of being elevated above life, of looking down on the plane, that site of disastrous exposure. This probably accounts for the appeal of the "old times" so cherished by Winnie in *Happy Days*, who passes her time recycling the debris of her life even as she sinks down in the interval between Acts One and Two, who tracks back psychologically even as the unravelling of events marks the pitiless progression of her misery, losing and finding herself back at the crossroads, in the provisionality of another happy day, "no better, no worse, no change" (*Complete* 139); like the "Click-Clack" girl who finds herself in the re-issuing of the old threat and so loses herself in the accomplishment of another social round.

Abjection, a Social Art

By subjecting the bodies of his performers to extreme conditions, while exposing them to the caprices of an apparently arbitrary fate, all under the scrutiny of a judging public, Beckett created an intermediary space between reality and representation, a place of abjection, defined by the intergeneric anxieties it stimulates. In *Not I* from 1972, the human body is reduced to a mouth speaking aloud these anxieties, constantly falling between statement and non-statement:

> found herself in the dark . . . and if not exactly insentient . . . insentient
> . . . for she could still hear the buzzing . . . so-called . . . in the ears . . . and
> a ray of light came and went . . . came and went . . . such as the moon
> might cast . . . drifting . . . in and out of cloud . . . but so dulled . . . feeling
> . . . feeling so dulled . . . she did not know . . . what position she was in . . .
> imagine! . . . what position she was in! . . . whether standing . . . or sitting
> . . . but the brain— . . . what? . . . kneeling? . . . yes . . . whether standing . . .
> or sitting . . . or kneeling . . . but the brain— . . . what? . . . lying? . . . yes . . .
> whether standing . . . or sitting . . . or kneeling . . . or lying . . . but the
> brain still
>
> (*Complete* 377)

More primal stress: absolute unknowing combined with the compulsion to search. There is no room for nostalgia here, only a breathless search for continuity, that pre-condition of rest. Being has been constrained into a useless attempt to say itself, compressed into a narrow space filled with dysfunctional language. As in *Happy Days*, we are still at an existential watershed where the subject as individual consciousness is about to be absorbed into the infinite abstractions of the universe or, conversely, where the impersonal calm of non-differentiation has been broken by a fuss of suffering subjectivity. The stress is on the lungs here, as they work overtime to power the voice in its effort to say itself and cease. The abjection of useless saying is the essence of life, its duration dependent on the power of the heart and lungs to pump enough air. One speaks, in a sense, against one's body, in order to end the doubt as quickly as one can. Speech, at least as Beckett conceives of it, is by definition a social act, and the staging of speech in the theatre only serves to confirm this. The saying away of the subject takes place in public, under a spotlight, the abjection is, inevitably, social.

It is at this point that Beckett's work has affinities with body art, crossing over from theatre into performance, as the idea of an actor with a role is replaced by the presence of action, that is, of an acting body, or a body performing acts, or, in the social context, of a *behaving* body. We can go back to Captain Beefheart's "Click-Clack" (*The Spotlight Kid*) for a formulation of the social rationale of body art: one behaves in order to get oneself lost and found, just as the voice in *Not I* behaves linguistically (i.e. speaks) in order to cease being itself and to become something other. The basic physical process which makes all behaving possible is, of course, breathing, and here we can identify a link between performance art and music, since both are pitched against that same bottom line of bodily being. Music, like the stressful song of the abject voice, is framed by the silence of non-being, a condition which both forms of noise, in certain instances, seem to covet; while in the in-and-out of respiration we can hear and feel the grim alternation of loss and reclamation, as the body gets itself lost and found.

Beckett explored this territory with *Breath*, written in 1968, a theatrical performance which collapses the distinction between reality and representation in order to test the interdependence of being and behaving.[4] Such works, which compress the experience of living into reductive structures of repetitive physical acts, imply an equivalence between conception and death. Being, at its simplest, is not capable of changing anything, and so death is no different from conception, since both are located at the unchanging interface between being and non-being. Birth, in this sense, is the first and most tragic disappointment, since it is the moment when we emerge into fully-fledged independent being, all capable of action, only to find that, like the sun at the beginning of Beckett's *Murphy*, we have risen to shine, "having no alternative, on the nothing new" (1). Birth is the birth of the abject, as Julia Kristeva noted:

> The abjection of self would be the culminating form of that experience of the subject to which it is revealed that all its objects are based merely on the inaugural loss that laid the foundations of its own being.
>
> *(Powers* 232)

In *Waiting for Godot* Beckett wrote about "[giving] birth astride the grave" (*Complete* 82), and the trauma of birth (often evoked through memories of infancy) haunts his work as a pre-experience of death. We are led, then, to interpret that first gulp of air which, as in Beckett's play, is accompanied by a cry, as a fall into abjection, into the in-betweeness of conscious being, equivalent to that panic-stricken moment of exposure on the plane, or the agonising hesitation at the crossroads.

The British artist Stuart Brisley, has devised a number of performance and video pieces which use respiration as a basic structural and thematic element, while evoking the abjection of pre-natal being through more specific arrangements of imagery. In *Arbeit Macht Frei*, a film from 1972, we first see the artist vomiting copiously in a bare impersonal setting. We then find him lying in a bath of water, alternately immersing himself and coming up for air to the sonic accompaniment of the over-amplified sound of his raucous breathing. The title refers us back to the Nazi death camps, a subject which, as we shall see, Don Van Vliet was also willing to address, and Brisley's vomiting in the cold institutionalised setting certainly evokes the gas chambers, while the immersion scene reminds us of *la baignoire*, preferred torture method of the Gestapo. According to Kristeva: "The abjection of Nazi crime reaches its apex when death, which, in any case, kills me, interferes with what in my living universe is supposed to save me from death." (*Powers* 232) The unnaturalness of death-in-life, that *sine qua non* of the gothic which we, following Kristeva, can reach by way of abjection. Brisley's repeated immersions effectively present this interference of death with life, as the air supply is cut off and then restored, cut off and restored. Simultaneously, of course, it re-enacts that first breath of the infant emerging from its underwater world into a life of loss, a situation more nakedly symbolised by the vomiting prelude which presents us with an irruption of death in the form of ingested food, a classic *mise en scène* of the abjectly repellent which takes us back to Zappa's theatre of the repugnant.

Like Brisley and Beckett, Don Van Vliet is acutely sensitive to the process of breathing and its existential implications, and, in his own way, has also made the link with maternity. The terms he chose to describe his own memories of birth trauma seem especially abject: "I remember when the jerk slapped me on the fanny and I saw the yellow tile and I thought what a hell of a way to wake somebody up" (Barnes 2). The doctor or midwife is a "jerk", a fool, but also somebody who has jerked a reluctant infant out of the womb: "I was born with my eyes open—I didn't WANT to be born—I can remember deep down in my head that I fought against my mother bringing me into the world." (Barnes 2) Violence, then, a struggle against the mother's body, culminating in a slap on the "fanny" and a first glimpse of that nauseating tile. An echo of this scene crops up in "The Dust Blows Forward 'n' the Dust Blows Back" (*Trout Mask Replica*), where the Roundhouse Man wakes up "in vomit and beer in a banana bin", an image which brings together the nausea and birthing bath of Brisley's *Arbeit Macht Frei* and the bilious glow of that yellow tile. As Kristeva remarks, in a line which recalls Beckett's image of the mother squatting over the tomb, "I give birth to myself amid the violence of sobs, of vomit" (*Powers* 231). When the birth trauma returns the mother has been abjected, and so one gives birth to oneself, closing the circle of violence and despair. Instead of ice and intestines, Brisley might have filled his bath with his own cooling excretions.

Motherlove is Animal

Don Van Vliet's musical defiance of maternity and the trauma of the yellow tile took the form of an assault on the "moma heartbeat" of rock 'n' roll.[5] As Marcia Tucker reminds us, "Man alone among animals is able to symbolize, to respond not only to the direct effect of a stimulus on his body, but to a symbolic interpretation of it" (quoted in Warr 207). In the context of rock 'n' roll, the stimulus of a regular beat, normally provided by the drummer, is symbolically interpreted as a heartbeat, the pulse of life which registers our emotional responses to the world and the workings of our physical apparatus. In rejecting this regularity, the mystifying mythopoeic ecologist in Van Vliet attempted to slough off the human consciousness of body and its psychic load through a blissful return to the body innocence of the animals. By breaking up the "moma heartbeat", Van Vliet hoped to break the hysterical power wielded over the body by the unconscious. Irregularity of rhythm was heralded as an instrument of devolution, capable of unpicking the symbolic threads of subjectivity and unveiling a state of grace where the personal coincides perfectly with the natural, where behaving is subsumed back into being. In his interviews, VanVliet frequently claimed to be immune to influence, arrogating to himself an authenticity of being, where the subject, animal-like, exists both for itself and as a fully functional, fully integrated part of the ecosystem. The nearest the human being gets to this state is, of course, the utopia of the womb; so the animal in Van Vliet's system is also the embryonic, where the "moma heartbeat" is lived rather than heard in an undifferentiated unity where experience is not yet stalked by interpretation, where there is no possible hesitation between the real and the represented.

"Wild Life" (*Trout Mask Replica*) expresses this urge pretty clearly, where a return to the wilderness is, paradoxically, a matter of survival:

> Wild life wild life wild life
> I'm goin' up on the mountain along with m' wife
> Find me uh cave 'n talk them bears
> In t' takin' me in
> Wild life along with m' wife
> Wild life
> It's uh man's best friend
> Wild life along with m' wife

I'm goin' up on the mountain fo' the rest uh m' life
'fore they take m' life
'fore they take m' wild life

It is touching and perhaps typical of Van Vliet's lyrical environmentalism that he should imagine his mountain bears to be open to verbal
persuasion. This is the wilderness at least twice removed, filtered
through Kipling and Walt Disney, and rendered even more benign by
Van Vliet's consistent refusal to speak about predation (even in *The Jungle
Book* there was a villainous tiger and a sick snake).[6] Reading his texts and
interviews, one would think that there was no such thing as a carnivore;
the wolf with his claws worn down in "When it Blows it's Stacks" (*The
Spotlight Kid*) is a predatory male human "as cold as ah snake sleeping in
the shade". The savage traits of the animals survive only in metaphorical form, transferred to human beings, underlining once more how
birth, in the Van Vliet scheme of things, is seen as an eviction from the
Edenic womb of nature into the lapsarian wilderness of human society,
where the beast roams upright through culture. This duality informs
the poem "You Should Know By The Kindness Of A Dog The Way Uh
Human Should Be" where we can read:

'n the snake's in shape
He rattles like uh baby wears his diamonds
Better than a fine lady's finger
'n his fangs are no more dangerous
Than her slow aristocratic poison[7]

As in "Wild life" (*Trout Mask Replica*) the human world is discontinuous with nature, here the only link is simile, the dominant rhetorical
device in Van Vliet's poetry. Comparisons are made between the snake
and two human beings, a baby and a fine lady, a mother and a child,
perhaps. A measure of the snake's shapeliness is that it can incorporate
traits from both the human subjects without suffering division. It seems
to be a repository of forms, a signified of which the two humans are
mere signifiers. In setting up this hierarchical distinction, Van Vliet
bears down on his anthropomorphism, indicating that while animals
can be compared to humans one must never lose sight of their ethical
and aesthetic superiority. If left unchecked, anthropomorphism quickly
slides into the shocking abjections presented by H.G. Wells in *The Island
of Dr Moreau* and in numerous films by Walt Disney, of which *Bambi*
would stand as a fair example. Ezra Pound debated this issue in his

poem "Meditatio":

> When I carefully consider the curious habits of dogs
> I am compelled to conclude
> That man is the superior animal.
>
> When I consider the curious habits of man
> I confess, my friend, I am puzzled.
>
> (111)

In contrast to Van Vliet's strident advocacy of the animals, Pound's hesitation leaves the door open to an abject anthropomorphism which, in the end, is perhaps the inalienable fate of any dog which finds itself caught at the crossroads of semi-domestication.

Two of Van Vliet's paintings might be cited at this point. "Pig Erases A Statue In Passing", which dates from 1985, seems to pit nature against art and to assert that the pig, in its sheer ontological integrity, has the power to eclipse human creations. This may be seen as a corrective to the *Book of Genesis* where God takes credit for the snakeiness of the snake:

> And the LORD God said unto the serpent, Because thou hast done this, thou art cursed above all cattle, and above every beast of the field; upon thy belly shalt thou go, and dust shalt thou eat all the days of thy life:
> And I will put enmity between thee and the woman, and between thy seed and her seed; it shall bruise thy head, and thou shalt bruise his heel.[8]

By fixing the form of the snake in an arbitrary act of revenge, God makes nature the signifier of which he is the signified, thus reversing Van Vliet's scheme of things while preserving the divide which separates man from the animals (charging it with enmity in fact).[9] The serpent which slithered into Eden was formless, before God's curse it both was a snake and wasn't a snake at the same time. In this sense it was abjection itself, and quickly made its presence felt, muddying the pristine waters, mixing up the divine and the diabolic, the natural and the unnatural, the spiritual and the profane, raising *the* question of precedence ("who created whom?" or "who signifies whom?"), which rewrote itself as the question of existential doubt ("for whom should I be?"), in short, introducing desire. Eve got herself lost and found by the serpent and God, working together as a uniquely malevolent double act, and the moment of maximum abjection, when Adam and Eve discover their nakedness and hide in the bushes as a wrathful God hunts them down, is another of those crossroads, where humanity finds itself caught on the plane with the sun sinking down.

Van Vliet's pig is manifestly going about its business, trotting across the picture plane, and reversing in the process man's potential to molest the animals with his creations (which, from an agnostic perspective, would include God). An earlier painting seems to go even further; "Saint Dog", from 1976, canonises the animals in protest against the Christian creation myth, re-sanctifying nature within a Christian hierarchy. This gesture enacts two possible blasphemies: it idolatrously blends pre-Christian animal deities with Christian iconography, counterbalancing the fate suffered by the post-lapsarian snake; and, if we continue to extrapolate from the bear's cave in "Wild Life", it hints at mariolatry. By erasing the statue in passing, the pig proves itself capable of dissolving the world, as the phallic erection collapses into formlessness. It is an apocalyptic pig which, in wiping out everything that we have experienced since birth, can take us all the way back to the womb, that maxi-minimalist matrix of conception and death. The saintly dog, by equating mother-worship with the animal kingdom, also points to the womb, that realm where the maternal could be experienced naturally: motherlove, it seems, is animal.

For Whom Should I be? For Mother or Me?

Critics have sometimes qualified Van Vliet's genius as "primitive",[10] and the devolutionary thrust of his aesthetic ideology might lead to comparisons with that most celebrated of naif painters, Henri "Douanier" Rousseau, who also had a thing about animals. In a painting entitled "Heureux Quatuor" Rousseau seems to anticipate Van Vliet's utopian vision of mankind modelling itself on the unspotted nature of a friendly dog, and living in harmony with nature. A man, woman and child leap and gambol through a luxuriant glade while a flop-eared hound attends them submissively. The couple are linked by a train of ivy, symbolising fidelity, and the man translates the moment via his flute into notes of consonant joy. How could it be otherwise, given the musical title, and the apparent felicity of the four beating hearts? The semi-naked couple inevitably recall Adam and Eve, and the baby suggests that the Fall has occurred at least once, yet instead of enmity there is love between the humans and the animals. Taking a cue from the animals, the couple have cheated God's curse, and the music-making celebrates an unexpected victory over abjection and guilt: they have learnt how they should be from the kindness of a dog, and we are to imagine a traumatic expulsion into a world of dividing structures which, through the passing of a pig, begins to run in reverse, starting with the erasure of the structures and ending with re-entry into the womb of nature. The four-in-oneness of Rousseau's quartet is equivalent to the bodily unconsciousness of Adam and Eve before the Fall, the undifferentiated being of the embryo, which is both animal and human. The saintly dog is now part of the family group, it sits there implying a repertoire of sexual moves which has emerged backwards from the shadow of the taboo.

Rousseau, however, unlike Van Vliet, was willing to stage scenes of predation, both animal to animal ("Le Lion Ayant Faim", "Un Cheval Dans La Jungle") and animal to human ("Nègre Attaqué Par Un Tigre"). The intrauterine togetherness of "Heureux Quatuor", where nature feeds itself, is constantly menaced by the violent separation of birth, which is figured as nature feeding *off* itself. In the sexual sense, we are talking about the difference between consensual loving intercourse and rape (which Rousseau's predatory scenes strangely evoke). In "Wild Life" (*Trout Mask Replica*) Van Vliet imagines a dialogue between man and nature, as the fugitive speaker negotiates his future with the bears; will they agree to take him into their cave? It is a tense moment, as Van Vliet's persona waits to find out if he will be accepted back into the animal kingdom, sucked back into the natural womb:

> They got m' mother 'n father
> 'n run down all my kin
> Folks I know I'm next

In another extraordinary painting, entitled "Mauvaise Surprise", Rousseau stages a drama of triangular predation, which anticipates the dilemma of Van Vliet's wombseeker by pitting the animal against the human in a situation reeking with the potential for sexual transgression. In a rocky landscape a woman is surprised by a bear who is surprised by a hunter pointing a gun. But whose exactly is the *bad* surprise? Is the woman frightened of the bear or the man or both? Is the bear frightened of the man and disappointed by his intervention, or is it the presence of the woman which it finds disturbing? And where do the hunter's real desires lie?[11] Something, at least, has been interrupted, and in the circulation of this question through the wiles of the image we can hear again that plaintive query of the social subject at the cross-roads—"for whom should I be?" The static quality of the painter's style only serves to emphasise the hesitation inherent to the moment of abjection.

"Mauvaise Surprise" is, perhaps, Rousseau's riskiest image, in which he seems to deconstruct the pan-pastoral fantasies of the "Heureux Quatuor". It is a work which rigorously excludes any question of inno-cence; any unity here will be tainted with the violence which brings it about. The "bad surprise" of the title refers directly to the narrative moment where the loss of innocence is staged on a number of levels: the hunter and the bear seem to be about to engage in mortal combat over the right to enjoy the lady's favours, but how do we know that this is not already a *ménage à trois* and that what we are witnessing is the last bloody act of some intergeneric Wellsian love drama? More indirectly, we might take that resonant title as another reference to birth and the bad surprise of emerging into the world, and view the painting as a figuration of the trauma to stand alongside Van Vliet's evocation of the yellow tile. The lady's scream would now be the vagitus of the infant badly shaken by a first glimpse of the social perils it must learn to survive as it steers a course between the angry bear and the murderous gunman.

To speak of a "primitive artist" is to dally with the oxymoronic, since the primitive who ventures into the symbolic languages of art has exchanged his claim to naturalness against the possibility of self-expres-sion, with that crucial interstice between "self" and "expression" making room for the fatal intervention of culture. Failure to spot this subtle transaction has often led to a confusion between the primitive and the merely childish; and it is worth considering, as we reconsider his aversion to the "moma heartbeat" of rock 'n' roll, that Van Vliet has more of the big kid about him than the noble savage, more of the Alfred Wallis than the Forrest Gump?[12] His tantrums and manipulative struc-ture at least suggest this; while his urgent need to detach himself through music from the imago of the mother is more reminiscent of the adolescent. Which is to suggest that Van Vliet's engagement with rhythmical form is informed by that classically human dilemma: where to situate oneself in relation to the mother? Which is a narrower though hardly more answerable version of the question "for whom should I be?"

His reverence for the animals, we have seen, is also a nostalgia for the womb, and this complicated situation is rendered musically by his replacement of one form of regularity with another: the "moma heart-beat" is broken up in favour of a kind of melodic commentary to be played on the drums,[13] and this new irregular pattern is then to be *learned by heart* and reproduced for every new performance. Fear and desire return as a fresh symptom, and Van Vliet's rejection of influence (including the influence of basic beat) is vitiated by his insistence that regularity must be conquered without resorting to improvisation. This is the classic excremental hesitation of the child on the potty—"Am I to let it go? Am I to hold it back?", which is yet another avatar of the cross-roads.

The discovery of a form of regular irregularity in Van Vliet's musical practice demonstrates the pervasiveness of the oxymoron, that linguistic impasse which sends the subject doubling back on itself in search of an alternative issue, and then confronts him again with his lack of creative resources. What Van Vliet really wants to do is to regress to the womb and then beyond, to slip the shackles of the unconscious by turning the symbolic against itself. Another 19th century French painter might help us to understand some of the darker implications of Van Vliet's bid to break the oxymoronic bonds of culture.

Gustave Courbet's painting "L'Origine du Monde" depicts the lower torso, thighs and exposed genitalia of an anonymous woman. The viewer, one feels, is being lined up in front of the vagina, pushed head-long into the opening and down the channels of the female body, all the way back to the womb. Let us, then, imagine Van Vliet taking up this painterly invitation and worming his way in, back towards the mother's heartbeat in its literal reality. For all its realism, Courbet's painting (and our creative embellishment) is a symbolic interpretation of the woman's body, and therefore not for the animals. Which is why Van Vliet, even curled as he is now in the womb, is still *hearing* the mother's heartbeat as noise and not *experiencing* it as being. What he is realising in his dim lizard brain is that he must press on in his navigation and actually get into the heart, where the beats are beating. If he wants the symbolic to cease he must get into the heart and *become the beats*, tapping on the walls, working the clappers. To unite the personal and the natural, to close the gap between self and expression, in short, he must become a matricidal animal, the farrow that eats its own pig.

There is a moment in Joseph Conrad's *Heart of Darkness* where Marlow finds himself at a crossroads, and strangely anticipates Van Vliet's struggle with the beat. Having left the steamer during the night to search for Kurtz, who has fled towards the native drums, Marlow finds himself facing the wilderness. Suddenly, it is his crisis of self-possession, the moment when he must decide if he is part of nature or separate from it. The time for being in between is no more. A series of "imbecile thoughts" culminates in the image of himself "living alone and unarmed in the woods to an advanced age"(93). At the height of his crisis Marlow seems to lose a sense of the separateness of his body, confounding for an instant "the beating of the drum with the beating of my heart" (93). He passes, briefly, beyond the symbolic, and then immediately recovers his loss, declaring himself pleased with his heart's "calm regularity". While the crisis seems to have passed, his choice of metaphors to describe the pull of the wilderness reveals the precise nature of the symbolic frontier he has just transgressed: the wilderness has "drawn Kurtz to its pitiless breast by the awakening of forgotten and brutal instincts, by the memory of gratified and monstrous passions." The drum beat of the jungle comes from behind the "pitiless breast" of this mother, and Kurtz it seems is already there, at one with the pumping organ at the intersection of conception and death. He cannot be reasoned with, symbolic forms of communication are of no use anymore: "There was nothing either above or below him, and I knew it. He had kicked himself loose of the earth." He has reached his heart of darkness by predating the mother. In Conrad as in Rousseau, then, the jungle operates as a metaphor for the womb, a prime site of abject hesitations where the subject is beguiled into confronting the terrible and terribly tempting imago of the mother.[14]

Courbet's title "L'Origine du Monde", together with the cropping of the model's head, universalises the body he displays, inflecting the viewer's response towards the structural, away from the personal. At the same time the shock of black pubic hair, the precise weightiness of the thighs and awkward swivel of the pelvis, the position held at whatever cost to a set of uniquely taut-slack, worked-wasted muscles with a history all of their own, sufficiently reminds us of the real body beyond the representation, the performer beyond the form. In defiance of the title, we can read in the image the signature of an individual live body. Courbet, then, like Van Vliet is using art to explore the tensions between the symbolic and the real, and if Van Vliet's struggle against the beat can be interpreted as a drive to regress to a pre-individual or animal state of existence, then Courbet's image, in the special context of its title, seems to allude to exactly what he is looking for: the vagina as a porthole through time to the origins of everything, the very beginning of nature, the ecologist's pristine dream. In this way, the woman's body becomes a kind of time machine transporting the voyager back beyond the foetal stage to the moment of conception itself, the moment of transition between the world-without-you and the world-with-you.

For the purposes of Van Vliet's ideal human regression, then, the problem with conception is that there was nothing before it, just as the problem with death is that there may be nothing after it. Which further complicates our relationship to images of the female body, be they pictorial, like Courbet's, or musical, like the rock 'n' roll beat Van Vliet was revolting against. The mother's body, by conceiving us and at the same time conceiving our death, creates the double bind of symbolic representation and the matricidal urge that it, in turn, unleashes. In *Unmarked*, Peggy Phelan suggests that it is the primal scene which operates as "a screen memory for the always lost moment of one's own conception. . . . a psychic revisiting and anticipation of the world without oneself" (5). Somehow, in Van Vliet, the primal scene has been displaced by the birth trauma, which, in delivering the infant over to the social world, is the first and most radical consequence of conception to register on the new individual.

In a 1973 interview with Eliot Wald, Van Vliet confessed to a preference for the animal over the human in him:

> I'm an animal. A human animal, but the animal may be better than the human in my case.
>
> It's the animal that paints, the animal that makes music. The human part is me losing one of the best groups that ever was by being an art-statement-oriented fool.
>
> (unpag.)

This avowed preference reinforces the suspicion of a matricidal urge lurking behind his loathing of the "moma heartbeat", since ultimately it is the mother who separates him from nature. The only way to recover the real through the symbolic is to kill it, this is the revelation waiting for Van Vliet in the cockles of his mother's heart. Listening to those apparently chaotic rhythms of *Trout Mask Replica* and *Lick My Decals Off Baby*, we might thus imagine an impotent Van Vliet inside his mother's heart, tearing murderously at the ventricles, like some kind of cardio-psychopath. A symbolic assault on the symbolic, of course, is bound to fail, and as Captain Beefheart's aberrant rhythms resolve themselves through repetition, we can feel the maternal heart shrug off the assault and pick up its pulse, incorporating the syncope into the beat and heading for the euphoria of syncopation.

As aesthetic contexts shift around it, Van Vliet's music may seem to undergo a transformation, evoking the classic horror device of delayed interpretation, where the elements of a baffling situation suddenly click into place, and the danger which we had vaguely sensed leaps out at us, real and immediate and overpowering. The crepuscular terror of our crossroader caught on the plain is at the origin of this device. As the sun goes down the shadows enter the abject territory of the is-it-or-isn't-it, and the mental faculties are keyed up to a pitch of fearful interpretation under the maximalist stress of the anything-is-possible, the critical intelligence running on a pre-panic of pure adrenaline. In his explorations of the gothic recesses lurking in the blues, Van Vliet concentrated on those moments of agonised hesitation where, confronted with the transformation of the natural into something wholly other, we hold on as long as possible to the world we know and in which we know ourselves to be sane.

The Blues-Gothic of Abjection

In "Glider" from *Spotlight Kid*, that bluesiest of Beefheart albums, we move through just such a moment of chthonic terror predicated on monstrous transformation:

> Into the sun in my glider
> There's a shadow beside her

The pilot is alone with a girl and immediately notes the reassuring shadow which she casts, the sun is there to keep everything on an even keel, to suppress the powers of darkness, and one can imagine that the pilot is up in his glider to chase the sun around the world so that he will never have to experience the night and its terrors. The shadow is mentioned again as the pilot takes his "silent cues" from the clouds. Is he nervously bent on seducing his passenger, timing his moves to the arbitrary changes of the weather? The suspense is sexual, as it so often is before the shocking revelation. A classic horror film scenario, then, with a boy in an isolated claustrophobic space beginning to suspect that there is something uncanny about the beautiful female who has invited herself into his life.[15] Then it gets worse:

It begins to rain on her window pane
Up in my glider
There's no shadow beside her
Thundering 'n' lightning
Gettin' pretty frightenin'
I feel like an outsider

The sun disappears and her side of the cockpit is showered with rain, and we can feel the boy ransacking his memory for details of those rumours he dismissed in his super-rational arrogance and urgent desire to get her on her own. The sexual tables have been turned, however, and he begins to fear this girl as an animal surprised by darkness fears its predators. Will he ask her a question or two, or take a nervous peripheral peek to see if anything is changing, to see why she hasn't answered, to see what she is waiting for? As his fear increases, Van Vliet's pilot "feels like an outsider", his sense of isolation pitches to a panic as his companion flirts weirdly with the light and the shadows, as the storm brews up and the sun is blotted out. As in Rousseau's painting, this *mauvasie surprise* also carries connotations of the birth trauma, as the vampiric woman reduces the boy to the abject fears of infancy. Suddenly he "feels like an outsider", thrust from the womb into the horrors of social being, the pitfalls of misinterpretation.

The pilot is relieved when the sun comes back out and casts a shadow off the girl, scotching his fantastic fears, bringing him back within permissible bounds of reality. As the monstrous threat of the castrating female recedes, he celebrates with a burst of sexual arrogance: "me and my baby ain't never gonna bring my glider down". But is his jubilation premature? Is this another of those stock horror devices—the false alarm? What happens, for example, when the sun goes in again? As an unwritten ending of this song one can imagine the aircraft crashing mysteriously, and persistent rumours of a pale young woman emerging from the wreckage, or a large dog, or a bat, or a strange maleficent light.

Van Vliet explored another dimension of blues-gothic transformation in his version of Robert Pete Williams's "Grown So Ugly" (*Safe As Milk*). Williams's song commemorates his release in 1959 from Angola State Prison Farm where he had served three years on a murder conviction. The years of abject incarceration have wrought changes in him which he discovers in a moment of shocking alienation: He has grown so ugly that he is no longer himself. Suspense is created as he searches for his shoes then washes his face before picking up his comb and moving to the mirror, that instrument of terror, of self-love gone bad. Williams has woken up changed in a world where his old self is no longer feasible; like the new-born infant, he has been pitched into a challenging new environment which he must somehow learn to master:

> I made a move
> Didn't know what to do
> I tipped way forward
> Got to break and run

His first impulse is to run, but how can you flee from yourself? This is the extra turn of the screw, as the outsider becomes an "insider" locked into one body with the monster incorporate.[16] The hesitation here is pure intergeneric abjection as the speaker seems to lose a sense not just of who he is, but of what he is. Like Kafka's Gregor Samsa or Roth's David Kapesh, he must re-learn how to be, and we see this traumatic process begin with that indeterminate "move" he makes in the confusion of unknowing. The slow-gathering sludge of blues unease accelerates then into a moment of cinematic shock: "Got so ugly I don't even know myself", as the social stresses of being with others is sharpened into the existential stress of *being other*.

It would be difficult to exaggerate the importance of the mirror in the gothic tradition as the hinge between the social and the psychological, the means by which we acquire the shocking knowledge of change, the brutal reflection of an irruption of the unreal into the real, an appalling transgression of all that we had considered solid and dependable—Frankenstein's monster, Jekyll and Hyde, Harker in castle Dracula, the Elephant Man (who preferred to gaze at the angelic portrait of his mother, as if practising a form of radical nostalgia for the prelapsarian world before the fall of his disastrous conception), Dorian Gray and the devolving mirror of the portrait, and now Mr Ugly, who suffers the destructive shock of becoming other in an unchanged world. The regularity with which mirrors and reflections occur in Van Vliet's lyrics offers us a secret passageway into the hidden chambers of his gothic sensibility.

The theme of transformation informs "Mirror Man" (*Strictly Personal*), with its obsessive sequence of bizarre permutations: "Mirror girl mirror boy / Mirror frog mirror man / Mirror worm mirror worm / Mirror bird mirror germ". The mirror seems to offer a way out of linear temporality, a reversible perspective in which one conquers anxiety by becoming the other: "Lead me to your mirror now / Lead me to your mirror then /

Mirror man mirror man / Mirror you mirror me". The mirror here is a porthole to an alternative existence, rather than a reflective device which reveals and enforces the catastrophic discontinuities of one's present condition; it offers a new space rather than the horribly compromised environment which Mr Ugly has to cope with. In "Steal Softly Thru Snow" (*Trout Mask Replica*) the speaker laments: "The black paper between a mirror breaks my heart that I can't go", and if "Mirror Man" suggests that one can flee oneself by treating the mirror as a door of perception and breaking on through to the other side, here the speaker is tragically excluded from such an issue. He cannot pass through the mirror into the utopia beyond (which, typically for Van Vliet, is figured as an Edenic wilderness of swans, geese, and fruitful hills), he is excluded from nature, confined to the narrowness of his species, a prey to anxiety and death. In the poem "Three Months in the Mirror",[17] Van Vliet imagines a "moth pup" which flies through a soft mirror, leaving a smell of "burnt powder". This strange ceremony, performed with the help of some socks and light bulbs, again evokes the idea of a parallel world beyond the mirror and the existence of certain hybrid creatures which have the power to pass from one side to the other, irrupting into the real as emissaries of the maximalist anything-is-possible. Such creatures (and the tradition of the fantastic in litera-ture and film is full of them) remind us simultaneously of the prolifer-ating possibilities on the other side and the strictures of our present confinement. While the "moth pup" can fly through the mirror at the cost of a little burnt powder, the couple who release it remain subject to the mirror's reflective power, pitilessly defined by their image and the primal curse of humanity which roots them to the spot, wingless under the sun. Through the potent (if slightly hackneyed) motif of the mirror, then, Van Vliet creates suggestive parables which tap into the utopia/dystopia dialectic, the social imperatives and stresses which inform so much of the gothic and fantastic traditions. The mirror objectifies this dialectic as it beguiles us into imaginings of the beyond even as it casts us back into the pit of social reality, mocking us with an image of ourselves as others see us.[18] Mr Ugly's trauma is precisely this abject in-betweenness of "what am I?", as the change he has seen in the mirror is reflected back on him and redoubled by his woman's scorn when she refuses to recognise the sense of personal continuity he feels beneath the transformation, and casts him into the social abyss.

Horror films pay close neurotic attention to the dynamics of space, twisting tension out of degrees of distance and proximity, raising a frisson by the sudden unnaturally rapid contraction of the buffer zone. The best soundtracks mirror and extend this effect, abutting the ghostly whisper and the scream, extruding silence into a sudden bang. In their manipulation of the sonics of anxious space, werewolf films rely on the transition from the howl to the growl, as the far away incongruity is all of a sudden imminently intimate. The most obvious link between the tradition of gothic transformation and the blues is the figure of Chester Burnett, the Howlin' Wolf, the blues lycanthrope himself. We have seen how "Glider" plays with the possibility of transformation as a prelude to attack, and how it relies on the dynamics of a restricted space to set up a hesitation between sexual intimacy and predation; at the other end of *The Spotlight Kid* we find a terrestrial version of this situation as Vital Willie takes Weepin' Milly out for a drive. "I'm Gonna Booglarize you Baby" is a lycanthropic fantasy set to music, a masterful employment of the Wolfian blues timbre in the gothic manipulation of sonic space. The title establishes an initial uncertainty: is it a threat of violence concealed behind a promise of sexual thrills? Or is the lycanthrope, sickened by the violence he is bound to commit, trying to warn off his victim? The ambiguity of "booglarize" suggests metaphor rather than simile as the dominant rhetorical mode, the presence of one thing in another rather than two separate entities linked by similarities. In this it prefigures the concrete anthropomorphism of the monster; a lycanthrope, like a vampire, is a kind of metaphor sprung into life. Van Vliet here takes a decisive step beyond the hierarchical similes deployed in "Wild Life" (*Trout Mask Replica*) and "Kindness of a Dog", and conjures a scene closer to the seduction of Eve in the *Book of Genesis*. The lycanthrope, like the snake before the curse, represents a confusion of the natural and the unnatural in which any clear precedence of signified and signifier is lost. It represents a third term, which, in signifying itself, achieves enormous potency. As in the garden of Eden, this powerful presence instigates the desire which becomes its hallmark. The primal stress of this seduction is replayed endlessly in the blues, and we can hear it again in "I'm Gonna Booglarize you Baby" as Van Vliet's anthropomorphism devolves into abjection. When the song is over we have the distinct feeling that another episode in the eternal struggle has played itself out. For the first time, perhaps, popular music takes on something of the eschatological.

The song begins with a guitar riffing dark funk from a swamp boogie with some oddly turned accents, an otherworldly groove; a second guitar arrives to slash out a chord in the other speaker and open the gothic agenda of stereo sound: whatever it is it's coming from over there *and* over there. A single bass note of plunging amplitude suggests something rising from below like Tennyson's Kraken (that evil thing under the bed which hid there waiting for the light to go off, that urge, that thing imprisoned in the cellar). The second time it sounds there is a voice there too, an extra-grammatical utterance which sounds, incongruously, like a deformed "hurrah"; more likely it is an "aahh" of anticipation, a creature sound of inhuman understanding. By this time the hi-hat is thin and busy and irritating, pulling a quicker tempo out of the nasty bass which grooves in a very narrow range, as if unwilling to probe into those darker harmonic corners, scared of what it might find there, conjuring horrors through its refusal to dissipate stress. And then the singing begins: "The moon was a drip on ah dark hood / 'N they were drivin' around 'n around". The reflection in the wet car's bonnet is an obsessive detail worthy of J.G. Ballard's *Crash*, the slick bodywork of the "machine" mirroring the gothic emblem of a bulbous moon as night falls on the urban jungle.[19] This oblique imagery combines with Van Vliet's wolfish growl to raise the expectation of some erotic horror show of sexual predation—straddling and kicking, stiletto heels tearing the upholstery, blood spraying onto the windscreen, a limp arm dangling across the sill as the vehicle is abandoned. Vital Willie is going to "booglarize" Weepin' Milly if he can find a secluded spot out of town, but Milly suggests that they go back to her place where she will "slow [his] machine right down". Is she manoeuvring him onto safer ground, or is she, as Mina does in some versions of the Dracula story, contemplating a sacrificial surrender to his predatory lusts?[20] Vital Willie's sexual threat is explicit in his name, and his power is present in that irreducible term "booglarize". What does he mean by it? To burglarize and bugger in the form of a boogie? To seduce his victim into the chaos of sexuality and the curse of death? Is it the prelude to some kind of blues-inflected *danse macabre*? Whatever we imagine, by the end of the song Van Vliet's articulate growl has devolved into a howl, the very distillation of the blues-gothic. The field holler of the solitary sharecropper has been abjected and let loose in the city. It is more than enough to bring tears to the eyes of Weepin' Milly.

Interpretation Versus Appeasement, Maximalism and the Absurd

Let us revisit and extend our response to the sentence by Kristeva cited above: "The abjection of Nazi war crimes reaches its apex when death, which, in any case, kills me, interferes with what, in my living universe, is supposed to save me from death: childhood, science, among other things." (*Powers* 232). Nazi terror succeeded in rendering deathly all of those things which define life as an energetic system opposed to death. It perpetrated a massive irruption of death into life, drawing on the compulsive fears exploited in the gothic and converting its imaginings into stark political reality. Hitler, Himmler, Goering and the others were "monsters" who *existed*. Music is another of life's weapons against death which, since it expresses socio-political realities, is also subject to the morbid interference of abjection as perpetrated by the Nazis and identified by Kristeva. The blues-gothic, when stripped of its humour, or when pushed towards a hardly funny hysterical extreme of black humour, strays into the perverse territory of political abjection. Genocide occurs when a species turns murderously against itself, when it interprets the difference between strong and weak as a reason for eliminating the latter. The doubts and hesitations which reflect humanity's psychic legacy of abjection become at this point a principle of division, a prerogative of the weak. This is expressed through an asymmetrical distribution of knowledge: the strong know what will happen to the weak. The Nazis could, in some cases, keep their Jewish victims guessing and hoping until the last moment, withholding the rules of their language games and transforming the functionality of objects without telling anyone. The primal stress of the crossroads becomes an instrument of power through which the powerful may create for themselves the illusion that they are exempt from abjection; the possession of a victim frees one from that sinking feeling of exposure, the whirlpool of social angst, the maximalist interpenetration of inside and out. Led on, one imagines, by a coincidence of motifs (the train of the travelling bluesman suggesting Eichmann's trains of human freight) Van Vliet strayed into this dangerous territory with the song "Dachau Blues" (*Trout Mask Replica*) which surrenders itself to a kind of attraction of opposites, as the dirty blues soils itself with images of nazi "hygiene". The avant-gardism of its formal and generic deformations combines with its apparently misplaced humour, to suggest a rewriting of the rules of popular music, a musical victimisation of the listener who isn't in the know and who must consequently assume the full burden of doubts and hesitations generated by the piece. It is by far Captain Beefheart's riskiest song.

Houston Baker writes: "the dominant blues syntagm in America is an instrumental imitation of *train-wheels-over-track-junctures*. This sound is the 'sign,' as it were, of the blues, and it combines an intriguing melange of phonics: rattling gondolas, clattering flatbeds, quilling whistles, clanging bells, rumbling boxcars, and other railroad sounds." (8) Sure 'nuff, but since the Final Solution and the cultural response, a train is also Auschwitz-Birkenau, with a new vocabulary of sounds: wheezing coldbreath, moaning from heat and hunger, whispered prayers, the breaking of icicles, vomiting noises, weeping, the hush of fear and expiring hope, the noise of arrival (compounded of all of the foregoing) followed by the bark of orders and the barking of big dogs, the clash of tools, the click-clack of military heels, the shuffling of weak feet, the whimper of children and mothers, the cornered politesse of Eichmann in his glass box, the scary feedback and bouncing spring reverberation as the microphones are displaced in the courtroom. The deathliness of *Dachau Blues* is a an obvious aberration in the joke-rich often whimsical image-scapes of *Trout Mask Replica*; it is very serious, and it proposes the blues mood as somehow relevant to the holocaust, channelling its gothic undercurrent into that depthless reservoir of historical horror. It risks giving offence while attempting to clear a space within the emerging idiom of the blues-gothic for political commentary of the most urgent kind.

In a pointed criticism of Zappa's rock 'n' roll nostalgia, Van Vliet threw in the loaded word "appeasement", which suggests that the conflicting rhythms and disjunctive time signatures of his *Trout Mask Replica* music make it *more* rather than less capable of handling the weightiest and most controversial issues:

> Frank believes in time and we could never get it together. He writes all his music and gets sentimental about good old rock 'n' roll but that's appeasement music.[21]

The word that Van Vliet seems to be insisting on through its omission here is "down"—Zappa writes all his music *down*, fixing it in time and defining the way that it should be performed. To join the dots of this argument: fixed music eliminates spontaneity and deviance, it is "appeasement music" in that it meets the listeners' expectations about beat and measure. It is hard to think of Zappa's music in these terms, but perhaps we should give Van Vliet the benefit of the doubt, and accept that this is what it sounded like to him, or at least that this was one way in which he chose to define his own endeavours in relation to it. The distinction is something like that which Bamberger draws between country and urban blues:

> Bar lengths might change, the players speed up or slow down, verse lengths change. Country blues are a record of the motions and breath of a particular body. When the blues went to the city it had to conform, to become the steady pulse of a collective body electric. All of the players had to know what the music would do next.
>
> (35)

From this perspective we can see Zappa as a the city slicker, playing a regularised blues which is already more than half way to becoming rock 'n' roll, a music which betrays its roots in the primitive vernacular to win over (or appease) a mass market made up of listeners who also have to know "what the music will do next". Music that can be predicted is apt to convert real feeling into sentimentality, as it lulls us away from the actual moment of listening into vaguer and vaguer associations, peeling backwards through the memory until it beguiles us into a mood of fluffy infantile diffuseness. Van Vliet, by contrast, would retain a grip on the origins of the music in spontaneous body expression, and a claim to the reserves of folk wisdom which go along with it. We can detect in this stance a combination of the radical and the reactionary which leads back to the totalitarian undertones of "Dachau Blues". Van Vliet's determination to liberate himself from the collectivising heartbeat of the "body electric" seems to have led him into an authoritarian mode, where music, its composition, performance and reception, become issues of power. His blues would have it both ways, it would evoke the tradition while claiming the right to transgress its conventions at any moment; within a sado-masochistic dynamic of strength and weakness it would employ elements of ritual while eschewing the predictable as a source of sentimentality.[22]

Once again, in discussing blues, we encounter the problematic of authenticity, but here, as it is curiously conflated with the question of authority, we can see how it impinges directly on the content of the music in question, on the subjects that may be treated, on what the music may be allowed to say. Rather than offering the public what it wants to hear (and it is a fair assumption that most people most of the time do not want to hear about the extermination camps), Van Vliet will say what he likes about whatever he chooses, having won this freedom of speech through his radical departures from musical norms:

> Dachau blues those poor Jews
> Dachau blues those poor Jews
> Dachau blues, Dachau blues those poor Jews
> Still cryin' 'bout the burnin' back in World War Two's

This text is anti-genocide, but it is also a protest against the self-censorship of musical form, or the capitulation to market standards; if the form is felt to be inadequate to the subject-matter then so much the better, the point is the more forcefully made and the power of its maker by so much enhanced. And it is precisely in the exhilaration of rule-breaking that we can hear yet again that old blues strain of personal defiance, raised from the context of interpersonal strife to the bloody field of mass murder and human catastrophe "I ain't going to be your low-down dog no more." Somehow this was an extension which the best blues had always seemed to be crying out for, a transposition of personal virility into the realm of real political influence.[23] Eight years after *Trout Mask Replica*, we heard it again in Johnny Rotten's "God save the Queen, a fascist regime", although less powerfully, since by that time punk had already been formally commodified and was well on its way to becoming "appeasement music."

Nonsense Verse and Maximalist Resistance

Van Vliet's problem, while working on *Trout Mask Replica* was, if we run with Bamberger's categories for a moment, that of the Texan country bluesman arriving in the city and forming a group: how to hold on to those cherished irregularities of form when all the other players have to know what is coming next? In some ways it is the dilemma of the radical politician who must play the demagogue in order to realise his ambition of power. Zappa developed his famous lexicon of hand signals and rehearsed his bands to death as a way of squaring this circle, while Van Vliet, as we have seen, rushed dangerously into a mad paradox: he taught his musicians to play his irregularities in minute detail, evolving a dialectical method of structured spontaneity which was inimical to mental health and strangely reminiscent, in its oxymoronic perversion, of the stage-managed crowd of mass political gatherings. To avoid the sentimental slide into appeasement (one thinks here of Neville

Chamberlain's pathetic grin and fluttering scrap of paper) Van Vliet became a dictator; and in the trauma of this non-solution we can discover a formal explanation for the anger and bitterness that can be sensed so often behind the weirdness of *Trout Mask Replica*. A track like "Moonlight on Vermont", for example, sounds like an argument, an impossible social situation breaking out into music as the players work their frustrations off on each other, led by the heightened raging blues melancholy of Van Vliet's vocal delivery.

The blues train would carry you from a worse place to a better one, at least that is what you hoped, and the voyage at least was exhilarating; if you were disappointed, as you frequently would be, by the conditions awaiting you in the industrial north, you could take the train in the opposite direction, back towards the fields and the old folks, enjoying the return journey as an intermezzo of suspended nostalgia, you might even compose a song to commemorate the feeling: a having-it-both-ways-blues. The train promised mobility at least, and in the recent context of the no-choice fixed location of slavery, it could be said to be your friend. It inspired you with a certain life-rhythm, and taught you fluid form. As Houston Baker comments: "Even as they [the blues singers] speak of paralysing absence and ineradicable desire, their instrumental rhythms suggest change, movement, action, continuance, unlimited and unending possibility." (8). The African legacy, perhaps, the ability to repeat *and* accumulate effect. The deportees climbing aboard the Nazi trains were told that they were being sent somewhere better, or deported for their own good; they were probably terrified but clinging to the hope of a favourable issue, exercising their faith. Soon they must have realised that these trains were nothing but mobile prisons, a horrible contradiction-in-terms, which imposed a sickening rhythm of panic and tortured endurance, a narrowing down of form, a trauma too deep for the blues, for any form of creativity.

So what is Beefheart doing in rhyming "Jews" with "blues"? What else rhymes with these words? "Hues", "trews", "chews", "news", "flues", "didgeridoos"? Nonsense possibilities abound, so why "jews" and "blues" so contiguously? Could the blues have been a music for jews? How does the Afro-American experience of slavery match up to the Holocaust? Can we picture a ditch-digger or a member of the Sonderkommando sitting on the threshold of the blockhaus playing for the kapos?

Hardly.

Interpretation is liable to break down at this point, baffled by the unimaginable. Theoretical, pseudo-theoretical and aesthetic formulations can only approach the abject asymptotically. Van Vliet's song, however, like the events it evokes, provokes a maximalist backlash in the manifest absence of any single satisfying context. Better to keep saying than rest mute before the deathly absurd. To deny the unimaginable is an important ethical principle of maximalism.

So.

In the transition from the blues train to the Nazi train the faculty of representation is lost: the travelling bluesman may have been homesick, poor and anxious, maybe even desperate, but he was still able to sing *about* his feelings and incorporate elements of that experience into his performance. In the Nazi trains, one imagines, there was no possibility of an *about*. And here we experience the itch of connectivitis as the hint of another link suggests itself, not with "Dachau Blues", which is aberrant also in its un-Beefheart-like lucidity, but with much else on *Trout Mask Replica* and elsewhere, where Van Vliet's lyrics recall the Victorian counter-tradition of nonsense verse.

In a repressive society, Edward Lear and Lewis Carroll took to writing nonsense and one technical characteristic of such verse is that it abolishes the "as if", closing the gap between reality and its reformulation in figurative language, suggesting that there is in fact only one thing, an inclusive topsy-turvy world in which, without the faculty of figurative speech, we are roundly imprisoned in a vehicle which is also its tenor and a train which is just a train. Such work also abolishes the *about*, and this perhaps accounts for the nervy menace which lurks behind "Jabberwocky" and "The Owl and the Pussycat" — such works deny us space. "In Dachau Blues" Van Vliet opts for the anecdotal to tell his horror story, and the song is *about* the holocaust, defiantly annexing that space for reflection and form-finding, nudging us towards a saving style. It is blues, not Dachau. This leaves the possibility that it is perhaps Van Vliet's more nonsensical absurdist work which carries the atmospherics of the Nazi trains, where we have our faces (and minds) pressed up so closely to the experience itself that we cannot find the room for manoeuvre, to make *this* equal *that*, where we flounder in the annulment of style. Van Vliet's use of wordplay during interviews also sometimes carries a hint of fascist brutality in the sadistic alternation of sense and nonsense; interpretation is alternately encouraged and blocked as the good cop of maximalism and the bad cop of postmodernist relativity go to work on us, until we are forced to acknowledge (to the exclusion of everything else) the gigantic presence of the person who is saying these things to us:

> It's hard to use the English language. I'd rather play a tune on a horn but I've always felt that I didn't want to train myself. Because when you get a train, you've got to have an engine and a caboose. I think it's better to train the caboose. You train yourself, you strain yourself.[24]

The rhythm of this is like that of insensate cruelty, of a cat torment-ing a bird, or a child tormenting a cat. These nonsensical verbal substi-tutions function in the same way as Nazi euphemism, imposing assent by blocking interpretation. The nonsensicality of the statement "I think it's better to train the caboose" is worse than irritating, it carelessly dispenses with criticism, implying that, whatever one says, the quotient of meaning in one's words will never vary. While Van Vliet does seem to mount raids on the inarticulate, providing us for example with the intriguing vignette of a train undergoing training, the efficacy of the concept of the unimaginable as a motivating force and tool for apprais-ing and comparing our mental acts and experiences seems to have drained away. There is a promiscuity about the wordplay which brings with it a sense of political defeatism. If the unimaginable is redundant, then maximalism is finite, and we do indeed live in a post-modern age of relativity, pastiche and despair.

In a spirit of maximalist resistance, we could begin yet again, then, by proposing a committed juxtaposition of cultural forms: a reading of Lewis Carroll's "Jabberwocky" against the backdrop of, say, Felix Nussbaum's "Self-Portrait in the Death Camp":

> "Twas brillig and the slithy toves did gyre and gimble in the wabe, etc."

CHAPTER FOUR

Laughter Inside and Out:
The Subject-Object on the Edge

In 1942 Salvador Dalí reflected on the compositional problems involved in the making of his painting "Premonition of Civil War":

> In this picture I showed a vast human body breaking out into monstrous excrescences, arms and legs tearing at one another in a delirium of autostrangulation. As a background to this architecture of frenzied flesh devoured by a narcissistic and biological cataclysm I painted a geological landscape, that had been uselessly revolutionised for thousands of years, congealed in its "normal course." The soft structure of that great mass of flesh in civil war I embellished with a few boiled beans, for one could not imagine swallowing all that unconscious meat without the presence (however uninspiring) of some mealy and melancholy vegetable.
>
> (*Secret* 357)

And so, one imagines, the painting gained a second title: "Soft Construction with Boiled Beans", while the image itself hovers between the two, being both a "premonition" and a "construction" a political statement and a pictorial composition; the passage from one to the other being facilitated by the addition to the visual diet of some essential dietary fibre, a handful of magic beans. And Dalí is thinking too of his viewer, like a solicitous chef he adds a vegetable to make his picture more digestible; the "unconscious meat" of his surrealist dreams is leavened with the quotidian, a scattering of beans, a familiar element realistically painted, a reminder, perhaps, of the origins of this unpalatable new image-making method in the solid traditions of still life, where food sits inertly on the table in comforting abundance or healthy frugality. This hankering after antique fare both on the plate and in the picture hints perhaps at a conviction on the artist's part that a millennial constipation of "useless revolution" was crying out for the twin purgatives of surrealism and fascism. For Dalí, the aesthetic (and perhaps political) success of an image, we may even say its "beauty", was directly linked to how easily and pleasurably it might be consumed. Composition, here, is already akin to gastronomy.

This gustatory aesthetic was an expression of the ultimate desire to possess and, indeed, merge with the object through introjection. As Dalí explained:

> Our need of taking part in the existence of these things and our yearning to form a whole with them are shown to be emphatically material through our sudden consciousness of a new hunger we are suffering from. As we think it over, we find suddenly that it does not seem enough to devour things with our eyes, and our anxiety to join actively and effectively in their existence brings us to want to *eat them*.
>
> ("Object" 95)

The impulse can be a loving one, as in Dalí's professed intention to eat Gala after her death, or a more purely erotic one as in Zappa's "Jelly Roll Gum Drop" (*Ruben and the Jets*) where the teenage persona wants to take a "tiny bite" out of his baby, the eponymous Jelly Roll Gum Drop, the girl as confectionery. The title track of Captain Beefheart's *Lick My Decals Off Baby* is more explicit, passing beyond foreplay and teenage coulding to the act itself:

> Rather than I want to hold your hand,
> I wanna swallow you whole
> 'n I wanna lick you everywhere it's pink
> 'n everywhere you think

How exactly Van Vliet is going to lick a girl he has already swallowed whole is not explained in the song. The felicitous internal rhyme "She stuck out her tongue 'n the fun begun" suggests that the girl herself will also be doing some licking. To tongue, it seems, is also to be tongued, as the membranes come together in a natural act of fun which simply begins without any prior exertion of the will.

Like the futurist synaesthetics discussed in our introduction, Dalí's reflections also alert us to the proximity of looking and eating and the temptation to pass from the first to the second, while Zappa's sinister teenager begins his lovesong with the line "Jelly Roll Gum Drop, I've got my eye on you." The visual treat of looking at food we are about to eat is perhaps difficult to overestimate, if it doesn't look good it won't taste good, at least not at first. The visual shock of vomit makes the same point: as we turn away, disgusted and yet fascinated by our disgust, we are reacting to something which once was food, "hideously looking back at what once was beautiful", as Van Vliet has it.[1] Roadkill packs a similar punch, and the two are brought together in that inventive slang term "pavement pizza", which draws its force precisely from the suggestion that the vomit is still somehow a food item, something which might be re-eaten. The transition from looking to eating, according to Dalí at least, involves sudden discovery *and* posed reflection, an urge which is weighed in the balance. Why should there be this moment of tense hesitation? Why not simply tuck in? Perhaps Dalí is reluctant to surrender the advantages of the voyeur, his painter's privileges, and is testing himself against that primeval tension between holding back and letting go, the richness of self-possession calculated against the risks of self-investment; which takes us back to the infantile potty dilemma discussed in Chapter Three. When the voyeur cracks and reaches out to touch it is, after all, a moment of high maximalist drama,[2] which can turn to tragedy if, as he fears it might, the visceral contact turns out to be a literal disillusionment. We can imagine on the one hand the food voyeur hoarding comestibles, maybe even painting them with frigid fascination like Paul Cézanne or Wayne Thiebaud, and on the other the disillusioned gourmand satiated with participation, slave to the machine, lacking distance, living it out, all body. The erotics of this dichotomy are complex and perverse, and include the bulimic trying to get back "to what once was beautiful", the Roundhouse Man from "Orange Claw Hammer" (*Trout Mask Replica*) bingeing on beer and bananas and waking up inside the bin, covered in vomit, a failure again, ready to beget seven babies on the "soft lass with brown skin", a spectacular self-investment in the visceral. In Van Vliet's image the Roundhouse Man is both inside and outside, both a fœtus coming to after a difficult passage back into his mother's womb, and an instrument of fecundation ready to fill the belly of the soft lass. While incorporated into the objective world, he remains capable of acting on it from the outside. His inside-outsideness is, as we shall see, typical of the maximalist body and the contending pleasures and pains it arouses and is subject to.

Earlier in "Orange Claw Hammer" there is another tense and transgressive confrontation which revolves around a "suffering hunger" and the perilous question "To eat or not to eat?":

Lic-licorice twisted around under uh fly
'n uh youngster cocked her eye
God before me if I'm not crazy
Is my daughter
Come little one with yer little dimpled fingers
Gimme one 'n I'll buy you a cherry phosphate
Take you down, to the foamin' brine 'n water
'n show you the wooden tits
On the Goddess with the pole out s'full sail
That tempted away your peg legged father

The "lic-licorice" is coiled up like a snake in Eden and the Lear-like father who has been beguiled once is tempted again. And what about that "lic-licorice"? The only moment on *Trout Mask Replica* when Van Vliet's faultless delivery seems to falter; and it is a risky passage of poetry: father and daughter gather around the coil of licorice, which, thanks to the attendant fly, reminds us of other things which flop and fall in coils. The daughter is young enough to have "little dimpled fingers" and yet the father wants to embark on her sexual initiation after an exchange of sweetmeats, the poisoned chalice of sexual knowledge symbolised by that attractive-repulsive sounding "cherry phosphate". As in the reconciliation of Lear and Cordelia (not to mention the word association of "Neon Meate Dream of a Octafish" [*Trout Mask Replica*]), there is at least a suggestion of incestuous hunger. Sweetmeats and shit, incestuous desires and poison, no surprise, perhaps, to hear that guilty stutter which isolates the "lick" in "licorice". And there is a tragic end to the piece as the "foamin' brine and water" begin to flow from the father's eyes as he cedes to his daughter's sugary charms or confronts the impossibility of doing so:

'n here it is I'm with you my daughter
thirty years away can make uh seaman's eyes
Uh round house man's eyes flow out water
Salt water

Sugar and salt, the alpha and omega of taste, and the phonetic pun on "seaman" alerts us to the blues origins of Van Vliet's fraught lyric. In Willie Dixon's standard "Spoonful", that masterpiece of equivocal flirtation, it is an open question whether we are dealing with a spoonful of sugar which stands for the metaphorical sweetness of love, or a spoonful of sperm which stands instead for the salty practicality of sex. Perhaps in the end we are simply dealing with a spoonful of sex, a blues measure.

In Captain Beefheart's "Neon Meate Dream of a Octafish" (*Trout Mask Replica*), we have a stark and paratactic reminder of these antinomies:

> Squirmin' serum 'n semen 'n syrup 'n semen
> 'n serum
> Stirrupped in syrup

The repeated "and", abbreviated to an urgent apostrophe, expresses the rapid oscillation between the salt-sexy and the sweet-sexy which are fighting it out perhaps in some kind of oneiric belly, where the serum has been added as an additional neutralising agent. A reconciliation of these dyspeptic elements occurs in the frankly erotic "White Jam" (*The Spotlight Kid*):

> She serves me flowers 'n yams
> 'N in the night when I'm full
> She brings me white jam
> 'N I don't know where I am

Sperm *as* jam, but what exactly does the verb "to bring" mean here; surely the speaker is already in possession of the white jam which he "serves" to the woman in exchange for the flowers and yams? Apart from this transitive oddity which seems to be another manifestation of the body's inside-outness, there is the problem of repletion— how can the speaker go on eating when he is already full? Perhaps the swoon at the end of the song is induced by bulimic nausea or a burst blood vessel rather than the overwhelming sweetness of orgasm. What on the surface appears to be a romantic ballad in the risqué tradition of the blues becomes at this point an essay in the repellent, a mode, as we have seen, which Van Vliet and indeed Zappa found irresistible.

The Erotics of the Hypertrophic Edge

During rehearsals for the Ensemble Modern *Yellow Shark* concerts in 1992, Zappa was so amused by the grotesque gargling sonority of the didgeridu played through a "partially-filled coffee pot" that he had to leave the room. Why?

> You know the noise that comes out of a didgeridu, that kind of circular-breathing-type low droning noise? If you plunged anything that would

make that noise into a liquid, you get the tone and the bubbles at the same time. It's pretty nauseating, but fascinating.

(Menn 45)

"Nauseating, but fascinating", air down a tube into liquid, the noise we all like to make with our first milkshakes, an imitation of involuntary body noise pitched against the parental taboo. What Zappa stumbled across and took such obvious delight in staging was the music of the digestive tract amplified, externalised and performed by a serious and dedicated musician for the pleasure of a note-attentive discerning public. His hysterical outburst consecrates another exemplary release of maximalist excess, as the intestinal form of the didgeridu symbolises and performs the merger of the musician (subject) with the musical instrument (object). While every musical performance is a confrontation of subject and object, as the performer attempts to communicate through sound by observing or transgressing certain established conventions, Zappa's scene aptly focuses attention on the instrumentality of the body as the key element in this synthesis. By externalising the sounds of the digestive tract, the didgeridu objectfies the subject who plays (and digests): as the body is turned inside out through the sonorisation of its vital processes, the embodied subject, whose sense of identity is co-terminous with the body's fixed limits, is forced out into the objective world where the body is co-extensive with all matter. The bourgeois myth of the subjective body, existing for and in itself, gives way to the modernist postulate of the objectified subject, which exists precisely on the edge. From the subjective certitudes cultivated by the arch individual of the 19th and early 20th centuries, grounded in a secure sense of the usefulness and passivity of its objects, the modernist and post-modernist subject enters a crisis of cross-contamination with the objective world, where the buffer zone is increasingly populated by transitional phases of the object-subject relation. The riotous overanimation of objects in Alice's looking-glass prefigures the irreducible anxieties of metaphysical painting,[3] while the fragmentations and interpenetrations of analytical cubism and the machine men of Léger and Boccioni are so many symptoms of the permeability of the edge: as the objectified subject merges with the subjectified object, the edge expands until it threatens to engulf the entire cultural field. This image of the hypertrophic edge is an expression of the "new hunger" noted by Salvador Dalí, and it stands as a figure for maximalist epistemology.

A visual arts equivalent to Zappa's discovery might be Mona Hatoum's optic fibre videos, mentioned above in Chapter Two, where the artist turns herself inside-out and takes the viewer on a tour of her body's channels and chambers.[4] The subjectivity of the artist is again thrown into question by a staging of the materiality of her body, and the viewer may undergo a concomitant shock of objctification when exposed to this violation of the conventional parameters of cultural (and social) exchange. Like the insertion of the optic fibre, Zappa's technical move was invasive and highly significant, taking the physicality of close-miked recording technique one speculative step beyond, actually into the body and out again. Such artistic processes, relying on the spectacle of the body's objectification, create an hysterical seam where performer and audience meet as subjects thrown into crisis by the loss of the subjective body. Such performances imply not just that one body equals another, but that body itself is mere matter, that the embodied self is meat.

In his performance piece, "Hotdog", the artist Paul McCarthy offered another staging of the loss of subjective control over the body. After cramming his mouth with hotdogs, he taped it shut, exposing himself to asphyxiation if he should vomit in response to the audience's retching.[5] The performance here is menaced by the infectiousness of the bodily spasm, the involuntary response of the body as object, and Zappa's *mise en scène* runs a simlar (though less dangerous) risk, playing off the sympathy between bodies, how convulsions in one may set off convulsions in another by hitting those resonant frequencies of humour, disgust, lust, grief and so on. Body may act on body as matter acts on matter, and Zappa's objectification of his musician's body through the special amplification of her blowing may be seen as an externalisation of musical performance. As his player internalises her instrument, so her playing externalises her body, provoking the bodies in the audience into a parallel response of agitated viscera. Zappa described the sound of the treated didgeridu as "nauseating", and if one takes this as a primary source of disturbance to the listening body (one in which the subject can participate), equivalent to the sight of McCarthy with his mouth full of hotdogs, then the scondary, and much more problematic wave of nausea, arrives with the subject's realisation that the body is laughing or retching *automatically*, in response to the material behaviour of another proximate body. The Roundhouse Man in his puke-stained banana bin could be re-staged as a performance piece by McCarthy or Hatoum.

This externalisation of musical experience, which threatens to annihilate the subject, might be seen as another episode in Zappa's research into the objectification of the individual by the crowd, which began with his critique of fashion conformism in *Freak Out, Absolutely Free* and *We're Only In It For The Money*. On the political level, the subjective body as a site of resistance to mass psychology intrestingly bridges the ideological divide between the Marxist critique of capitalist alienation and Zappa's libertarian-inflected concern for indiviual freedom.

In Ovid's *Metamorphosis*, as we have seen in Chapter Two, Marsyas is punished for his inferior musicianship, and the horror of his fate derives not just from the physical violence of the flaying itself but from the exposure of his insides:

> Why do you tear me from my self, he cries?
> Ah cruel! Must my skin be made the prize?
> This for a silly pipe? he roaring said,
> Mean-while the skin from off his limbs was flay'd.
> All bare, and raw, one large continu'd wound,
> With streams of blood his body bathed the ground.
> The blueish veins their trembling pulse disclos'd,
> The stringy nerves lay naked, and expos'd;
> His guts appear'd distinctly each expressed,
> With ev'ry shining fibre of his breast.

(182–183)

What a recording it would have been if someone had been on hand to mike up Marsyas during his agony and to capture the music of his body's special trauma! And what *kind* of a recording would it have been? As funny as the didgeridoo player? Funnier? Thomas Mann gives us a clue in *The Magic Mountain* when a character describes his experience of the "pleura-shock": after pinning back the skin of the breast, the physician palpates the pleura with a blunt instrument, looking for the point at which the pneumothorax may be performed; the patient is under a local anaesthetic only and can feel the transgressive touch on his vitals, his insides are exposed and his shocked response is a blend of horror, nausea, and hilarity:

> The pleura, my friends, is not anything that should be felt of; it does not want to be felt of and it ought not to be. It is taboo. It is covered up with flesh and put away once and for all; nobody and nothing ought to come near it. And now he uncovers it and feels all over it. My God, I was sick at my stomach . . . never in my life have I imagined there could be such a sickening feeling outside hell and its torments. I fainted . . . with all that I heard myself laughing as I went off—not the way a human being laughs —it was the most indecent, ghastly kind of laughing I ever heard. Because,

when they go over your pleura like that, I tell you what it is: it is as though you were being tickled—horribly, disgustingly tickled—that is just what the infernal torment of the pleura- shock is like, and may God keep you from it!

(310)

A hellish hilarity, the desperate mirth of the torture victim whose body has become an instrument for violating the strictest physical and psychological taboos; the hysteria of the subject living through its transformation into object. Notice again how the objecitification of the subjective body is a social phenomenon (as torture always is), a flouting of convention: "nobody and nothing ought to come near it". Marsyas particularly laments the loss of his skin, the removal of which leaves "one large continu'd wound", an undifferentiated mass of inside-outside which anticipates, perhaps, Dalí's "soft structure" torn apart by a civil war of the flesh. Protecting the taboo of the body's insides from the rest of the world, the skin is both the body's edge and its euphemism, to penetrate or remove it is to expose the subject to that-which-must-not-be-said; an exposure screened by the kind of desperate hilarity we note both in Zappa and in Mann's unfortunate invalid, whose nausea is a response to the body's abjection, its entry into a world emptied of distinctions.

Unwittingly or unconsciously, then, Zappa commits an Apollonian violation of his musician, turning her inside out, flaying her for public consumption. The didgeridu as optic fibre or palpating finger objectifies the insides of the player, instrumentalizes her, as if it is she who is being played by the didgeridu, or as if she and it, under Zappa's direction, have become inseparable in ambiguous objecthood. The sado-masochistic undertones of this scene are obvious, as the serious musician transmitting the music of her body is physically restrained from sharing in the joke; while the objectification of the human body suggests, more generally, the pornographic. As the boundary between subject and object dissolves, a double transfer of attributes takes place which implies a range of perverse possibilites. The woman blowing air down a tube into water becomes a woman blowing herself, a woman blowing air through her rectum becomes a woman blowing on a penis planted in her own stomach, a woman blowing through an extruded vagina into her vagina becomes a woman farting wetly through a penis-vagina-rectum into an agitated all-stomach. Where does the woman begin and end, where does the object take over, what does *it* feel? Reading such a complex is a free-for-all of symbolic exchange, interpenetration explodes interpretation as the edge expands to incorporate the elements it once held apart. We can glimpse here an erotics of maximalism as the merger of the subject-object takes us beyond penetration and the model of one thing acting on another, into a world where everything is everything else, where the erotic coincides with the ultimate expansion of significance. Perhaps, then, there is also an element of embarrassment or alarm in Zappa's laughter, since the instrumental woman is also an instrument of sonic seduction; perhaps it is the laugh of a subject which feels itself threatened with objecthood while simultaneously sensing the purer eroticism of the expanding edge; the hysterical outburst of a wavering subject?

The precise promiscuity of this wind-blowing subject-sucking instrumental woman raises the status of the human body in art to a rich and dynamic dialectics of inside and out, furthering the modernist line of research while intersecting with some of its later manifestations. The cubist assault on the integrity of the picture plane led to a revision of the relationship between object-matter and pictorial space, so that one may become indistinguishable from the other. The determination to see in the round loosened the hold of those binary groupings which had so far governed the relationship of subject to object, the visible could now be reconciled with the hidden, the surface with the interior. A desire to see differently produced different things to be seen, which were different precisely in their refutation of established visual logic. Applied to studies of the human form, this new episteme makes itself felt at the level of the skin, which can no longer fulfil its function of holding the body in and demarcating it from the rest of the world. Boccioni's striding figure which constitutes the sculpture entitled "Unique Forms of Continuity in Space" drags through that space some shards of the objective world adhering to its calves and head; or perhaps its skin cannot free itself from all of the space it travels through in such haste, some of which has solidified into fin-like chevrons and incorporated themselves into the body. In Picasso's late female portraits the body seems to interpenetrate itself while its corporeal limits leach definition: ambiguous passages which might or might not be skin (or the inside of skin), baffle the eye, while unfurling orifices suggest that the body, for our pain or delectation, to our disgust or amusement, is about to turn itself inside-out. The "Weeping Woman" etching from 1937, a variation on the painting of the same name discussed in Chapter Two, anounces this discovery, with the lips curling back to reveal the gums, a patch across the chin where the skin seems to have been peeled off Marsyas-like, an eye which might be its socket, and the great rhinoceros nose leaping out of the forehead and bringing part of the brain with it in a splurge of aquatint. In weeping, the inside grief erupts onto the surface and the dissimulating skin is scorched by rivers of lava tears, the configurations of the face are biffed about, swollen and crunched by the boulders and gases of volcanic distress. The subject has failed to keep up appearances.

The Australian performance artist Stellarc has theorised the metaphysics of the skin:

> I think metaphysically, in the past, we've considered the skin as a surface, as interface. The skin has been a boundary of the soul, for the self, and simultaneously, a beginning to the world. Once technology stretches and pierces the skin, the skin as a barrier is erased.
>
> (quoted in Warr 184)

What Picasso began with his etching needle Zappa continued with his recording techniques, getting under the skin of his players for intrusive musical effect, abolishing the tentative dialectics of the interface and laying open the body's sandwich, letting the world rush in. With his didgeridu experiment Zappa hit upon a form of musical piercing, which radically changes the status of the player: the pierced musician becomes one with his or her instrument, coterminous with the world, phenomenological, no longer a body trained to play. The craftiness of technique is abolished when the musician is obliged to play as he or she is obliged to live, inside is also outside and vice versa, the grief or hilarity of the world mesh with and detonate the feelings of the individual. There can no longer be a debate about the sincerity of the performance since hierarchical notions of the depth and shallowness of expression are untenable in this reconfigured musical space. Expression involves externalisation, but how can anything be externalised where inside and outside are one?

We should be careful not to confuse this process with free improvisation, where, even though it may be impossible to decide whether the improvisation has been played with sincerity or not, the player still generates material *via* the instrument, where a skin still exists between player and world allowing the music to begin and end as manufactured phenomenon: the filling of the sandwich is open to extremes of innovation and subjective choice where the player may seek to outflank his or her musical identity, but the sandwich is still closed. And this may account for that awkward fall at the end of the improvisation where observance of the edge is re-imposed and the world lapses back into abuttment and a strict segregation of art from non-art, subject from object.

At this point it might once again be useful to compare Zappa's aesthetics with those of Don Van Vliet, who spoke of his approach to painting in terms borrowed from the old heroic struggle of the abstract expressionists, for whom sincerity was all: "I'm trying to turn myself inside out on the canvas. I'm trying to completely bare what I think at that moment" (Barnes *Captain* 330). This one-way narcissism of self-expression prompted the feminist critique of abstract expressionism, where the dominant gestural metaphor is that of penetration rather than piercing. The formal embarrassment of this mode of picture-making again derived from the edge, or, more precisely, the corner, where the closing down of space restricted the free flow of expressionist gesture, raising the following awkward question: how can I maintain my sincerity when the corner is narrowing down my motifs? The formal response to this was the shaped canvas as pioneered by Frank Stella, which immediately created a dialectic between work and world. Where the edge between motif and support collapses, the inside-outside trajectory is doubled and reversed by an outside-in. The picture pulls away from the picture-making subject as it takes on objecthood. Van Vliet has so far eschewed the use of the shaped canvas, preferring the strictly delimited four-cornered receptacle of self.

Information, Ignorance and the Muff in the Muffin

In the collapse of the distinction between subject and object which, by analogy to the human body, we have figured as a flaying of skin or dissolution of tissue, the euphemism stands as a transitional phase on the way to the promiscuous interpenetrations of maximalist style where what is revealed does not depend on what is concealed. The euphemism holds the subject and the object in a titliating tension by allowing the literal to co-habit with the figurative, the decent with the indecent; it introduces the body as brute matter through a delicacy of rhetorical manner which simultaneously transfigures it into pure style, or almost. To employ a euphemism is not just to admit and deny the body in a single verbal gesture, it is also to imply that the body may be conceived of differently. Just as the unconscious takes its own figurations literally, so the euphemism proposes an equivalent symbolic exchange whereby the body which is concealed possesses and is possessed by the figure which conceals it. This effect is more apparent in the innuendo, that evil twin of the euphemism and favourite device of sex comedians, which, through a perversion of the euphemistic equation, reveals what it purports to conceal and reshuffles the relationship between the subjective body and its objects, producing in the process the maximalist remainder, that something extra which is left over after the working out of the rhetorical equation "By A I really mean B". In this way, the "pencil" which stands for a penis may stretch its powers beyond evocation and actually become the penis. Beyond this substitution lies a madness of additional displacements, since a penis which has mated with a pencil is unlikely to resist further interpenetrations.

Playing on analogies between eating and sexual intercourse, comestibles and genitalia, comedians have often used food as the perfect vehicle for the innuendo. Beyond the obvious parallels revolving around penetration and sensual pleasure, the process of interpenetration triggered by the innuendo finds its own analogy in the processes of ingestion and digestion, through which the body once again suspends its integrality and meets the objective world half way. A food item which reproduces the inside-outness of the innuendo and the body it inscribes is the sandwich, as Graham Greene acknowledged by choosing the phrase "onion sandwiches" as his preferred euphemism for sex.[6] The sandwich combines the explicitness of the innuendo, revealing the filling or body, whose inside is visible all along its edge, with its logic of compromised concealment, since the precise content of the filling is not always to be determined by the content of the edge. Like the innuendo, the sandwich may conceal a supplement at its core, a maximalist corrective to the reductive logic of equivalence. Such edgy rhetorical devices as the euphemism, the innuendo, and the paradox, which depend on an open-closed model of meaning, set up a dichotomy of ignorance and information which often draws attention to the political tensions in a discourse, the moments when power is distributed through the sharing, witholding or manipulation of knowledge. A work which masterfully exploits the erotics of the food euphemism while inscribing it in discourses of authority is Oscar Wilde's *The Importance of Being Earnest*.

At the beginning of the play, Algernon and Jack are expecting Lady Bracknell and Gwendolen, the atmosphere is thick with sexual longing and Algernon is working his way rapidly through a plate of cucumber sandwiches. He can permit himself this indulgence since Lady Bracknell is his Aunt Augusta, just as he can refuse Jack his consent to marry

Gwendolen since she is his ward. There is bargaining to be done, and his greedy consumption of the sandwiches, edge and all, expresses his confidence in the strength of his position. Aunt Augusta, after making a brutal witticism about the rejuvenating effects of widowhood, turns to the sandwiches and the business in hand: If she is to hear a suit for the hand of Gwendolen, it will be with her belly full of bread and cucumber.[7]

The sandwich here is the currency of the matrimonial bid, the stake offered against Gwendolen's body. When Lady Bracknell has taken her collation, Jack may look foward to a taste of Gwendolen's filling. By consuming the stake, however, Algernon arrogates to himself the right of veto over Jack's claims—he can cancel the order. If sex is the motive behind the meeting, then food and its consumption establish the relative strengths of the players. Jack must wait to enjoy Gwendolen because Algernon has overenjoyed the sandwiches; Greene's onions have been replaced by a slice of cucumber. The exchange value of the food is underlined by butler Lane's duplicitous announcement that there were no cucumbers to be had at market that morning, "not even for ready money". The phallic potential of the market has been bought up and consumed, and it is Algernon who holds the key to Jack's sexual ambitions quietly digesting in his stomach. The homoerotic undertones of this are hinted at by Lane's "I went down [to the market] twice", a splendid innuendo to set alongside the euphemism of the sandwiches. The understanding between master and servant perhaps goes beyond the social manipulation of their guests and extends from the drawing-room to the bedroom, and into the territory of Robin Maugham's "The Servant".[8] Notice also how Wilde's social power games turn around an asymmetry of information and ignorance: Algernon sets up his coup by eating the cucumber sandwiches ordered for his termagent Aunt and then consolidates his position through the barefaced lie, obviously prepared in advance with the butler. This is designed to reduce the authority of the matriarch, who clearly believes that she has the right to choose Gwendolen's sexual partner, while cowing Jack with a demonstration of his superior audacity. The social value of the innuendo lies in the creation of a group of initiates who define themselves in opposition to the ignorance of the excluded. Jack, like Algernon, is in the know, but the information he holds is useless since Algernon has shredded the evidence with his teeth. He is the subordinate initiate who may not act on his knowledge. The hierarchy is subtly enforced.

While waiting for the arrival of Gwendolen and her aunt, Jack must make do with bread and butter; deprived of the phallic vegetable, he must satisfy himself with a sandwich without a filling, a sandwich that isn't. He is told by way of consolation that "Gwendolen is devoted to bread and butter", upon which he applies himself with some vigour, drawing the comment from Algernon: "Well, my dear fellow, you need not eat as if you were going to eat it all. You behave as if you were married to her already" (Wilde 255). Aunt Augusta, meanwhile, is able to magnanimously forgive the want of cucumber since she has just risen from a feast of crumpets with Lady Harbury, who, with her husband freshly filling his grave, has rediscovered her appetite for sensual pleasure.

Thus we arrive at the crumpet, or "Crumpet" when used euphemistically, decoded by Eric Partridge as "women viewed collectively as instruments of sexual pleasure", and dated to the late 19th century (228). If Algernon and Lane are engaged in some kind of foodsex conspiracy, then aunt Augusta's unconscious innuendo reasserts her matriarchal authority over Gwendolen's sexual future, by indicating to the company that she is also one of the initiated. This is one of the moments when the poise of Wilde's comedy wavers, as if it is about to be swamped by a tidal wave of wit. One innuendo provokes another and the action of the play begins to seem like a pretext for making jokes, an hysteria of hinting, as if the social comedy is about to be swallowed whole by the comic impulse itself.[9] Aunt Augusta's innuendo (if we agree to let it stand as such) is rather lame (or should that be "Lane"?), and this may be attributed to the social pressure she is under: better to make a bad joke than to risk exclusion by making none at all. Wilde's risky fondness for the innuendo exposes the viscious hypocrisy lying behind the self-censorship of the taboo-ridden high society of the 1890s; the infectiousness of the foodsex trope is symptomatic of the twisted sublimation of repressed sexuality into social politics and beyond.

When Cecily and Gwendolen contest the hand of Mr Ernest Worthing, Gwendolen refuses sugar in her tea on the basis that it is "not fashionable any more" (293); Cecily sugars the cup with four lumps, wielding the tongs with a vengeance. Given the choice between cake and bread and butter, Gwendolen again refuses the sweet option, remarking that " cake is rarely seen at the best houses nowadays" (293). The girls are playing an intricate game of one-up-womanship, trying to outrank each other on the social scale; the winner will gain the rights of possession over Ernest and his sexual organs. In Samuel Butler's *The Way of All Flesh*, a similar situation is resolved by a game of cards,[10] while

Wilde settles the connubials through an appeal to food-fashion, where the trick is not to betray one's vulgarity by eating the wrong thing. The girls are at each other's throats because of a misunderstanding, a fatal lack of information exacerbated by the text's wilful dallying with euphemism and innuendo, but they are not so much squabbling over a man (even less a body) as over a romantic ideal connected with the word "E(a)rnest". The name, according to Gwendolen, "has a music of its own", which "produces vibrations" (264), and the sexual innuendo here offers a timely reminder of the body which still underpins the surface play of verbal fantasy. Misunderstanding, of course, is a stock in trade of comedy, and Wilde's model for the hopeless entanglement of words, bodies and social imperatives may well have been Shakespeare, and that masterpiece of euphemistic structure, *A Midsummer's Night's Dream*, which, through its admixture of the unconscious, gestures towards surrealism. Or we might ask how close Gwendolen and Cecily are in their squabbling petulance to the Mad Hatter and the March Hare, and in their confused ignorance to Alice, who is left wondering "Why is a raven like a writing desk?" (Carroll 60–61). Carroll's remarkable question seems to investigate the fitness of the first term to stand as a euphemism or innuendo for the second; it presupposes a radical expansion of the edge and a loss of distinction between the literal and the figurative, the object and the subject. It is a despairing attempt to impose hermeneutical logic on a world already given over to interpenetration. When the euphemism begins to conceal more than it reveals, the body behind it recedes, and Wilde's competing females would do well at this point to ask themselves "What *is* the importance of being Ernest?" A dysfunctional euphemism is more repressive than a functional taboo, as we see in the ludic refinements of Wilde's style as the nominative function of "Ernest", which initially occludes the body capable of producing the all-important vibrations, is itself occluded. How can the same Ernest be engaged to two women? And if he can't, then who is Ernest and who isn't? If the nominative function of the signifier is blurred, what happens to that throbbing body it once purported to signify? A riddle without an answer is like a sandwich without a filling, a sexless body; and if Wilde proposes an equivalence between ignorance and celibacy, then perhaps he also suggests, contrariwise, that information is sexy.

Gwendolen and Cecily's predicament is soon resolved by an avalanche of answers as the coincidences tumble out, redeeming the promise of those suggestive tea-time delicacies, and pointing, perhaps, less towards Lewis Carroll and his obscure experiments with confessional nonsense and euphemistic taboos, than towards Willie Dixon and his spoonful of sex or Captain Beefheart and his "Sugar Bowl" (*Unconditionally Guaranteed*). Cecily handles the sugar tongs with cunning aplomb, and Van Vliet's lyric taps into this moment when sugar and sex glide into each other:

> They reach their fingers in that ole sugar bowl,
> Lick 'em and sweeten their souls.
> Little girls and little boys never get old,
> They know they're being naughty
> But they love that sugar bowl.

The riskiness of the song is that it purports to be about children, and their pre-adolescent intimations of sexual excitement, which leads us back to Carroll and the Mad Tea-Party, where Alice, like the teenage daughter of a PMRC puritan mother, is left bemused by the Dormouse's open-ended story about the three little sisters who live at the bottom of a well from which they draw treacle.

During his testimony at the Senate Hearing on "Porn Rock", where he was defending his use of explicit lyrics, Zappa responded to Al Gore's questioning with a plea for information instead of ignorance on sexual matters:

> And I think that, because there is a tendency in the United States to hide sex, which I think is an unhealthy thing to do, and many parents do not give their children good sexual education, in spite of the fact that little books for kids are available, and other parents demand that sexual education be taken out of school, it makes the child vulnerable, because if you do not have something rational to compare it to when you see or hear about something that is aberrated you do not perceive it as an aberration.

> (Kostalanetz 200)

Children who lack "something rational to compare it to" might find themselves, like Alice, confronted with an impossible question. To be informed about sex is not just safer, it is also sexier, to judge from the example of Wilde's ignorant maidens; not least because it allows the innuendo to be handled in a way which concentrates rather than dissipates the eroticism in language, which erodes rather than reinforces the taboo. The penetrating innuendo, then, may stand as a corrective to the obfuscating frigidity of the euphemism, and Zappa's preference is clearly for a rhetoric of information.[11]

Before the dénouement of Wilde's play, and the reconciliation of divided bodies proper to comedy, Algernon and Jack are left in sexual suspense as the disgruntled girls remove themselves from the scene. In accordance with Wilde's system of foodsex substitutions, Algernon immediately starts eating, filling himself with muffins instead of filling Cecily's muff with himself. The intricate reversal of outside and in, as Algernon symbolically swallows the body he wanted to penetrate, may remind us of Zappa's didgeridu imago where rhetoric passes into style as the two terms which the innuendo would confront across an eroti-cised edge interpenetrate and precipitate a maximalist expansion. In Zappa's tableau the raven *becomes* the writing desk and the unanswer-able irrationality of Carroll's question overbalances into an anti-logic of the unaskable: "Why is a woman like a didgeridu?" is not even nonsen-sical when the subject and the object are one. We have passed over into the realm of the *hors sens*, where the neurosis of rhetoric becomes the psychosis of style, and the expansion of the edge coincides with an eroti-cisation of everything. Algernon has become a muffin man, and Zappa's song of the same name stages another interpenetrative moment as a man, in the manner of Archimboldo's cook (see our discussion in Chapter Two), becomes what he eats, and then seems to mutate one step further into a bird-man-muffin who eats what he is:

> Girl, you thought he was a man, but he was a muffin.
> He hung around till you found that he didn't know nothing.
> Girl, you thought he was a man but he only was a puffin.
> No cries is heard in the night as result of him stuffin'[12]

Algernon and Jack perform their own version of Cecily and Gwendolen's tea-time spat where abstemious observance of food-fasion decorum has given way to the virile rivalry of an eating contest. The muffin functions as a kind of secular host, standing in for the girls' absent bodies; the projected incorporations of sexual intercourse are represented by this unholy-communion of the muffin, and the men are determined to eat as much of it as possible. It is significant that Lady Harbury's crumpets have mutated into muffins, now that the prospect of sex has receded.[13] Both men refuse the non-consolation of the tea-cake, which clearly has no symbolic value. The snack becomes a binge with Algernon determined to finish off the plateful, just as he has polished off the cucumber sandwiches in Act 1, when hopes were still high. The women's bodies remain remote in their objecthood, and the muffin, whether we consider it as a euphemism or an innuendo, stands for this separation. By eating the muffins, then, the men are trying to eat the edge; they are trying to eat their way into the female body. Algernon's excess stands as desire's protest against the restrictions of sexual and rhetorical convention. It is a bid for knowledge in a world of imposed ignorance; and female sexuality, in Wilde's play, stands as that something extra which can be eked out of euphemistic structure when equivalence is edged out by identification, when the raven becomes the writing desk and the muffin becomes the puffin.

On one level Zappa prefers information to interpretation, arguing that ignorance allows you to be taken advantage of; and his preference for the clarity of the obscene over the obfuscations of euphemism might seem to be endorsed by the real stresses engendered by Wilde's sweet and sour tea party, which the relentless summer comedy fitfully exacerbates.

Is it an indication of Don Van Vliet's relative indifference to political matters (with the exception of his ecological concerns) that his work should rely so heavily on a mystique of obfuscation in which the euphemism plays a pivotal role? Is this also, perhaps, a question of his lineage in both blues and surrealism, where the euphemism keeps company with other such edgy devices as the *double entendre*, the pun, and the preposterous juxtaposition? A line like "making love to a vampire with a monkey on my knee" from the song of the same name (*Doc at the Radar Station*) differs usefully from Zappa's "I fucked this dyke by the name of Freddy"[14] in terms of its rhetorical means and aesthetic aims. The predominance of a semi-abstract aesthetic in Van Vliet's paintings, where something might be or might not be, also serves to illustrate his affiliations. These paintings, like the first generation abstract expressionism they derive from, are, to apply the criterion derived from Zappa's testimony, supremely uninformative.

The foodsex rivalry between Wilde's competing males reduces social relations to the slogan "eat or be eaten"; the subjective body resists objectification by consuming other bodies. Promiscuity, on the social and sexual levels, is akin to cannibalism, and Wilde's orgy of wit is a sublimation of the primal urge to eat one's enemy. One avoids being swallowed by swallowing the other, one objectifies the body of the other by consuming it. For an allegory of this process we might turn to a classical image from the early Northern Renaissance. Pieter Breughel's drawing "The Big Fish Eat The Little Fish" presents an orgy of ingestion and regurgitation, a levelling vision in which every body is linked to every other in hunger and fear: fish, man, manfish, birdfish, mollusc and crustacean slog it out on the riverbank for the laurel of the gob-conquering glutton. The visual field of the picture is organised around the corpse of a giant fish which is bloated with the bodies of smaller fry; these too, in infinite regress, are bloated with the bodies of smaller fry. Breughel, like Zappa and Wilde, grapples with the special dialectics of the inside-out, and in the middle ground of his picture a diminutive figure in outsize and inappropriate armour carves into the flank of the biggest fish with a giant table knife, opening up the inside-outside dynamic as he releases the contents of the overstuffed belly. The body threatened with eversion can rescue the edge between inner and outer, subject and object, by eating the world. By presenting his "delirium of autostrangulation" as a well-balanced meal to be consumed by his viewer, Dalí suggests that the exemplary eater is he or she who can stay outside; and Breughel's struggling fish-butcher is determined to distinguish himself as subject by maintaining his place at the top of the food chain.

Breughel's enterprising figure enacts the euphemistic fate of the human subject who erodes the edge which separates his subjectivity from the objective world at the same time as he seeks to reinforce it. In harvesting the objects he must eat, he lays bare the *mise en abyme* in which he is merely one link. His lack of mastery is cleverly indicated by Breughel who encumbers him with a knife drawn to the scale of the giant fish. This lack of proportion, where the objective world is too much for the subject, re-invokes dream and the experiences of Lewis Carroll's Alice.[15] The transition from gigantism to miniaturism in chapters one and two of *Alice in Wonderland* (Carroll 13–16) represents the fluctuating degrees of the subject's mastery over the objective world. The bottle of liquid makes her small, the cake makes her big and the fan makes her small again. Her body and its environment are locked into a dynamism beyond her control, she vibrates as one with the material world. Dream once again provides the model for subject-object interpenetration, and Carroll, like Breughel before him, evokes oneiric experience in relation to the inside-outness of eating. To formulate: if the subjective body can save itself by eating the world, the dream model suggests that autophagy is the steady state of the subject-object, which takes its place in a self-consuming world. In Breughel's drawing no human body is directly consumed. However, a figure walking out of the frame in the top left corner has been transformed into a monster of interpenetration, half human half fish. This hybrid figure objectifies the process of ingestion, whereby the fish eaten by the man becomes a man-fish. This extrusion of the stomach and phantasmic extrapolation of its contents recalls Zappa's didgeridu woman and the overdeterminations of the scene we have already explored. We might add to the growing portfolio of possible reasons for Zappa's laughter his understanding of how his musician might have saved herself by eating her instrument.

The Maximalist Fuck and the Subject-Object

The dreamwork of condensation produces overdetermined figures half-way between subject and object, where the lineaments of the body are transcribed onto the world we move about in, while brute matter quickens in turn with the palpitations of body and mind exceeding themselves. The pornotopic simultaneity of such figures may remind us of Zappa's theory of time:

> I think that everything is happening all the time, and the only reason why we think of time linearly is because we are conditioned to do it. That's because the human idea of stuff is: it has a beginning and it has an end. I don't think that's necessarily true. You think of time as a spherical constant . . . [in which] everything's happening all the time, always did, always will.
>
> (Menn 64)

If everything is happening at once, this includes all the fucking (not to mention the foreplay) that was ever done and ever will be. It is a major tribute to Zappa's aural imagination that he can glean something of the effect of this cosmic total intercourse from the intestinal burble of wind in water. We don't know what his theory of space was, but let us make the obvious leap and imagine all the fucking that ever was taking place at the same moment in time constantly and *at the same point in space*, no edges, no collage, just an inside-outside of hellish orgiastic togetherness. The best we can do, perhaps, are discrete images of confused erotica, feeble approximations of this maximalist fuck –Dalí's edible autostrangulation, the double lick of Van Vliet's decal fantasy, the foodsex frolics in Wilde's comedy, certain things by Picasso and Ernst, certain passages in *Finnegans Wake* such as the following:

> Can't you read by dazzling ones through me true? Bite my laughters, drink my tears. Pore into me, volumes, spell me stark and spill me swooning. I just don't care what my thwarters think. Transname me loveliness, now and here me for all times! (I.6.18–21)
>
> (Joyce *Finnegans* 145)

and Zappa's didgeridu player from the Ensemble Modern.

Maximalist style is set against the fixity of subject positions, it is the surrendering of self-definitions and the sacrificing of demarcations; it puts everything up for grabs, re-provisionalizes it, leaving the reader, listener or viewer with everything still to do. Style interferes with binary distinctions and pluralizes the options—the masculine can no longer exist apart from the feminine, the subject bleeds into the object, the fixed relations of old flounder in cross-currents of erotic anxiety. The exercise of maximalist style involves the suspension of the idea of self and a mobilization of the socio-psychological forces which contribute to the making of a subject. This is achieved not through some Jungian surrender to unconscious automatisms, but through a pan-psychic multiplication of expressive means, through which a "self" may be both subject and object, man and woman, attractive and repellent, true and false, alive and dead.[16] Style is a playground and a torture chamber, a prison and a laboratory, a dangerous kitchen; it provokes a promiscuity of identifications, in which the indefinite subject-object tries on/ is tried on by every available subject position, the sum total of which is constantly being raised as long as style continues. Zappa has tested this ground in songs such as "Sofa No 2" from the album *One Size Fits All*, where the speaker spreads its subjectivity round about and throughout the sofa, claiming to be its "secret smut and lost metal money", its "cracks and crannies", before arrogating to itself a total undifferentiated presence with a pantheistic arrogance worthy of the "Book of Genesis":

I am all days and nights
I am here
And you are my sofa
I am here
And you are my sofa
I am here
And you are my sofa [17]

This statement of proprietorial rights over the object, however, still relies on the categorical separations of stable grammar, and thus stops short of the fusions and fissures which are the norm in *Finnegans Wake* where the dominant process of the text (dominant enough to jam all other textual processes—narrative, evocation, argument, even expression) is superimposition, where grammar has collapsed into its singulartrity, leaving no space in which the subject and the object might accede to separation. Subjective reconstituiton along maximalist lines is fundamentally erotic, an inexhaustible source of "secret smut", and this is Joyce's great discovery, and the great imposition of *Finnegans Wake*: "Pore into me, volumes, spell me stark and spill me swooning." (145)

Since identification is polymorphous, polysemantic and polyvalent, it is also provisional, and this provisionality creates an infinity of interstices where the incompleteness of identification creates the illusion of differentiation. Thus, the subject/object division and all that it entails in terms of meaning, is constantly glimpsed but never grasped, and the hybrid forms which thrive on its suspension are free to prolong their preposterous existences:

> When he rolls over his ars and shows the hise of his heels. Vely lovely entilely! Like a yangsheepslang with the tsifengtse. So analytical plausible! And be the powers of Moll Kelly, neighbour topsowyer, it will be a lozenge to me all my lauffe. More better twofeller we been speak copperads. Ever thought about Guinness's?
>
> (Joyce *Finnegans* 299)

While the orchestrations of his texts and much of his instrumental music might bear comparison with Joyce's superimposition of subject and object positions, Zappa's speciality as a lyricist lies in the exploration of the cracks in the sofa, those interstices which interrupt the seamless fusion of subject and object. The song "You Are What You Is", from the album of the same name, plays on confusions of racial identity while incorporating into its title the grammatical indifferentiation of second- and third-person: *You* are what (*he, she* or *it*) is. The extended fade-out chorus utilises a form of textual xenochrony as the second voice articulates subject positions from elsewhere in Zappa's oeuvre, as if attempting to deconstruct the reductiveness of the main lyric and its brittle insistence on fixed definitions:

> You are what you is
> (I'm gwine down to de links on Saturday mornin' ...)
> An' that's all it is
> (Gimme a five dollar bill ...)
> YOU ARE WHAT YOU IS
> (And an overcoat too ...)
> AND THAT'S ALL THERE IS
> (Robbie take me to Greek Town)
> YOU ARE WHAT YOU IS
> (I'm harder than yer husband; harder than yer husband ...)
> AN' THAT'S ALL THERE IS
> (I'm goin' down to White Street, y'all ...)

YOU ARE WHAT YOU IS
(Gone down to the Mudd Club, 'n work the wall . . .)
AN' THAT'S ALL THERE IS
('N work the floor, 'n work the pipe. 'N work the wall some more . . .
And here we are at the Mudd Club, y'all . . .
I hope you enjoy yourself, cause the show's about to begin.)

The statement "You Are What You Is" seems to belong to a rhetoric of reduction, which refuses to enter into questions of subjective definition; it is as contemptuous of ontology as Iago is of epistemology at the end of *Othello*: "Demand me nothing. What you know, you know. From this time forth I never will speak word." (V.ii.300–301). The interlineations, however, explode this rhetoric by exposing its premise: identity is always more than one. It is as if Shakespeare (or somebody else) had interlineated the text of Iago's unconscious. Once again, then, Zappa's maximalism is to be found in the presence of its opposite, as repetition must contend with a segment of infinite variety. A devotion to the invariable is an act of minimal(ist) resistance to the maximalist onrush of style; a touchingly futile assertion of a remnant of control, a salvaging of the subject through a cricular reduction of its potential acts: "You are what you is, and that's all it is." By reducing the subject to a tautological next-to-nothing one can, in theory, similarly reduce the threat of its subjective dissolution. The tragic flaw of this strategy lies in the realisation that subjective repetition requires objects. What style must be kept out of is precisely this dangerously ill-defined territory which separates a subject from its objects, what we have been calling the edge or the crack in the sofa. Repetition, and here perhaps we can finally appreciate the severest stresses which animate minimalist practice, is a promethean attempt to render invariable this most variable of relationships; to seize the object in the same way time after time and so to seize it ever more closely. One thinks of Giorgio Morandi as a representative of this form of aesthetic brinksmanship, whose work either depicts a successful invariant of the subject-object relationship or defines itself as an unvarying bid to achieve this invariant. Though Morandi's paintings might be more closely defined as serialism, an attempt to delimit the subjective facets from which an object may be conceived, a manoeuvre which is hopelessly technical in its arbitrariness and as such alerts us to the rich paradoxes set in motion by the minimalist gambit. Again, we might imagine an attempt to empathise with the object, this time as it is stripped of its quiddity, reduced to a sequential sentence, seized by the subject and ravished by its serialist eye. Such a tableau adds to the connotations of the "anxious object",[18] that incomplete characterisation of modern art which refers us to the modernist period as the key historical moment in the transition from manner to style.[19]

If Morandi's work might be seen as an impossible attempt to forestall the process of subject-object identification by anticipating it from the perspective of the object, an antithetical approach, which will quickly bring us back to Zappa's didgeridu woman and the starting point of these reflections, is represented by that most hideous of Beefheartian miscegenations, the "Human Totem-Pole". If Morandi's jugs quiver at the limit of objecthood, Van Vliet's animated pole writhes in the panic of style:

> The pole was a horrible looking thing
> With all those eyes and ears
> And waving hands for balance.
> There was no way to get a copter in close
> So everybody was starving together. [20]

We are told that "excercise *on* the pole was isometric", but can we trust this preposition, which implies that the body of the pole and the bodies it incorporates are still ideally distinct? We are also told that the pole is "an integrated pole" which "didn't like itself", and these phrases suggest the animated object. Like Zappa's muffin man and the hybrid creations of Joyce's sleepy grammar, the human totem pole is a visitation from the crack in the sofa. At the end of Van Vliet's vision, a small child approaches "with Statue of Liberty doll", a sight which inspires "a gurgling and a googling" from the pole. As a reaction of the subject-object to the sight of a subject *and* an object, these baby noises might be heard as an echo of Zappa's maximalist laugh but from the other side; a gurgle and a google to complement the musical gargle of the didgeridu woman. The internecine disaster-movie horror of the pole, which is "starving together" beyond rescue, reminds us, inevitably, of Dali's "architecture of frenzied flesh devoured by a narcissistic and biological cataclysm."

Zappa's Hilarity of Forms

Zappa's important interview with Don Menn and Matt Groening ends with his serious-dismissive comment "So long as somebody gets a laugh out of it, what the fuck?" (64), which returns us to our original enquiry: why should all of this be so funny, especially if we credit the assumption that when Zappa uses the word "hilarious" he also means something like "ethically sound"? Is it the old "laugh or you cry" chestnut, that binary dyke raised and re-raised against the inundations of hysteria? Was Zappa's body trying to subvert the terminal dichotomy of healthy-unhealthy by laughing itself inside-out of its diseased condition? Or is this hilarity simply the ejaculation of Zappa's manic mood, a semi-coincidence of psychic vibes which dupes criticism into overdetermining the circumstances of its pre-determined peak? Is connectivitis, therefore, a symptom of the interpenetration of criticism and its objects?

On the musical plane, Zappa's theory of time as a spherical constant would break down into an attempt to render all sound audible at once; and this might lead us back to the "massive overdubs" indulged in at Studio Z and documented on the *Mystery Disc* album. On the psychoanalytic level, this overdubbing of experience (expressed physiologically by the over-consumption of coffee) might be conceived of as a desire to have it all at once and thus to subvert mortality and its incremental bit by bit. It is also very reminiscent of the high of the maniaco-depressive, who alternates between periods of pure desire when the ego discovers that it is identical with its ideal, and periods of irremediable melancholy when the subject turns against itself as the cause of its own dispossession. The maniaco-depressive, when things are on the up, empties his or her pockets of patience; everything appears creatable and there is a rush to create it while the power lasts, connectivitis runs amok, linear time is maddening. There is a sort of aesthetic panic and euphoria, an hilarity of forms. Perhaps the didgeridu experiment induced such a mood in Zappa where, by a magical acceleration of style worthy of Joyce, the creative ego attains its ideal, releasing a bark of jubilation before the fall, a highpoint of combination on the cusp of dissolution. Apparently freed from the constraints of the symbolic order, the maniaco-depressive proceeds with an unchecked over-consumption of his or her creative energies. The food metaphor returns us to Breughel's allegory: the big fish eating the little fish might be read as the struggle of the maniaco-depressive who is driven by desire to eat even as he or she is eaten into loss by the symbolic order.

In Samuel Beckett's *Watt* the eponymous character mixes up a dish for his patron Mr Knott, combining a maximum of ingredients, manipulating an over-sufficiency of materials:

The dish contained foods of various kinds, such as soup of various kinds, fish, eggs, game, poultry, meat, cheese, fruit, all of various kinds, and of course bread and butter, and it contained also the more usual beverages, such as absinthe, mineral water, tea, coffee, milk, stout, beer, whiskey, brandy, wine and water, and it contained also many things to take for the good of the health, such as insulin, digitalin, calomel, iodine, laudanum, mercury, coal, iron, camomile and worm-powder, and of course salt and mustard, pepper and sugar, and of course a little salicylic acid, to delay fermentation.

(84)

All of this, when boiled together for four hours in a pot produces a grey poss which is served to Mr Knott twice a day. The moment of creative potential is rendered down into an indifferent mess which, while failing to tickle the tastebuds is nutritious enough to sustain life with its incremental drip by drip. Watt in the kitchen with all these ingredients before him is the maniaco-depressive approaching his high, his ego and his ideal are gearing up to make a night of it; Watt collecting the remains of Knott's dinner and scraping them into the dog's dish is the maniaco-depressive at the other end of his cycle. Zappa's laughter is pitched to that peak of tastiness, the master chef of the Utility Muffin Research Kitchen is confident that his audacious new recipe will be a success. With the celebration of a serendipitous triumph, however, comes the recognition of the inevitable fall: it is easy to hear this laughter slipping into that register where all the symptoms of bodily mirth (the shaking shoulders, the reddening face, the running eyes) are equally those of the body weeping, a mood as indeterminate as Watt's slop and as colourless as Zappa's "what the fuck!".

CHAPTER FIVE

Unprincipled Pleasure

Maximalist Aesthetics and the Problem of Pleasure

As we approach what can only be the arbitrary end of this study it is perhaps time to boldly state what may so far have remained implicit: in responding to maximalist production, criticism becomes paracriticism, an experiment in critical form which proceeds in defiance of the obligation to provide definitive statements. In this way, maximalist art forces the hand of criticism, obliging it to multiply its means until it too becomes an excessive art of intellectual juxtaposition with no end in sight. Just as the attempt to name the source of anxiety in clinical psychoanalysis is a form of that anxiety, so paracriticism is a form of maximalism. In the absence of any real belief in the possibility of finally achieving The Big Argument (for example a universal theory of Zappa's Project/Object), paracriticism stakes its validity on the claim that it is a useful or inevitable activity of the mind. Beyond such sober jusitifications lies the problem of pleasure. Residing somewhere between language and experience, pleasure is notoriously difficult to describe, for this reason it has become criticism's anxiety, and, by the logic of repression, one of its taboos.[1] Paracriticism is heroic to the extent that it breaks with this logic, taking on the anxiety of maximalism and running with it, refusing to construct for itself a system of adequate understandings. The heroic, in its sacrificial acceptance of displeasure, is also tragic, and we shall see how paracritcism, in its refusal to think of pleasure and pain in terms of a categorical opposition, uncovers the melancholy of maximalism and its affinities with sado-masochism.

So, if there is such a thing as a maximalist aesthetics, and the aesthetic is a category of pleasure, what are the pleasures of maximalism and the paracriticism it fosters? In an essayist spirit of free enquiry, and as a culmination to this particular instance of paracriticism, let us try out some pseudo-solutions to these vital and neglected problems.

Subject, Meaning, Pleasure, Body

When in 1977 Roland Barthes announced the death of the author, the basis for his extrapolation was a sentence in a short story by Balzac, a would-be maximalist who wasn't. Writing, for Barthes, is "That neutral, composite, oblique space where our subject slips away, the negative where all identity is lost, starting with the very identity of the body writing." ("Death" 168). Neutral, bodiless, oblique, emptied of subject and identity, the death of the author would seem to render moribund the entire textual scene. Before Barthes resurrects the body of the author in that of the reader at the very end of his text, it is imposible to see in his vision how the literary exchange could be a source of pleasure, or of anything else for that matter. Critical premises are never innocent, of course, and the panache with which Barthes deconstructs the authorial subject seems in retrospect directly proportional to the crassly ideological sentence he cites from Balzac:

> This was woman herself, with her sudden fears, her irrational whims, her instinctive worries, her impetuous boldness, her fussings, and her delicious sensibility.
>
> (167)

If ever there was an attempt to write determinately, this must be it; and one can only sympathise with the desire to save this sentence as writing by expunging any traces it may harbour of an authorial subject. Suitably dehistoricised by the time Barthes has finished with it, the sentence-formerly-written-by-Balzac is ripe for repossession by the newly nascent reader. Now, if such a procedure makes satisfying sense in relation to a particularly strident example of nineteenth century "realism", how would it fare in the maximalist context, when confronted for example with something from *Finnegans Wake* or, to skip media, something from Zappa? And how would the transference of agency from author to reader work in such a context to impinge on the problem of pleasure?

We have been arguing that, as a maximalist paradigm, the body is immanent (and sometimes exorbitant) in maximalism. Without trying to say *whose* body is present *where*, such an assumption immediately seems to put us at odds with Barthes' vision of writing as disincarnate. Conversely, to accept the death of the author as implicitly true of maximalism would, we suggest, imply an inconceivable mastery of such art on the part of its audience. Or it would simply imply a neutrality of non-response equally difficult to conceive of in relation to the sublime irritant of maximalism. In the face of its excess, the reader of the maximalist text (whether literary or musical) *needs* a body, and this is the short explanation for why Zappa as author is ever-present in his work, while Joyce the author, with his bad eyes and perforating ulcer, is a cult amongst readers of Joyce. This need, of course, is a double bind: while the presence of the body in maximalist art may help the audience to take pleasure in the work, creating at the same time a sense of political agency, it may also contribute to the deferral of such pleasure. There is sometimes a feeling that our pleasure must wait until the body in the work has finished taking its own; that the work is a tireless body determined to pleasure itself endlessly. For Barthes, the death of the author would seem to precipitate a deferral of meaning and the pleasure which is traditionally contingent on it:

> In the multiplicity of writing, everything is to be disentangled, nothing deciphered; the structure can be followed, "run" (like the thread of a stocking) at every point and at every level, but there is nothing beneath: the space of writing is to be ranged over, not pierced; writing ceaselessly posits meaning ceaselessly to evaporate it, carrying out a systematic exemption of meaning.
>
> (171)

This sounds suspiciously like the postmodern sprawl which may offer us a mild and strangely technical amusement even as it teaches us indifference. Maximalism is a much more confused and urgent situation, where it is no longer certain whether pleasure is contingent on meaning or the other way around. Under such conditions, nothing is exempted, everything accumulates, pullulates. It is as if maximalism had taken root during the interval between the death of the author and the birth of the reader as Barthes conceives of them. The body of maximalism is heavily pregnant with a meaningful pleasure that is also a pleasurable meaning, and it is with this unwieldly body that the audience must grapple. The space of this massively overblown interval is the crossroads of the body pinpointed in Chapter Three and figured as the subject-object in Chapter Four, and, as we have seen and will see, it echoes with disturbing laughter.

Barthes attacks the author as a final signifier which caps meaning, the demise of this authorial subject, however, does not in the first instance produce a wild expansion of sense; rather it unravels meaning to its degree zero, the point at which it has been rendered "systematically exempt". While one formulation of this particular emptiness might be the depthless surface of the postmodernist text, another might be something much closer to classical minimalism as articulated in the 1960s by figures such as Frank Stella, Donald Judd, Steve Reich or Terry Riley, where unravelling is to be viewed as reduction, and the author is just one more element to be forced out of the text (once again, to be understood as literary, musical or visual). One of the fascinations of minimalism is its determination, against all the philosophical odds, to make nothing, an aesthetic strategy which pits art against death. And one of the key discoveries of minimalism is that dead art doesn't exist: one can only reduce up to a point. If we think of this point as a Barthesian degree zero of meaning, it is very difficult to answer the question: "What limits reduction?" One would need to consider how it is exactly that a code is wrested from a subject. If, however, we think of the minimalist point of maximal reduction as coincident with the maximalist double contingency (the point at which the aetiology of meaning and pleasure becomes impossibly ambiguous), one can indeed posit an answer. Just as the last redoubt of subjective experience is the body, so the degree zero of meaning is also the body, somehow a transference is effected between the symbolic links in the signifying chain and the somatic significance of the body. One can kill an author, but a text (that is *something* rather than nothing) will always have a body. The minimalist body residing at the point of double contingency is, as we have suggested above, pregnant with its own maxima. The maximalist anatomisation of the body produces a body-in-progress to set alongside the "Work in Progress" of Joyce and Zappa's Project/Object. Even though it was intended as an act of revolution, Barthes' execution of the Author, as we have seen, runs the risk of installing a neutral territory empty of meaning and thus void of political discourse. The maximalist body-in-progress, by contrast, functions as a guarantor of political content. It is clear, for example, in reviewing Zappa' work that its political content has always depended on its physicality and that this has much more to do with its maximalist credentials than a few references to blow jobs.

Maximalism is politically embodied and thus stands as a vital check on the bodiless ideology conjured up by Barthes and translated into the anti-practice of political quietude by certain strains of postmodernism.

The degree zero of meaning lies beyond the body in an unimaginable nothing, it is bodilessness, and, in the light of this discovery, the Author may begin to look like something of an Aunt Sally. With this in mind perhaps, Barthes wrote an essay on the French painter Bernard Réquichot,[2] which goes a long way to ackowledging this body beyond the author and its crucial location at the crossover point between the impossible zero of minimalism and the inconceivable everything of maximalism. Before considering some of the implications of this essay for our comparative inquiry into the aesthetics of Zappa and Captain Beefheart, let us briefly explore another model of maximalist composition which offers an alternative account of the origins of the body-in-progress as immanent and exorbitant pleasure system.

Maximalism and the Baroque Fold

> "Matter that reveals its texture becomes raw material, just as form that reveals its folds becomes force. In the Baroque, the coupling of material-force is what replaced matter and form."
> —Gilles Deleuze

> "La vie dans les plis"
> —Henri Michaux

As suggested at the beginning of this essay, one of the most visible contemporary avatars of musical maximalism is the "new complexity" school of contemporary British music (a term which was itself coined against the "new simplicity" of the minimalists), a style shared by composers who sought to push the limits of instrumental virtuosity, rhythmic structure and polyphonic models. To some extent, Zappa's taste for extremes of register, his penchant for density and abstraction and his increased performance demands (as well as his constant search for methodological and technological procedures devised to cope with problems beyond the reach of traditional performance) allies his works with those of Brian Ferneyhough and Michael Finnissy, to name but two of the godfathers of the new complexity style. There is no reason to believe, however, that Zappa had any specific interest in the works of these composers. By contrast, his admiration for Pierre Boulez, which culminated in his collaboration with the French composer on *The Perfect Stranger* (1984), points to his affinities with an art which would be more aptly described as neo-Baroque rather than as merely promoting various forms of "density" and "complexity". In *The Fold: Leibniz and the Baroque*, Gilles Deleuze cites Boulez, the author of the Mallarmé-inspired *Pli selon pli*, as a continuator of the Baroque style, with its emphasis on virtuosity and eccentricity and its tendency to create a mass of curves, convolutions, and folds that, according to Deleuze, "[unfurl] all the way to infinity" (*Fold* 5).[3] By citing Boulez as an example of a neo-baroque tendency in modern music—one which signals the birth of an "extended chromatism" and a "polyphony of polyphonies" (112)— Deleuze invokes a major interface between Zappa and the realm of "official culture"[4]. But perhaps the best way to do justice to the infinite compositional foldings of Zappa's works is to resort to an architectural model. According to Yago Conde, the effect produced in architecture by folding is "the ability to integrate unrelated elements within a new continuous mixture" (253).[5] While the preceding chapters have shown that it would be a mistake to reduce the maximalist quality of Zappa's oeuvre to his penchant for density and exuberance, it is the fluid, seamless character of his later transgeneric experiments (which began after the merz-inspired "collagist" period that ended more or less with *Weasels Ripped My Flesh* in 1970) that allies him with the efforts of other neo-Baroque artists who attempt to discover "new ways of folding, akin to new envelopments" (Deleuze 189) and which reflect the composer's desire to privilege process and mobility over juxtaposition and rupture.

This tendency is most apparent in the Synclavier compositions, whose entry into the Zappa catalog was marked by the publication of *The Perfect Stranger*, in 1984. The album contains three orchestral pieces conducted by Pierre Boulez and four electronic pieces including "The Girl in the Magnesium Dress," a piece adapted eight years later by Ali N. Askin for the Ensemble Modern's *Yellow Shark* concert. From Zappa's sleeve notes to the album, one understands that the light, ductile, silver-white metal dress is only the prelude to a bizarre *dance fatale* whose outcome will be the death of the lover, who is destined to be impaled upon the lethal spike that adorns the girl's plate armor:

> "The Girl in the Magnesium Dress" is about a girl who hates men and kills them with her special dress. Its lightweight metal construction features a lethally pointed sort of micro-Wagnerian breastplate. When

they die from dancing with her, she laughs at them and wipes it off.
(sleeve notes to *The Perfect Stranger*; unpag.)

But if we dare to look up the girl's deadly dress and try to make sense
of the inner dynamics of the piece, we cannot but be reminded of the
conversion of rhythmic digital "dust particles" into pitched sounds
(discussed in the introduction to this book) which is yet another manifestation of Zappa's maximalist fold, one which delights in questioning
the boundaries between matter and sound, the literal and the figurative, the real and the virtual. The seemingly infinite polyphonies of the
piece, the irregular rhythmic groupings and the overall absence of
symmetry, combined with the strange phrasing of the lead melody all
help to blur the outer limits of the piece as well as those of the girl's
body. Typically, the function of the Baroque fold—in Zappa's music,
Bernini's sculptures and elsewhere—is to relay and prolong traditional
mimesis when the latter has reached its ostensible limits. Here, Zappa's
maximalist dress once again returns us to the body (and to the folds and
circonvolutions of the skin) only to disrupt our most ingrained assump-
tions about how to deal with the opposition of inside and outside, both
of which are subsumed into a reversible plication which comprises an
"inside as the operation of the outside" (Deleuze 112).

In the same way as the true subject of Zappa's piece becomes not the
girl itself but the dress she is wearing, the unfinished body, eventually
confronted with its own absence of limits, gives way to the aesthetics of
the baroque garment, which detaches itself from its instrumental
destiny and is no longer subordinated to the body that wears it.[6] The
baroque costume ceases to translate or even prolong the shapes and
movements of the body and becomes its own movement, "wrapping the
body with its autonomous, always multipliable folds" (164). The baroque
fold and its sculptural extension in, say, Bernini's Saint Theresa is in
turn interpreted as a body of infinite folds, curved lines and surfaces
that twist and weave through the changing conditions of time and
space. Whereas Bernini's goal was to give three-dimensional expression
to the body possessed by religious ecstasy (and in a state of abandonment often interpreted as a form of eroticized suffering), Zappa's "Girl
in the Magnesium Dress" is an example of a secular baroque art that
seeks to conquer formlessness by allowing a profusion of matter to
overflow the frame (166).

For Deleuze, the baroque embodies "the law of extremum of matter,
i.e. a maximum of matter for a minimum of space." In a footnote to the

closing chapter of his study, he claims that there are therefore a lot of affinities between the baroque and certain kinds of minimal art where "form no longer limits itself to volume, but embraces an unlimited space in all directions" (168). Deleuze cites Robert Morris's felt folds and Christo's wrapped buildings as examples of minimalism's "constant confrontation with the baroque." The complex and often paradoxical dialectics of minimalism and maximalism in their relationship to time will be addressed in the following section of this chapter. At this stage, one must point out that Zappa's Dyonisian aesthetics, constantly return us to the carnivalesque body, remain radically opposed to the more austere, Appolonian landscapes of architectural minimalism. Zappa's performance of John Cage's "4'330", in which he let the composition sheets fall from the piano, once again allows the body to interrupt the illusion of absolute silence and timelessness created by Cage's blank intervals.[7] Ultimately, however, as Yves Bonnefoy remarks, the Baroque is "neither illusion nor insight"; instead, it "puts illusion to the service of being" where illusion is converted into "a space of hallucinatory presence" (quoted in Deleuze 170), a tendency reflected in Zappa's interest in the physicality of sound and the creation of material musical objects. Like Bonnefoy's baroque, which exists at the paradoxical conjunction of maximum presence and extreme absence, the "G numbers" of Zappa's magnesium dress can be seen as so many interacting prototonal microevents that signify both the absence of matter and the essence of immateriality. They are, to quote Deleuze on Leibniz, very similar to the musical monad, "an eternal object of pure Virtuality which actualizes itself in the [sound] sources . . . pure Possibilities which realize themselves in vibrations and fluxes" (109).

Applied to the field of language, the poetics of the Baroque fold can help us to make sense of Zappa's decision to write a whole Broadway-style musical composed in the "pseudo-negrocious dialect" discussed above in connection with "You Are What You Is". In *Thing Fish*, the grammar and vocabulary of dominant, standard English is challenged by the infinite possibilities provided by the folding and unfolding (which are here typographically rendered by means of hyphens) of letters and phonemes that result in a complex network of semantic disruptions and phonetic turbulences.[8] *Thing Fish* is Zappa's *Finnegans Wake*, a work that takes us to the imaginary periphery of the English language, dissolving familiar words into strange combinations of sound and sense. In the song "Brown Moses", for example, the characters' malapropisms and hypercorrections result in an irresistible musical idiom, a lettrist festival of micro-linguistic events:

Dey callin' me BROWN MOSES,
Fo' dat id sho'ly what I am,
Ancient an' re-lij-er-mus
Solemn an' pres-tig-i-mus
Wisdom reekin' outa m
'Long wif summa dis baby pee
'Minds me of dem River Weeds
'N all dem ignint Bible deeds

Drawing simultaneously on the singular ontology of Leibniz's monad and Hans Arp's claim that in poetry, as in nature, "a tiny particle is as beautiful and important as a star" (McCaffery xviii), Steve McCaffery has argued that the clinamen[9] (a central concept in Alfred Jarry's pataphysical writings) "helps formulate a Poetics of the Particle" (xviii) or "micropoesis" (xxii).[10] For McCaffery, the combination of the clinamen and the fold creates an infinite number of protosemantic turbulences disrupting linguistic systems and urges us to "rethink what guarantees stability to verbal signs" (xix). The political implications of this are apparent in Zappa's choice to dismantle Western culture and history through linguistic parody; while his own particular brand of lettrism displays itself in one of the most unusual (even by his standards) songs of *Thing Fish*, a Negro spiritual retelling of the Moses story, sung by Johnny "Guitar" Watson. The song is actually about the Crab-Grass Baby, a minor character in Zappa's musical, who has been abandoned by his parents, a (literally) inflatable woman named "Artificial Rhonda" and a televangelist named "Quentin Robert De Nameland" (of the "VIDEO CHAPEL FOR ECONOMIC WORSHIP"). Brown Moses discovers the infant and begins by rebuking his parents for abandoning their baby in "a cardboard nativity box on some Italian's front lawn":

What wickedness id dis?
De way you's carryin' on.
Dis pygmy I be clutchin'
have been lef' out on de lawn.

De daddy were ne-GLIJ-ible,
De mama were de-FLATE-able,
De trauma to de imfunt
Be mostly not ne-GATE-able

As explained in the first chapter of this study, Brown Moses' dialect was inspired by Tim Moore's character Kingfish in the "Amos & Andy" series. But contrary to the original character of the TV programme, which veered dangerously in the direction of the minstrel show tradition, Zappa's uncompromising satire of mainstream white culture in *Thing Fish* restores the dignity of the "pseudo-negrocious" dialect. As linguistic eccentricity becomes the mark of political deviance, Zappa delights in the power of the individual graphemes and phonemes to undermine from within the political ramifications of late XXth century Western US English. Critics and listeners who were (and still are) baffled by the "childishness" of Zappa's linguistic games inadvertently put their fingers on the prime mover of the composer's design, which builds upon what Barthes described as the alphabet's power "to rediscover a kind of natural state of the letter. For the letter, if it is alone, is innocent: the Fall begins when we align letters to make them into words" (xix). The suggestion that humanity's linguistic fall originates in the aligning of letters into words and sentences is particularly appropriate in a song dealing with one of the most famous episodes of the Old Testament. If Zappa does not put too much hope in the prelapsarian babble of infants (the crab-grass baby only manages to produce "computerized vocal sounds" which already mimic his parents' selfish and superficial concerns), the song nonetheless deals with the loss of innocence and the general potential for corruption of a world ruled by greed, ambition, and political and religious hypocrisy. In fact, "Brown Moses" seems to hesitate between different themes, including child neglect, Eurocentrism (Brown Moses himself stands as a reminder to white Christians that the characters from the Bible were dark-skinned people) and the corruption of the Church (eventually Brown Moses's own morality is questioned as he seems more interested in money and gin than in the baby's fate). Finally, the closing part of the song suggests that the parents' negligence will not go unpunished and that the illiterate orphan will take his revenge on the people who hurt him (the song concludes that "Sho'ly one day he will grow, / 'N put some shit / In yo' sack o' woe").

It was also in 1984 that Zappa became interested in the music of late-Baroque composer Francesco Zappa, a contemporary of Haydn and Mozart who, according to the New Grove Dictionary of Music, "had a reputation among his contemporaries as a [cello] virtuoso and . . . toured in Germany in 1771, playing in Danzig and Frankfurt". Entirely executed on the Synclavier, *Francesco Zappa* is an "album of 'digital baroque dinner party music'" which enacts the technological fold effected by Zappa's increasing fascination with Synclavier programming. Zappa's special affinities with Baroque music were later exploited by the Helsinki-based Ensemble Ambrosius, who applied the concept of *basso continuo* to their interpretation of (and improvisations around) Zappa's works, a feature especially suited to the intricate contrapuntal structures of pieces such as "Night School," *"Uncle Meat"* and "G-Spot Tornado."[11]

We have seen that Zappa's eagerness, in "The Girl with the Magnesium Dress", to let the hardware of the computer generate the basic parameters of his compositions recalls and reconciles the contemporary avant-garde's attention to the material conditions of art production and the baroque's tendency to "foreground matter" (166) to the detriment of (traditional) form. But the technological fold effected by Zappa's electronic compositions also raises the question of the contributions the Synclavier made to Zappa's maximalist art. Was Zappa using the Synclavier as a maximalist "desiring machine" liable to multiply the conceptual vectors of his oeuvre *ad infinitum* by combining "various elements and forces of all types" (Deleuze and Guattari xxiii)?[12] At this point the question recurs as to whether Zappa's work should be regarded as a late modernist collage or a postmodern "rhizomatic" assemblage of heterogeneous genres and styles (which would therefore exemplify what Deleuze and Guattari have described as a reworking of traditional notions of subjectivity into a network of multiplicities, a heterogenous aggregate of parts functioning in "social and natural machines")? But these considerations are finally, perhaps, less important than the suggestion that Zappa's investment in Synclavier technology was a necessary stage in the folding and unfolding trajectories of a transmorphic art which has confounded several generations of listeners and left them speculating about the origins, influences and limits of his work. The next logical stage in the construction of the Project/Objact was the creation of music that coalesced the technical infallibility of the machine and the personalities of live musicians. In this respect, the coexistence of Synclavier pieces and works written for and executed by Boulez's Ensemble InterContemporain on *The Perfect Stranger* (1984) anticipates Zappa's later mixed experiments which typically hesitate between the gestural and the mechanical, the "authenticity" of "organic" execution and the necessities of accurate performance (in the sleeve notes, Zappa thanks Boulez for "having the patience to demand accurate performance of the *killer triplets* on page eight").

Minimalism into Maximalism Will Go

In saving us from the infinitesimal, our senses cede the field to the fairies. William Blake, who articulated the coincidence of minima and maxima with his famous quatrain:

> To see a world in a grain of sand
> And heaven in a wild flower,
> Hold infinity in the palm of your hand
> And eternity in an hour. [13]

was visited by them, and, as a child, Salvador Dalí would press on his eyeballs to make the angels come, imitating the gesture of the human fœtus and countering his fear of the dark with benign intrauterine hallucinations. That we are all relatively myopic is clear from the paranoid imaginings which begin where the penetration of our senses tapers off, when one sight, sound, smell, taste, or touch fails to suggest another, thus creating a maximalist concentration of focus and endurance, which is also a nexus of pleasure and pain. It is no coincidence perhaps that Dalí, as the most paranoid of surrealists, was also its most maximalist.

Minimalism in painting and the minimalist use of repetition in music seek to restrict our sensory receptions and test our aesthetic tolerance. How can one go on listening to the same thing? For Vico and Nietszche and any other philosopher of eternal return, repetition does not pose a problem, since its pulse is so infinitesimally slow; in the absence of an enduring observer, objects and events can pass themselves off as unique. History itself would be a minimalist work if its pulse were accelerated to a rate which allowed us to experience it again and again; if we could be outside it and eternal. Since we are within it and finite, history for us is too full, and must remain for the time being a maximalist paradigm. Music, however, is there to be endured.

In his essay on Bernard Réquichot, Barthes argues that "quite often in a single painter [there is] a whole history of painting" (*Responsibility* 228); by changing the levels of perception, for example with the aid of a magnifying glass, "Nicholas de Staël is in three square centimetres of Cézanne" (228).[14] What determines our experience of a work is the level at which we perceive it: "isolate, enlarge, and treat a detail, you create a new work" (223).[15] Minimalist music, according to Jonathan Bernard, can induce its listeners to effect a similar perceptual shift:

... the small number of events over time tends to focus the listener's attention intensely on each event, in all its particularity, thus resulting, from the minimalist point of view, in a music of parts rather than a whole.

(quoted in Potter 5)

This is not pointillism, where each constituent dot remains a functional part of the whole, submissive and superficial; no, minimalism (an)atomises its material, distilling particles which have *different* properties, which *depart from* the original unity. In this way, each particle may be a composition, or something else. The minimalist cell is a new maximalist body.

With typical raw intuition, Don Van Vliet may have stumbled across this process and formulated it for the amusement of his musicians in what he called his "exploding note theory". When learning "Flavour Bud Living" prior to the recording of *Doc at the Radar Station*, Gary Lucas took for his model John French's performance of the piece on the *Bat Chain Puller* tapes. Van Vliet wasn't pleased and sent Lucas back to re-learn it according to his new theory: " ... you play every note as if it has only a tangential relationship to the preceding note and the note that follows." (Barnes *Captain* 273). Each constituent part of the piece becomes semi-autonomous, it may detach itself from its syntagmatic functionality and become a tiny but expanding centre of new experience—a paradigm. One could knuckle down at this point and bash out some formal philosophy on the warring themes of monism and monadology, Spinoza and Leibniz. Each note in "Flavour Bud Living" if played according to Van Vliet's exigencies would perhaps be a monad, not "windowless" as Leibniz suggested, but separated from its neighbours by a transluscent veil, rendering relations oblique at best. Spinoza's monism admits only one substance: God.[16] Everything else is merely a mode of this oneness: "Whatever is, is in God, and nothing can either be or be conceived without God." (*Ethics* I.xv). In our musical model, God would be the unified work which imposes modality on its parts and arrogates to itself the exclusive right to exist. In critical parlance, this may be what we mean when we say that a work is "self-contained". In Leibniz's "best of all possible worlds", by contrast, God has created a maximum of independent substances; the world is exemplary precisely because it has been created on maximalist principles. In criticising John French's performance as "too religious", Van Vliet may have thought that it made his composition sound too monistic (or even monastic), too much like a substantial God who is ineluctable essence and cannot be subdivided. He must have heard too much veneration in French's playing, a worshipful submission to a single sprit in the piece which checks its capacity to stimulate the ear in and into detail.

This theological cleavage is again audible in "Peon", which was performed by Bill Harkleroad and Mark Boston for *Lick My Decals Off* and then re-recorded by the same duo in 1976 for the debut album of Mallard. In the *Decals* version one of the first things we notice is how loud the bass is in relation to the guitar; they are not playing on the same dynamic level and this discrepancy tends to emphasise both inexactitudes of timing and the piece's asymmetric intervals, opening up a space for the ear to engage in creative decomposition. It would be interesting to know how deliberate this mixing strategy was and at whose insistence it was allowed to stand. The guitar itself sounds excessively dry and trebly, with a lot of muting to cut off its resonance. There is a staccato sinfulness about the unison bends which appear after a definite pause about three quarters of the way through the piece; and when Harkleroad plays the final descent each of its eight notes sounds as if it has something separate to say. The Mallard version by contrast is ushered in with a few seconds of twittering birdsong, like some kind of relaxation cassette purchased at a headshop along with the cannabis chocolate and peppermint essence for the pillowcase. This pastoral backing continues throughout, filling in the gaps between the notes, rounding off the edges, lubricating the jerky listen, appeasing the body. The guitar and the bass are mixed together now and the former has a mellow jazz tone traceable to the soft-stroking fingertip rather than nit-picking nail. The reverb is up and those unison bends are played with a tasteful tremolo. Glissandi are introduced to spread the notes into the gaps with a mollified attack, most notably on the fourth of those last eight notes, which slips self-effacingly into its neighbour, executing the self-sacrifice of melody, an offering to the oneness of the whole. The overall effect is like the bogus Mexican melancholy of Bob Dylan's incidental music for Sam Peckinpah's "Pat Garret and Billy the Kid", a film about the ritual extinction of the individual. Don Van Vliet said that French's "Flavour Bud Living" "put the whole thing in heavy syrup" (Barnes 273),[17] and with the Mallard "Peon" we have a second helping of the sticky.

If the mechanical aid to the shift of perceptual level in painting is the magnifying glass, in music it is the tape recorder, which not only records sequences of sound but allows them to be played back at different speeds, helping the ear to focus differently.[18] Don Van Vliet's assessment of *Decals* pinpoints the link between its aesthetics and the speed at which it is perceived:

> What the music is going at is complete absence. That's the way we did it. You can't think about that music. That music is moving so fast that if you think about it it's like watching a train go by and counting the cars.
> (Barnes *Captain* 336)

Here there is no danger of minimalist endurance and the consequent effect is one of "total absence". Except it isn't of course, Van Vliet is indulging in hyperbole; though there is an accelerated rate of event in the music, which certainly runs ahead of our ability to concentrate on any one moment. It is like the scary succession of ideas during insomnia, which defeats our efforts to pin down a single thought or image and endure it long enough to enter the expanded realm of dream, to count sheep for example rather than those impossibly speeding railway cars. It is very difficult to shift the level of our perception of *Decals*, perhaps even more so than was the case with its predecessor, *Trout Mask Replica*. This music is antithetical to minimalism, and it is therefore very intriguing that Van Vliet should associate it with an experience of emptiness, "total absence". If slowed down maybe it would begin to provoke those minimalist moments of escape into new plenitudes, or at least some odd points of access for the ear's proactive penetrations. Or perhaps we should think of it rather as fairy music, that is to say the kind of thing we might hear after shifting our level of perception of something which has been pressing on our eardrums, a minimalist piece for example. Could Captain Beefheart be a sonic equivalent of Dalí's angels?[19] Perhaps it is *coming from* as well as "going at" absence, revelling in what Samuel Beckett has called the "cyclic dynamism of the intermediate" ("Dante . . . " 16), a phrase which might be usefully set alongside Van Vliet's definition of painting as "fulfilling the absence of space between the opposite meanings," (Barnes *Captain* 331) and which also suggests the technical phenomenon of interference, caused by the intersection of two or more wave systems. In any case, we begin to see here the logic of repetition within the minimalist aesthetic, for what better way is there to slow down the rate of progression of a piece of music than to begin to repeat its parts?[20]

The close scrutiny of minimalist repetition invites the listener to re-hear music. After a certain number of habitual expectations are confounded, the listener and the music arrive at the point of double contingency, where art is reduced to art matter and incorporated into the body-in-progress. Moving from Vico to Bruno the Nolan and still concerning himself with the poetics of *Finnegans Wake*, Beckett reminded us that "the maxima and minima of particular contraries are one and indifferent" ("*Dante . . .*" 6). Joyce's writing, like *Lick My Decals Off Baby*, moves too fast whereas minimalism moves too slow, but both are maximalist in that they tap into frequencies beyond the normal perceptual range, at the low end or at the high end, where extremes of contraries meet and structured response collapses into an urgency of matter. Blake's fairies, Dalí's angels, and the dreamer of *Finnegans Wake* are all avatars of the body-beyond-the-author which presides over this point of double contingency, plying its excrutiating pleasures. They are not metaphors, since they inhere at a point of concentration, equivalent to Zappa's Big Note, where the space and time necessary to see one thing in terms of another is no longer available. The shift of the level of perception is now revealed to be a re-materialisation of the language, of the music, in which what you hear is what you hear *and* everything else, miraculously disrobed of the acculturated vestment (which certainly includes Barthes' author and may even include his reader) designed to fast-track pleasure at the expense of its painful other. It is the "special art [made] in an environment hostile to dreamers" announced by Zappa in the communiqué published by the *International Times* in 1971,[21] and its dreamer, along with everything else, is to be taken as literally as possible.

Pleasure and Power

As it seeks to define and transcend its condition, maximalist art is subject to a special *dédoublement* in the staging of its own thematics. Maximalism is fated to undertake a futile inquiry into the theoretical possibility of meta-maximalism. *Finnegans Wake*, for instance, reflects on itself constantly, trying out strategies of circumscription in a mode of automatic (i.e. authourless) self-parody as it seeks to decide whether it is an object or an experience or both. Its psychic stresses regularly suggest a desire to breach its own limits and become something else, as it fantasises about delivering itself as a letter, or tries to pass itself off as a piece of mad machinery, a pleasure receptor perhaps which would allow us to have our fun and be done with it (until the next time):

> Our wholemole millwheeling vicociclometer, a tetradomational gaze-

> bocroticon ... autokinatonetically preprovided with a clappercoupling
> smeltingworks exprogressive process ... receives through a portal vein
> the dialytically separated elements of precedent decomposition for the
> verypetpurpose of subsequent recombination
>
> (614)

Zappa's work is likewise full of dramatisations of the maximalist
wager, limited or parodic formulations of the problem of pleasure
which might be seen as dysfunctional attempts to exert some kind of
categorical control. "FREEDOM," wrote Zappa in one such formulation,
"IS WHEN YOU DON'T HAVE TO PAY FOR NOTHING OR DO NOTHING".[22]
In the hostile environment of maximalism, which imposes its rigour on
the subject through a conflation of pleasure and pain, passivity would
indeed be a kind of freedom, a release from the clamant obligations of
response. The freedom to tell enjoyment from its opposite is, then,
perhaps, the control which maximalism seeks to exert on itself through
its self-reflexive stagings. How witty of Zappa, then, to have invented the
Central Scrutinizer narrator on *Joe's Garage*, who, as a personification of
the totalitarian state, would discipline all unruliness and dismiss any
doubt by imposing a definition of pleasure as that which is good for you.
In practice this means, passive conformity to the law: Freedom is to be
told when you are having fun. Zappa's maximalist point seems to be
that any attempt to circumscribe pleasure risks unleashing a political
nightmare: meta-maximalism is fascism.

The Central Scrutinizer clearly evokes Jeremy Bentham's panopticon.
The all-seeing eye, like the all-knowing author or the all-enjoying reader,
is a maximalist myth, posited on the false postulate of the all-encom-
passing point of view.[23] From the perspective of the scrutinized subject
(Joe, for example) the eye stands for everything which restricts creativity,
from the inherited philistinisms of the socialised ego to the body's
inherent insufficiency and its unshakeable economies of time and
energy. In this way the Scrutinizer's need to keep an eye on Joe while he
succumbs to the inevitable pressures of life and lives out his creative
failure represents the maximalist transition from criticism to paracriticism. While the former would place the artist under twenty-four hour
surveillance, the latter would recognise the futility of such a move while
at the same time maximalising its means; how minute an attention is
implied by the word "surveillance", how broad a consideration? Isn't
there always an obscure region inaccessible to the sweeping eye?
Doesn't the eye create such regions? The artist in the meantime, may
have perceived the asymmetry between what has been done and what

there may be still to do, and, unless he or she also happens to be a para-critic, may well have perished of the insight. The panopticon is apt to become a *huis clos* in which the artist and the critic meet in failure. Zappa captures this moment at the end of *Joe's Garage* when the scrutinizer reverts to his "regular voice", joining spent forces with Joe, in order to sing that anthem to the capitulation of art "A Little Green Rosetta". Like Chaplin's "Modern Times", this song presents a vision of the foiled individual or the artist intimidated into silence, whose normalization is expressed through the mechanical tasks his body must perform. The repetitious nature of the composition picks up where the proto-minimalism of Chaplin's soundtrack leaves off. Each rosetta that Joe applies to a muffin (one of Zappa's favourite symbols for the interplay of aesthetic and olfactory pleasures) and each revolution of the refrain is a test case for the maximalist incorporation of minimalism we have argued for above. Having sold his guitar and taken up a "proper job", Joe has opted for regularity, his social conformism finds a physical analogue in the monotonous nature of his work. Like Chaplin's production-line wage slave, he trembles on the brink of reification, his last hope is a subjective revalorization of his objectification as excess; if he can become an expression of his condition (as Chaplin's character seems to do when he personifies the machine running out of control) art will have been saved. Every blob of icing that Joe applies to his muffins is fraught with the future of human subjectivity.

The garage, as Zappa's album underlines, has become a symbolic site of resistance, a place to unmake dreams and literalize metaphors. At the other end of the scale of technical sophistication to the Utility Muffin Research Kitchen, its function is basically the same: it is a place for discovering ways of being active, for exploring the body and enhancing the subject's potential for survival in a world of dictated pleasures. *Joe's Garage* is one of the great concept albums in rock history, and it pursues its chosen problematic with great tenacity, repeatedly setting up scenarios in which the subject is required to defend itself or not against the forces of dehumanisation. "Sy Borg" (*Joe's Garage*) is another song which promotes pleasure as a force for counter-reification.

In "Modern Times" Chaplin chases a woman with a spanner, attracted by the buttons on her dress, like Wyndham Lewis's Kreisler, this is the machine as rapist.[24] Zappa reverses these terms and pushes the futurist eroticisation of the machine to its limits, as Joe discovers the pleasures of "oral sex with a miniature rubberized homo-replica" before turning his attentions to Sy Borg. Joe is so turned on by the complicity of the machine-lover that it is he rather than the Gay Bob doll who goes "all the way". He is so empowered by his pleasure that he fucks the Sy Borg to death. The object succumbs to the subject's excessive desire, which paradoxically humanises the technology by killing it. The return of the Central Scrutinizer at the end of the song recalls the shocking moment in George Orwell's 1984 when the telescreen from behind the picture chimes in with "You are the dead" (199), a nonsensical line which at the same time is true enough to suppress Winston's and Julia's revolution of pleasure. During the symbolic power games of their sado-masochistic sex, Joe's golden shower "must have shorted out" the Sy Borg's "master circuit". For this mistake Joe is to be punished, and now it is he who must submit to a higher power as the state exerts it control. We begin to discern at this point a repetitive succession of terms:

> power = pleasure = guilt = punishment = power

The problem is that we don't know whether the Central Scrutinizer is having fun, whether the panopticon harbours a voyeur, or whether he embodies the nightmare scenario of the authority which takes no pleasure in its power, which functions like a machine. The bleakest implication of Orwell's dystopia might, in the end, be the thought that Big Brother is immune to enjoyment.

Pleasure and Pain

While writing songs such as "Sy Borg", and deploying his Central Scrutinizer, that totalitarian tease, Zappa seems also to have believed in the existence of a pleasure unadulterated by pain:

> "I don't understand people who think of art as an antidote to entertainment, something that should not give you a pleasurable experience ... the idea of punitive art—that sounds like something from the East Village."
>
> (Menn 34)

Perhaps "music is best"[25] precisely because it can give pleasure without involving its listeners in a complicated dialectic of authority and transgression. This one-way guiltless pleasure was theorised by Terence Penelhum in an essay first published in 1956: "Enjoyment ... is an effortless form of attention, a response which is drawn *by* something and not directed *to* it." (246). If this is so, then, in order to be pleasurable, music must relieve the listener of the effort of concentration; it must, in a sense, listen to itself through the listener. But can this model be applied to maximalist art? Zappa's analysis seems to reject the "no pain, no gain" theory of aesthetic pleasure: why should pleasure be the dividend paid on a prior investment of pain, it seems to ask.[26] A good question, and an objection well worth making, but we are still left with the problem of accessibility. Art appreciation may imply a variety of displeasures, from the uncomfortable chair at the cinema, to the overheated opera house, to the effort of concentration which is required to receive the work before us. All of these must be surmounted if we are to accede to the pleasures the work has to offer. Zappa's comment is clearly intended to debunk the masochistic approach to art appreciation, which assumes that the greater the displeasure incurred, the greater will be the pleasure derived; a perversion which has become a durable critical misconception, lambasting artists for presenting work which bears no trace of inconvenience during the making, and which requires no suffering on the part of the adience during the process of appreciation. If taken in more absolute terms, however, the dismissal of "punitive art" seems to suggest that accessibility is not a problem, that pleasure begins when the senses first pick up data from the work, that no tedious or uncomfortable "tuning in" of the faculties is necessary, that enjoyment, as Penelhum suggests, is "effortless". If this seems an unlikely claim, not least because it leaves out all the environmental factors of art reception (hangovers, stress, the presence of other people, the ergonomics of the hi-fi or concert hall, etc.), perhaps we should try out another way of reading Zappa's comment. If art appreciation is neither punitive nor immune to those multifarious conditions of life which make it an effort, then perhaps we should think of the pain involved (which in practice might be anything from a slight inconvenience to a burgeoning agony) as an integral part of the pleasure rather than anterior or accessory to it. This would overturn an Epicurean or Benthamite view of pleasure as the absence of pain, and help us to field the following objection: if a certain type of music is not pleasurable, why listen to it, why not simply ignore it?

On side three of Captain Beefheart's *Trout Mask Replica* we can hear a broken attempt to recite the following absurdist dialogue:

Fast and bulbous.
That's right, the Mascara Snake, fast and bulbous. Also a tin teardrop.

Bulbous also tapered.
That's right.[27]

What is the meaning of this? Firstly, it clearly relates to the statement made at the opening of side two of the album: "A squid eating dough inside a polyethelene bag is fast and bulbous." But again, what is the meaning of this, and how can it be enjoyed? Finding no explanation, but somehow being drawn to the imagery and the conviction with which it is performed, we might content ourselves with the thought that the meaning is a secret, a complex of private associations which we can emulate but never reproduce. If the mystique of this appeals to us, we have already accepted a pseudo-solution to the problem of meaning which has a direct bearing on the quality of the aesthetic pleasure derived from the composition. Meaning is repossessed by the imagination, where it can thrive in any number of forms, verbal and non-verbal. The displeasure of deferral ("What does it mean?") now coincides with pleasure ("Whatever it means is for me") in an act of personal re-signification involving incalculable loss and gain ("It means I it"). In the instant of appreciation, pleasure and pain are one and indifferent: the squid in question is fast and bulbous and so am I, so is everything. And this is one posible account of how a maximalist aesthetics might function.

"Pleasure hurts" is a very different kind of slogan to "no pain, no gain", and it evokes a very different kind of aesthetic tradition—that of the Sublime and its psycho-sexual inscription as sado-masochism—a more promising framework for any attempt to define the pleasures of Zappa's art and those of maximalism in general. We have seen how Don Van Vliet theorised his deconstruction of the mama heartbeat as an attempt to deny the listener an easy listen. His rhythmic ideas were designed to "break up the catatonic state";[28] a strategy which seems to fall squarely within the punitive tradition of "no pain, no gain".[29] While for Zappa, listening to the Big Note (an ideal aesthetic perception of all time happening at once) is supposed to be *the* sublime entertainment, where the experience of pain as pleasure is a mode of maximalist being.

In its capacity to exceed the perceptual capacities of the subject it contains, the maze stands as a symbol for maximalist art. A system which may initially be approached as a game, a source of pleasure, the maze is apt to revert to the classical labyrinth, and mutate into a source of anxiety and terror. The formal and generic manipulations of maximalist art similarly scramble the faculties of reception, pitching its audience into an intermediate terrain between the maze and the labyrinth. Listening to Zappa or reading Joyce, for example, our sense of pleasure may suddenly begin to question itself under the influence of all those factors mentioned above plus a more specifically maximalist strain of displeasure which we might think of as a form of alienation. It is as if maximalist art deconstructs the aesthetic pleasure it arouses, making it impossible for the subject to identify with his or her enjoyment and rais-ing the curiously insistent question: "Where am I in relation to this pleasure?" This alienated pleasure hovers somewhere between the subject and the work, purporting to be a property of both but never actually becoming a property of either. It is worth noting that even Theseus, slayer of the Minotaur, escaped from the labyrinth not by finding his way out but by retracing his way in. This undoing of the act translates the labyrinth into a psychological scene where the subject is likely to lose its sense of agency in the double movement of making and unmaking. The subject, like Penelope at her loom, is stranded between the death of the author and the birth of the reader (to re-apply the Barthesian formulae introduced above); and it may be that this ambigu-ous placement of the audience in relation to the work is at the root of that special anxiety one feels, for example, when reading *Finnegans Wake*, the feeling that somehow something is having fun but that this mysterious pleasure cannot be pinned down either as a product of one's agency as reader nor as a direct effect of the text. Attempts to give an impression of the sensation of alienated pleasure might well refer to a sense of instability, of rapid change and expanding scale, of sensual overload and epistemological crisis where what we think we know recedes behind performative and necessarily unsequential acts of know-ing, instantaneous thoughts which accomplish little more than the registration of their own existence as acts of response, or the traces of such acts. Alienated pleasure fails to accomplish itself, and while it is clear that such an experience may be worse than uncomfortable, the subject at some level always wants more. One of the less alienated pleasures that maximalist art has to offer its audience is, in fact, the knowledge that there will always be more.

As if commenting on the capacity of his art to push these limits, Zappa adopted the iconography of alienated pleasure as one of his favourite themes—from the sadean paraphernalia of the "Torture Never Stops" (*Zoot Allures*) to the prosthetic sexuality in "Sy Borg" to the "brief-case" episode in *Thing Fish*, where Rhonda's pleasure and Harry's pain confront and condition each other through the mediation of the valise as transitional object.[30] Scenarios such as this suggest a way of theorising the object in maximalist art as a repository of alienated pleasure: Harry's briefcase is not a means for Rhonda of transferring the erotic charge of Harry's body onto a less threatening object (as it would be in fetishism), but a way of ceding neurotic control over her subjectivity precisely through the experience of pleasure and pain as *one and the same thing*. An object, it seems, is indispensable to this process. In this instance it is a briefcase which functions as a vehicle for maximalist alienated pleasure, elsewhere in Zappa's oeuvre it is a penguin in bondage (as opposed to a squid in a bag) which fits the bill. On stage at the Roxy, Zappa approached the evocation of this object with a passage of "circumambient peripherization"[31] worthy of Joyce:

> The name of this song is "Penguin in Bondage" and it's a song that uh deals with the possible variations on a basic theme which is ... well you understand what the basic theme is, and then the variations include uhm manœuvres that might be executed with the aid of uh extraterrestrial gratification and devices which might or might not be supplied in a local department store or perhaps a drugstore but at very least in one of those fancy new shops which they advertise in the back pages of the free press. This song suggests to the suggestible listener that the ordinary procedure uhm that I am circumlocuting at this present time in order to get this text on television is that uh if you want to do something other than which what you thought you were going to do when you first took your clothes off and you just happen to have some DEVICES around, then it's not only ok to get into the paraphernalia of it all but ... hey ... What did he say? You ready?[32]

This text, as Zappa acknowledges with his reference to circumlocution, is radically decentered, and, like all such texts, it puts an exaggerated premium on objects or, perhaps we should say, their possibility. If continued much beyond this point, it would risk provoking the alienation of its own pleasures, the maximalisation of its rhetorical status as joke.

For Michel Foucault sado-masochism was a form of disciplinary displeasure designed to enlarge the subject's capacity for liberty or pleasure. As Ladelle McWhorter explains:

> Instead of an increase in docility, then, we might seek out, create, and cultivate disciplinary practices that produce an expansion of behavioural repertoires, practices that increase the range within which we exercise our freedom and within which freedom plays itself out beyond who we

currently are. Most likely, those practices will in themselves be intensely pleasurable and will also increase our capacity for pleasures of new sorts.

(McWhorter 182)

It is in this sense, surely, that Zappa's devious introduction recommends the object as a device for radicalising the "ordinary procedure" or "basic theme" of sex. If this is so, then in the song that follows the circumlocution we can only marvel at the expansion of behavioural repertoires that has been achived through the application of a little S and M:

> She's just like a Penguin in Bondage, boy
> Shake up the pale-dry ginger ale
> Tremblin' like a Penguin
> When the battery fail.
> Lord, you must be havin' her jumpin' through a hoopa real fire
> With some Kleenex wrapped around a coat-hang wire.[33]

Could the alienated pleasures of the penguin in bondage also be those of the maximalist subject stepping beyond what it currently is into a world of dynamic (dis)pleasures, while paracriticism stands as its disciplinary other, given over to the futile but indispensable bid to restore order? Every and any order, that is, which it can discern or create.

The "terrible screamin'" of the anthropomorphised "Penguin Bound down" might recall the experiments of H.G. Wells's Dr Moreau, who also contributes, albeit in a deeply disturbing way, to the reconfiguration of the body as a body-in-progress. During his attempts to justify his work to the castaway Prendrick, the mad doctor admits that on one occasion he exceeded his vivisectionist brief, fabricating a hybrid creature in the spirit of pure research:

> "The fact is, after I had made a number of human creatures I made a thing -"
> . . . .
> "We chased it for a couple of days. It only got loose by accident—I never meant it to get away. It wasn't finished. It was purely an experiment. It was a limbless thing with a horrible face that writhed along the ground in a serpentine fashion. It was immensely strong and in infuriating pain, and it travelled in a rollicking way like a porpoise swimming. It lurked in the woods for some days, doing mischief to all it came across, until we hunted it, and then it wriggled into the northern part of the island, and

we divided the party to close in upon it. Montgomery insisted upon
coming with me. The man had a rifle, and when his body was found one
of the barrels was curved into the shape of an S, and very nearly bitten
through .... Montgomery shot the thing ... After that I stuck to the ideal
of humanity—except for little things."

(Wells 75)

Beyond the "ideal of humanity" Moreau's imagination perceives a
world of unmade but makeable "things", generic miscegenations which
provoke the curiosity to "pass beyond the bounds of permitted aspirations". The phrase is from Joseph Conrad's *Heart of Darkness*, a text which
has many structural and thematic similiarities with Wells's novel, not
least the presence of a narrator who is forced to confront a man of
monstrous ambition. Kurtz, like Moreau, has a maximalist vision, a will-
to-excess, as Marlow, Conrad's narrator, explains:

Since I had peeped over the edge myself, I understand better the meaning
of his stare, that could not see the flames of the candle, but was wide
enough to embrace the whole universe, piercing enough to penetrate all
the hearts that beat in the darkness. He had summed up—he had judged.
"The horror!" He was a remarkable man.

(Conrad 101)

And, evidently, a maximalist. While some of Wells's Beast Folk seem
to tempt Moreau's wayward assistant, Montgomery, into exceeding
"permitted aspirations"and expanding his behavioural repertoire
beyond sexual norms, Moreau's experiments, which are social as well as
biological, suggest that we should recognise teratology as one of maximalism's darker arts. The fascinations of pure research have caused
Moreau to recreate himself as a monster, since this is surely Wells's
point, and Kurtz has evidently done something similar by expanding his
perspective to the point at which it embraces the world and reduces it to
the "horror". Or perhaps the horror is Kurtz's recognition of himself in
the world as a monstrosity, as a subject of monstrous pleasures contingent upon horrific pain. Moreau's theological take on Darwin allows
him to dismiss pleasure and pain as equally irrelevant:

Then I am a religious man, Prendrick, as every sane man must be. It may
be I fancy I have seen more of the ways of this world's maker than you—
for I have sought his laws, in *my* way, all my life, while you, I understand,
have been collecting butterflies. And I tell you, pleasure and pain have
nothing to do with heaven or hell .... This store men and women set on
pleasure and pain, Prendrick, is the mark of the beast upon them, the

mark of the beast from which they came. Pain! Pain and pleasure—they are for us, only so long as we wriggle in the dust . . . "

(Wells 72)

What is left out here, of course, is the body. Moreau, the mad vivisectionist has forgotten the body; or perhaps his "ideal of humanity" is precisely that, a bodiless humanity. There are limits, then, to his interest in the body-in-progress, and it is at this point that his true profile emerges—that of a mere religious fanatic. If we substitute Nazi party ideology for theological Darwinism (a very minor conceptual leap), the affinity between Dr Moreau and the real life Dr Mengele becomes clear. Fascism, as apocalyptic science, practices an eschatology of the body, diametrically opposed to the body-in-progress of maximalism.

Zappa is also a monster; a producer of shocking generic mixes and a transgressor of permitted aspirations, whose addiction to pure research is also a programme of ceaseless self-re-creation. Zappa's penguin, like Moreau's puma, whose distress is so vividly communicated by Wells, is a subject of sadism, and it is probably worth noting that Zappa's later teratological dabblings, for example the creation of the Mammy Nuns in *Thing Fish*,[34] are also associated with discourses of power and punishment. While Wells reveals the mostrosity of Moreau's scientific pretensions, however, Zappa exposes the eugenicist thinking behind the mass incarceration of African Americans in the United States,[35] linking it with the Broadway tradition of racial stereotyping. Zappa is maximalism's *moral* monster, and it is no coincidence that he was so bitterly opposed to contemporary America's unholy alliance of Christian fundamentalism and extreme right politics, a coalition which is eminently capable of endorsing the beliefs and practices of doctors Moreau and Mengele.

If we try to think of a practice diametrically opposed to those imagined by McWhorter and Zappa, which instead of "expanding our behavioural repertoires" reinforces their ancestral limits and reconfirms the subject in its original configuration by convincing it of the continuities of its past pleasures, we would be hard pressed to find a better candidate than nostalgia. If maximalist pleasure is alienated and unstable, the pleasures of nostalgia are self-present and distinctly docile. If sado-masochistic practices involve a loosening of the bonds of pyschic structures through the acceptance of pain as pleasure, nostalgia is a form of determinism which serves only to tighten the bonds: one is what one is, as defined by past pleasures, and that is for the best. Zappa's stagings of notalgia thus stand as some of his riskiest and most radical maximalist gestures. In *Ruben and the Jets*, for example, he seems to take on the ultimate compositional challenge, in seeking a way to make nostalgia function within a maximalist aesthetic. The result is an original perversity, where a vehicle for docile pleasures is hijacked by maximalism, and the listener is forced to submit to its alienating rigour couched in a formal language which, while it is constantly familiar, is never reassuringly so. In *Ruben and the Jets* the body-in-progress meets the body-regressing, and this can be heard as the musical gestures of the musicians' bodies strain against the bondage of the hackneyed forms: Roy Estrada's bass experiments with displaced accents during the saxophone solo on "Anything", raising the issue of polyrhythms at an indiscrete moment; on "No, No, No" it plays some slap figures which fail to distract from the aggravated monotonality of the composition, the sense it gives of being stuck in the middle, of being unable to move either forwards or backwards. While the lyrics throughout the album are quite basic, doggedly returning to the theme of adolescent love, the close harmony parts are consistently bizarre, as if the singers are trying to find a way out of the form and its narrow thematics through a deconstruction of its vocal conventions. The body-in-progress is trying to warble its way out of trouble. A final flexing of the "magic muscle"[36] is Art Tripp's use of the multiple paradiddle, which is especially apparent on "Any Way the Wind Blows". These extended rolls are a physical protest against the tendency of nostalgia, represented here by the 1950s rock 'n' roll ballad, to fix parameters for the future of pleasure based on the compromised standards of the past. It is debatable whether *Ruben and the Jets* is Zappa's most difficult album to enjoy, but it is certainly one of his most divisive, in its problematisation of the progressive pleasures of the maximalist body.

Time, Pleasure and Style

Appreciation of maximalist art is conflated by the audience with its sense of itself as enjoyer, which is conflated in turn with a sense of the material still available for enjoyment. The audience's doubts about the limits of the artwork infect the work itself which incorporates them before re-infecting the audience with doubts over the content of the work and the mode of its appreciation. Conflation and contagion are terms which might initiate a revision of the simplistic concept of "response", as the audience takes responsibility for the configuration of the work *from* the work and cedes responsibility *to* the work for the configuration of his or her world. Maximalist art subverts the notion of the artefact and exceeds the taxonomical schemata of consciousness; it goes further and takes liberties with our conceptual vocabulary, generating scepticism about the validity of terms such as "enough", "complete", "full". The maximalist œuvre is thus pregnant with an asymmetry between the sensually experienced fragment and the ever-materialising limitless whole. We have seen that Zappa employs technology to maximalise his means, but the idea of art appreciation technology attuned to the human unconscious (electrode impulse machines and suggestive low-frequency subliminal emitters?) remains a sci-fi or Joycean fantasy. While paracriticism, in attempting to discuss the spectacle of maximalist art, is inevitably confronted with its phenomenological and metaphysical lacunae, it finds qualified solace in melancholy, that antique distraction crucially divided between pleasure and pain.

When Shakespeare's Richard II contemplates the waste of his life during the Pomfret castle scene in Act Five, his melancholy revolves around a sense of having failed to meet the maximalist challenge of time:

> I wasted time, and now doth time waste me
> For now hath time made me his numb'ring clock:
> My thoughts are minutes; and with sighs they jar
> Their watches on unto mine eyes, the outward watch.
> Whereto my finger, like a dial's point,
> Is pointing still, in cleansing them from tears.
> Now, sir, the sound that tells what hour it is
> Are clamorous groans which strike upon my heart,
> Which is the bell. So sighs, and tears, and groans,
> Show minutes, times and hours; but my time
> Runs posting on in Bolingbroke's proud joy,
> While I stand fooling here, his Jack of the clock.
>
> (V.iii.49–60)

Richard has been a bad listener and has passed his time heedlessly; he has been overtaken by the spectacle of Bolingbroke's opportunistic usurpation. His tragedy is conditioned by his failure to pay attention to time's minor units. He is a victim of the maximalism of history, and the melancholy of this soliloquy is precisely that of the subject intimidated by the sublimity of its own omissions, it is the authentic voice of the *artiste manqué*, the statesman as wastrel. The melancholic has a special talent for the imaginative figuration of his or her suffering and Richard understands his punishment as the objectification of his body as a clock, a mere instrument for measuring off the units of subjective time which are no longer his but Bolingbroke's. The implication might be that whatever we cannot experience as pleasure we are bound to endure as pain; a pessimistic formulation of the maximalist predicament, which paracriticism seeks to resolve, as we have seen, by cultivating a melancholia in which pain becomes pleasure. Richard is forced to live out the time he can no longer use, and if the intensity of this torment recalls that of Prometheus, the fiendish device of making the body a vehicle for the inscription of the crime anticipates Kafka. It also antici- pates Zappa, who made direct reference to Kafka's "In the Penal Colony" on the sleeve of *We're Only In it For the Money*. The last of six "instructions for the use of this material" warns the listener that "At the end of the piece, the name of YOUR CRIME will be carved on your back." Richard uses a musical metaphor to articulate his sense of remiss:

> How sour sweet music is
> When time is broken and no proportion kept!
> So it is in the music of men's lives.
> And here have I the daintiness of ear
> To check time broke in a disorder'd string;
> But, for the concord of my state and time,
> Had not an ear to hear my true time broke.

(V.iii.42–48)

It is possible that the crime Richard convicts himself of in the above passage is the same as the felony anticipated by Zappa in instruction number six, namely inattention. And while Zappa's "instruction" is also an invitation for the listener to enter into the sado-masochistic dynam- ics of qualified response, typical of maximalism, it is also, perhaps, a self-lacerating recognition on his own part that he will never have enough time in which to do his own work; that it is impossible to satisfy the daintiness of such an ear as his. Statements like the following, read alongside the numerous testimonies of Zappa's workaholism, suggest that the Big Note should be taken as Zappa's maximalist nirvana rather than a description of what he thought he had achieved:

> To be able to write music for that kind of sound universe offers some major opportunities if you have the time to do all the typing to manipu- late it properly. And there's never enough time at one sitting to finish something, because the more you get into it, the more you understand it

could sound a lot better if it only had this nuance or that nuance. And
every nuance you want to add takes hours, which then go into days which
go into weeks, and on and on.

(Menn 42–43)

The mood of such statements, emanating from the isolation of the
Utility Muffin Research Kitchen bears comparison with the melancholy
of Shakespeare's Richard languishing in his dungeon of despair at
Pomfret Castle.

The melancholy of maximalism, then, is that the bulk of its pleasures can only be deferred, its body remains in progress with no end in
sight. It is this provisionality of response which makes guilt one of the
psychic components of maximalist art. Pleasure deferred can lead to a
sense of political irresponsibility, to a feeling of suspended agency. The
degenerate luxury of the aristocracy is all about deferred pleasure, and
innumerable novels from *Tristram Shandy* to *The Great Gatsby* have
dramatised the perils of idleness. Fielding's *Barry Lyndon* depicts the
upward mobility of its eponymous subject as a progressive loss of
agency, an aristocratic accumulation of guilt. Maximalist art, like
inherited wealth, in denying us nothing, charges us with work that we
will never be able to do. The carnival is often seen as a popular form
dedicated to the people as a disadvantaged majority, in the context of
maximalist deferred pleasure, however, we can see it rather as a boon
for the aristocracy, who are offered the opportunity to assuage their
guilt in the restricted pleasures of work. The snag, of course, is that the
carnival can only function for a limited period; its pleasures are predicated on its reversibility and the inevitable reversion to normality. If
continued beyond a certain point it can only result in the restoration of
the system it had originally subverted. When work perceives itself as
recreation the game is up, afterwards one can only *play* at not feeling
guilty. As a solution to maximalist guilt, then, permanent carnival
could only function so long as the subject remains oblivious to its
pleasures. The vigilance of the superego being what it is, one might
conclude that in order to remain unconscious of its pleasures, the
subject would have no other choice than to become pure body. Carnival
imagines this erasure of the human psyche as the ultimate solution to
the problem of guilt, it's witless Rabelaisian republic would be a place
of human perfection.

In the absence of this lobotomised all-body, the deferred *jouissance* of
maximalism risks turning the body-in-progress into a deferred body.
Modernism produced a pseudo-solution to this problem in the figure of

the *flâneur*, who takes on this burden of pleasure and walks with it, maximalising his perspectives in an effort to defer the supension of agency. The *flâneur* is an aristocrat in motion dedicated to walking as an absurd form of work, an inverted aesthete who sneers at the world for its failure to take pleasure in his own supersensitive subjectivity.[37] The paracritic is similarly peripatetic in his or her undertaking to cover as much ground as possible through the accelerated *flânerie* of connectivitis. The body-in-motion, personified by the aesthete, the *flâneur* and the paracritic, is a literalisation of the body-in-progress designed to displace the guilt of deferred pleasure. From its incarnations we may deduce a notion of style as a prioritisation of pleasure over desire. Foucault's *askesis* "the exercise of oneself in the activity of thought" (McWhorter 184) conceptualises the style of the *flâneur*, whose bid to outrun his guilt depends on the taking of aimless exercise. The maximalisation of pleasure at the expense of desire, was Foucault's preferred solution to the waning of agency: "What we must work on, it seems to me, is not so much to liberate our desires but to make ourselves infinitely more susceptible to pleasure" (184). And Ladelle McWhorter shows how the desireless promenade of the *flâneur* may work out intellectually:

> Writing is simply a vigorous practice of freedom, an exercise through which thinking engenders more thinking, through which it becomes possible to continue to think. (186)

This statement is strangely reminiscent of the description Zappa gave Don Menn of his working practice:

> Usually, I just get up, get something to eat, go downstairs, and go right to the Sonic Solutions ... I'll transfer tapes onto the hard drive and start editing them, equalizing them, and building things. And then, after an album has been constructed, I'll dump it off, reload the hard disk, and keep going. (Menn 32)

To be absolutely free of maximalist guilt, it seems, one must defer desire with pleasure by practising *askesis*. The style of the *flâneur*, who roams the world on impulse taking phenomenological pleasure in what *is* might remind us of Zappa's chosen way of deflecting the charge that some of his lyrics are sexist:

> The songs I write about women are not gratuitous attacks on them, but statements of fact. The song "Jewish Princess" caused the Anti-Defamation League of the B'nai B'rith to complain bitterly and demand an apology. I did not apologize then and refuse to do so now because, unlike *The Unicorn*, such creatures do exist—and deserve to be commemorated with their own special opus.

> (*Real* 226)

Jewish Princesses, along with any number of other potentially controversial subject-matters, exist, they are part of the self-engendering world in which the subject must participate; to exclude them from art is to put desire before pleasure, to surrender to guilt. Anything may be subject-matter by virtue of the fact that it exists; and this statement harbours a seductive corollary within its structure likely to appeal to the maximalist *flâneur*: if anything may be subject-matter, subject-matter should be everything. In this licentious extrapolation we can perhaps detect the origin of maximalist style. If we formulate it in literary terms this style becomes a writing which undertakes the maxima of writing which is everything. Writing (and art in general) seems to provoke us constantly with what it can't do, hence the perceived discontinuity of art and life; a discontinuity which has always been denied by stylists, from Oscar Wilde to Michel Foucault to Frank Zappa, for whom art is a means of living pleasure limitlessly. Style may write any subject (or object) once it has become the reason to write, a truth demonstrated again and again by Gertrude Stein throughout her career but perhaps most eloquently in her "Studies in Description" from *Tender Buttons*:

> *Roast potatoes*
> Roast potatoes for.

> (*Writings* 339)

Maximalism is unfailing style.[38]

   The diachronicity of the human psyche, of course makes desire and its evil twin, anxiety, all but unshakeable. Which is the reason why maximalism, for all its proliferating excess, tends towards a singularity of pleasure, the Big Note, as Zappa conceives it. The body-in-progress of maximalism may be pictured groping its way out of a morass of diachronic neuroses towards the ideal synchronicity of everything, where there is no space in the euphoria of presence for a before and after of desire and guilt.

The Last Laugh

Responding to a question about his ability to combine emotion, political commentary, beauty and humour, Zappa replied: "You can reduce it to this—you can ask this question: Is it possible to laugh while fucking? I think yes." (Menn 38). And this image of the coordinated pleasures of mirth and sex re-centers alienated pleasure as a self-present maxima of joy. At the same time, we have seen in Chapter Five how the maximalist laugh is full of its own misery, how hysteria, like melancholy, depends on the interpenetration of pleasure and pain. Zappa's maximalist laugh, we have argued, is inspired by the spectacle of the subject-object, a version of the comic which chimes in with Henri Bergson's observation that:

> Les attitudes, gestes et mouvements du corps humain sont risibles dans l'exacte mesure où ce corps nous fait penser à une simple mécanique.[39]

(22–23)

Even funnier than the body as machine is the body as mal-functioning machine, where it is denied even the limited satisfaction of efficiency. This ridiculous body which lacks both the spontaneous grace of the organism and the coherence of pure technology, which flounders in a compromised state of imperfection, is a conception of the maximalist body-in-progress which holds out small hope of advancement. Zappa's key aesthetic question—"does humour belong in music?"—may be taken, then, as an enquiry into the capacity of the maximalist body to pass from its melancholy hysteria into a state of coordinated pleasure, a self-perpetuating *jouissance* of sex-laughs.

In his first four albums Zappa was determined to establish a distinction between freaks and hippies. By June 1967 and the release of the Beatles' *Sergeant Pepper*, the hippy ethic had reduced the body to an instrument of self-transcendence, sex had become peace and love and the immediacy of humour had been displaced by a drug-fuelled quest for spiritual "truth". *Freak Out, Absolutely Free, Lumpy Gravy* and particularly *We're Only In It For The Money* reintroduced sex and laughter in the form of satire. The musical laugh became an act of sociological aggression in "The Chrome-Plated Megaphone of Destiny", *Money*'s extraordinary finale. After two minutes of *musique concrète* and abstract piano, the track degenerates into a cacophony of forced hilarity which is not laughter, but the *sound of* laughter. Forced laughter literally makes a mockery of humour as spontaneous subjective expression, it is a social perversity which represses the body by depriving it of emotional content. This burst of anit-hilarity sums up the condition of the body in hippy ideology, which imposes an ethic of enjoyment. Staged laughter, like choreographed applause is a sure sign of political subjection. Zappa's satire attempts a subtle reversal of this situation by turning laughter into a joke. The body laughing at laughter updates Bergson's image of the ridiculous body as dysfunctional machine into a body enjoying its own social trauma. It hystericises hippiedom by reintroducing the principle of pain. Similarly, Zappa's sex satire might be seen as a reintroduction of sexual suffering into the ideology of universal love, which was and remains a nightmare of social conformism. Without pain, which is to say real pain and not just its theoretical possibility, pleasure is not pleasurable. In the light of this rediscovery, Zappa's coordinated sex-laugh appears as a *jouissance* of pain, hysteria brought to orgasm. Is this, in the end, what the maximalist body-in-progress is progressing towards?

The most disturbing laughs in "The Chrome-Plated Megaphone of Destiny" are those which seem to return to their point of departure after playing out a permutated series of pitches and intonations. Since self-accomplishment requires the bliss of selective ignorance, these serial laughs express deep scepticism in the ability of the body-in-progress to ever bring itself off. Maximalism, these laughs suggest, obsessionalises the subject at the same time as it hystericises it, undercutting the laugh which laughs at the forced laugh until it in turn becomes laughable. The very circularity of this reverberating laughter precludes the co-ordination upon which orgasm depends. Zappa's work, in defiance of postmodernist pastiche, insists that every act of satire it performs may become the subject of a similar act. In such a system the height of gratification becomes the successful avoidance of pain, characterised by the obsessional's delaying of orgasm until exactly the right moment. The prime moment to come is, of course, under constant revision, which is to say that orgasm is constantly deferred. The maximalist diffusion of significance across an ever-broadening mass of apparently significant detail creates the perfect context for these delaying tactics. While hysteria might be defined as a repossession of the body carried too far, the obsessional body must be held in abeyance, hovering somewhere between presence and absence; its pleasures can only be provisional. The psychosomatic symptom is held in check by something which might be called "symptomatic thought",[40] or bodiless anxiety, where the obsessional's need to delay the last laugh of hysterical orgasm encounters its powerlessness and enters a crisis. And this chaotic interplay of neurotic structures, where the laughing body slugs it out with the bodiless laugh, typifies the dialectical instability of maximalism and further differentiates it from the indifferent quietudes of postmodernism. The maximalist is like a gambler whose gains and losses follow each other so incontinently that they blur into an undifferentiated medium where the euphoria of victory co-exists with the misery of defeat driven by the double charge of excitement and anxiety. It is this overreaching wager of hysterico-obsessional creativity that the receiver of maximalist art plays out for real in his or her body.

The self-conscious humour of The Mothers of Invention fed and concealed Zappa's real interest in the aesthetic potential of the dysfunctional or hysterical laugh. The low-highpoint of this high-lowness was probably the "*Uncle Meat*" film where Zappa presides over a succession of insanely unfunny scenarios played out in large part by Don Preston and Phyllis Altenhouse. The film inaugurates an aesthetic category—maximalist boredom—which works by spinning out the impossibly inane and pointless through a technique of deferred gratification. Titilation is raised to the power of hysteria and then laboured obsessively. As Zappa pushes his juxtapositions through tedium, hysteria and beyond, one loses the will to recuperate detail, and still the film continues. The *Uncle Meat* film is a collage which raises key questions about that particular mode of composition. As handled by Zappa, it becomes incipient sprawl, and its maximalism emerges as precisely a failure to determine content, an aesthetic white-out played to a soundtrack of sonic irritants. The refusal to develop key phrases such as "using the chicken to measure it" and "it makes me hot" contribute to the effect of wastage, as if Zappa is squandering a whole aesthetic form in his pursuit of the epically unfunny. The feeling is that instead of composing in time, Zappa has thrown things together in an improvised arrangement designed to last forever, a procedure that seems to belie the minute accumulation of conceptual continuity in the Project/Object while mocking the transtemporal concentration of the Big Note.

The inside-outside on the edge laugh in Zappa, which encapsulates the maximalist body, represents the rhythm of response we have described above, with its vertiginous plunge from miraculous gain to catastrophic loss and back again, while at the same time mocking it with an audaciously recessive form of metafiction. In the light of this phenomenal laugh one might even be tempted to risk a universalising statement and suggest that the origin of maximalist art is the antisocial impulse to go on joking regardless of the potential for real or feigned amusement.

Notes

Introduction

1 See Watson 90.

2 Frank Zappa, "This Is All Wrong" (*Civilization Phaze III*).

3 On Zappa's relationship with the Synclavier, see *Real* 172–73.

4 "Outside Now" (*Joe's Garage*).

5 See Jameson's reading of Warhol's "Diamond Dust Shoes" in the opening chapter of his *Postmodernism, or, The Cultural Logic of Late Capitalism*.

6 Zappa's relationship with doowop was complex and ambivalent. Even though he never missed an opportunity to deride the "cretin simplicity" (sleeve notes to *Ruben and the Jets*) of the "dumb fucking love song" (*Real* 89), the conventions of doowop continued to inspire him throughout his career and he seemed to have some genuine admiration for the form. As Ben Watson notes, *Ruben and the Jets*, far from being a mere attempt to parody the genre, "delineated the pleasures and perils of nostalgia" (126). For more on the problematic aesthetics of *Ruben and the Jets* see our discussion of nostalgia in chapter 5.

7 The phallic noses of *Ruben & the Jets* echo Franco Fabbri's remark that "Nabokov inverted the medieval hieroglyph which saw the face as represented by a ?oo?, the name of man, and replaced it with oJo—so that the disappearance of the eyebrows and the extension of the nose turns the face of man into his genitals" (Brusatin 29).

8 Zappa's food fetishism also evokes connections with the Enlightenment figure of the libertine (Sade notoriously promoted the conflation of gastronomy and eroticism). In many ways, Zappa takes us from the prelapsarian Gargantuan feast to the regimented Sadian orgies. For a detailed analysis of Sade's "functional" use of food, see Barthes's "Sade, Fourier, Loyola."

9 Or Eugene Chadbourne's rendering of Johnny Paycheck's "Colorado Kool-Aid",

where the bellicose drunk's ear when separated from the head becomes another body, an amplifier without a socket. See Eugene Chadbourne and Jimmy Carl Black, "Colorado Kool-Aid" (*Locked in a Dutch Coffeeshop*; Fundamental Recording Co, 1995).

10 Frank Zappa, "Your Mouth" (*Waka Jawaka*).

11 To borrow Walter Benjamin's phrase (Miklitsch 15).

12 In the final chapter of *Poodle Play*, Ben Watson compares Zappa with the dying Socrates:

> Frank and Gail wanted me to read the *Apostrophe (')/King Lear* section, which I did. Matt Groening called it "demented scholarship". I followed it with the conflation of Plato's Phaedo and Fido the poodle dog. While Frank's feet were rubbed with tiger balm to alleviate the pain caused by his prostate cancer, I discoursed about the last days of Socrates and the mortality of the soul (when Socrates drank the hemlock as ordered by the court, he first felt his feet go cold, the coldness rose to his heart).
>
> (540)

13 Liner notes to "The Birth of Captain Beefheart" (*Mystery Disc*).

14 On the secret lines of descent that run from Dada to Situationism and punk, see also Greil Marcus's *Lipstick Traces: A Secret History of the Twentieth Century*, which the title of this study implicitly refers to.

15 One doesn't have to be a postmodernist, of course, to spot the problems with this philosophy. Lurking behind the narrative of Kerouac's *On the Road* is Sal's subtextual anxiety that Dean's discourse of "it" is a self-serving circularity.

16 For an overview of the history of food as a performance medium including a whole section on Rios and Antoni, see Kirshenblatt-Gimblett 1-30.

17 Dalí's paranoid-critical method develops another useful maximalist theory which, in the painter's oeuvre, goes hand in hand with a fascination with food and a desire to understand the visceral totality of art as a phenomenon which comprises all the stages of ingestion and peristaltic expression, tracing the aliment from the mouth along the alimentary canal and out through the anus.

Chapter One

1 Another character, Dr Jean Flamboyant, is described as possessing a voice that "sparkles / like a zircon" (135).

2 After his ten-day stay at the San Bernardino County jail and the evacuation of "Studio Z," Zappa was so broke that he resolved to survive on a diet consisting exclusively of rice and red beans. His stomach swelled up so much that it left him "writhing in agony" (*Real* 61). As for the *Trout Mask* Magic Band, they were required, according to John French, to subsist on a few soya beans as their daily diet. Note also Beefheart's song "Big Eyed Beans from Venus" and the "What Do

You Run On Rockette Morton?" sketch on *Trout Mask*, where Morton replies "I run on beans. I run on lazer beans". One could also cite the fascinating bean minimalism of "one red bean stuck in the bottom of a tin bowl" in "The Dust Blows Forward and the Dust Blows Back."

3 Or the famous farting scene in Mel Brooks' *Blazing Saddles*.

4 In *Thing Fish*, the Thing-Fish is disgusted by the sight of the Evil Prince eating raw chitlins. Later in the show, his voice appears to have changed as a result of "his previous raw chitlin' ingestion" and he now speaks the language of the Thing-Fish. See also the following exchange between Harry and the Thing-Fish in "That Evil Prince":

> HARRY: Just what are these chitlin's?
> THING-FISH: Dat dere is perhaps de questium most frequently posed by members of yo' species!

Another example of the oscillation between the salt-sexy and sweet-sexy occurs in "Chocolate," one of Prince's most sexist songs, in which a man asks a girl to give him some of her "Chocolate Candy" in exchange for his "Tootsie Roll". Chitlins and candy sweeet potatoes figure prominently in the list of food items he associates with the act of intercourse: "Mashed potatoes, gravy, cranberry sauce, stuffin', green beans / Chitlins, candy sweet potatoes, black.. black-eyed peas, grits / Cabbage and . . .". See also Zappa's "In France" which describes French girls as "all salty" and French boys as "all sweet".

5 Tom Phillips' *The Humument*, a volume consisting of 367 color plate reproductions of paintings done on the pages of Mallock's late Victorian novel, *The Human Document*, contains a homage to Erik Satie which also evokes Zappa's "Evelyn." The words, transposed from Mallock's original text through a process of selection and gradual erasure, read thus:

> the carpet
>
> was a
>
> the art
> of great
> art of the
> sofa,
>
> bass that
> would
> sing
>
> sing by art
> seated at the piano
> a well-bred
> rounded
>
> the
>
> art

voice
that seemed to vibrate in
surprise

art
audience listened
with admiration
asked for more;

his forehead was moist
and vociferously
polished

6   Burroughs' "U.D.T." ("UnDifferentiated Tissue") makes an appearance in *The Grand Wazoo* (see page 4 of the sleeve notes).

7   Zappa's use of the sofa as a central concept to the eponymous song on the album *One Size Fits All* returns us to the Dada-inspired humor of Francis Poulenc's ballet *Les Biches* (written for Diaghilev's Ballet Russe in 1923 and first performed in 1924), whose set features a single object in the form of a giant blue sofa, a symbol of bourgeois coziness and domesticity whose uncanny proportions and metamorphoses is put to the service of a playful and erotically-charged choreography.

8   In the sleeve notes to *You Cant' Do That On Stage Anymore Vol.* 1, Zappa remarks that his performance of "Torture" in Nurnberg in 1977 was given a "special 'flavor'" by the "high concentration of U.S. Service Men in the audience". This remark reminds one of the episode involving US soldiers dismembering a doll on stage in the early years of the Mothers of Invention. When the Marines arrived on stage, Zappa handed them a large doll and "told them to pretend that it was a gook baby and do whatever you do to people in Vietnam. They tore the doll apart, completely wasted it, with musical accompaniment. And then when they finished doing it, I picked up the doll and I think I said, 'Let's hear it for the United States Marines.' I held up the dismembered doll. There was weird, quiet music. People were crying. It was pretty heavy. And then after that was over, everybody clapped and I introduced the guys to let them take a bow. The first guy walked up to the microphone and said, 'Eat the apple, fuck the core,' and the second guy said, 'Eat the apple, fuck the core.' And the third guy said, 'Eat the apple, fuck the core, some of them love our mothers more.' I saw one of those guys again when we played Philadelphia. He was out of uniform by then" (unpag.).

Chapter Two

1   Frank Zappa, "Muffin Man" (*Bongo Fury*).

2   Think of young Hanno Buddenbrooks, who suffers from bad teeth and miserable digestion and eventually dies of typhoid fever, bringing the family line to an end.

3   George Sandy's translation, available on the University of Vermont's Web site at: http://www.uvm.edu/~hag/ovid/. Interestingly, at least in the context of this chap-

ter on facial poetics, Marsyas's flute was orginally invented by Athena, who discarded it after realizing that her cheeks were ridiculously swollen when she blew into it.

4 Mann also wrote on the aesthetic and emotional potential of the x-ray in *The Magic Mountain*, in which Hans Castrop falls in love with Claudia Chauchat's x-ray portrait showing the upper-half of her body and the organs of her thoracic cavity.

5 Zappa's appreciation of disco music as a meaningless and preposterous ritual ("Hey, they're really dancin' / they're on auto-destruct / On the floor / On the pipe / Bouncin' off-a the wall") is very close to Adorno's perception of the "dance" music of jazz as a debased expression of sociosexual desire, "copy[ing] stages of sexual excitement only to make fun of them" (Arato 292). However, this does not mean that Zappa was allergic to dancing. In a recent interview, Ed Mann reports: "In 1977 Frank Zappa liked to go out to clubs all the time after gigs, and it was almost mandatory for the new guys to come along. I always went. Frank liked to get out onto the dance floor—this was the Disco era. It was funny—he really liked to dance, but in his humorous way, and then everyone on the dance floor would kind of assimilate that—100 people all dancing like Frank Zappa . . . by 1981 Frank Zappa was not so much into that anymore . . ." (The full interview is available at http://www.nucleusprog.com.ar/ingles/r-edmann.htm.)

6 As we know, Zappa's complete disregard for his own health eventually led him to develop cancer. His diet—which seemed to consist mainly of coffee, cigarettes and fast food—is a symptom of another kind of workaholism, that of a life dedicated to art and in which every minute had to be used to expand and maximalize the possibilities of the Project/Object. Zappa the aging chainsmoker warning his listeners against the use of cocaine sounds like alcoholic *chansonnier maudit* Serge Gainsbourg singing about the evils of heroin in one of his last songs,"Les Enfants de la chance".

7 A passage from Adorno and Horkheimer's *Dialectics of the Enlightenment* brings together Zappa's satire of city joggers and the inventory of physical and libidinal functions fulfilled by Charlie's buccal orifice. Comparing the regimented system of modern sport—and by extension the bureaucratized organization of labour— with the sexual exploits of Sade's Juliette, they write:

> The strict regimentation of modern sport has its exact counterpart in the sexual teams of Juliette, which employ every moment usefully, neglect no human orifice and carry out every function. The architectonic structure of the Kantian system, like the gymnastic pyramids of Sade's orgies—the strict regimentation of the libertine society of *120 Journées*—reveals an organization of life . . . These arrangements amount not so much to pleasure as to its regimented pursuit, the schema of an activity.
>
> (88)

8 The second half of the song is about the speaker's attempt to smuggle a suitcase of "special tape recordings" through customs, which leads to his getting arrested and beaten by the police.

9 "Like two erect sentries, my mustache defends the entrance to my real self";

"Même par les moustaches, j'allais surpasser Nietzsche! Les miennes ne seraient pas déprimantes, catastrophiques, accablées de musique wagnérienne et de brumes. Non ! Elles seraient effilées, impérialistes, ultra-rationalistes et pointées vers le ciel, comme le mysticisme vertical, comme les syndicats verticaux espagnols" (Dalí, *Journal* 19).

("even with my moustache, I surpassed Nietzsche! Mine wouldn't be depressing, catastrophic, overwrought with Wagnerian music and fog. No! they would be groomed to a point, imperialist, ultra-rationalist and pointed towards heaven, like the vertical mysticism, like the vertical Spanish Trades Union.")

10 Ben Watson's October 1993 interview is a significant exception to the rule. Here, Zappa declares that "what was great about the 1920s" was "the way you could combine the concept of working class with dada" and adds that he has "always appreciated dada and [keeps] trying to get [his son] Ahmet to read about it, because that's him in the flesh, he's a genetic carrier of that particular gene that has been pretty much bred out of the species" (Watson 547).

11 Like Charlie Chaplin's Hitler moustache in *The Dictator*, it also clichés the above-mentioned connection between degenerate art and slapstick comedy.

12 After being successively owned by King Francis I of France and Napoleon, and stolen from the Louvre by an Italian thief who brought it back to Italy in 1911, Leonardo's Gioconda was nearly disfigured by an acid-thrower in 1957. Note that the painter's model was supposedly Lisa di Antonio Maria Gherardini, the young wife of a wealthy Florentine nobleman who was also a successful silk merchant. One would be tempted to conclude that she was "the daughter of a wealthy Florentine Pogen," had Zappa's song not been inspired by a brand of Swedish cookies once available in America under the name "Florentine Pogen" (the word "Pogen" is a corruption of the Swedish "pagen" meaning "the boy's [cookies]").

13 "Frank Zappa's Got Brand New Shoes." Hustler interview (August 1974). http://home.online.no/~corneliu/hustler.htm

14 The appearance of Zappa's "official" bootlegs (15 CDs in all), released by Rhino Records under the title of "Beat the Boots" (1991-1992) more or less coincided with the release of the six double CDs of the *You Can't Do That On Stage Anymore* series (1988-1992). Both series grew out of Zappa's impatience with the worldwide commercialization of live-performance bootlegs. The very title of the series is a tribute to the "inimitable" styles and idiosyncracies of the musicians and bands Zappa played with from 1967 to 1988. It is also a reminder of Zappa's nostalgic attitude to live recordings, one that privileges the genuine, aural singularity of individual performance over its subsequent transformation into a printed work.

15 Once again, the example of Salvador Dalí comes to mind: Avida Dollars was always willing to lend his mustache to wine bottles, perfume, furniture and other commodities.

16 The film was originally intended as a critique of Thatcherism and the brutality of the new entrepreneurial spirit of the 1980s. See Smith 55.

17 See also the popsicle fun episode of Greenaway's *Drowning By Numbers*.

18 Psalm 51:7.

19 *The Lost Episodes* version of "Wonderful Wino," as sung by Ricky Lancelotti. According to Zappa, Lancelotti, an unknown maximalist artist, "had a cassette in which he imitated 100 cartoon voices in 60 seconds" (sleeve notes to *The Lost Episodes*). At a 1972 Hollywood Palladium concert, Zappa used him as an extension of his performing body: "Frank would open and close his hand in a gesture symbolizing a talking mouth, and Lancelotti would magically appear on stage and begin bellowing".

20 Our translation. "Casquette / de moire, / Quéquette / d'ivoire, / Toilette / très noire, / Paul guette / L'armoire, / Projette / Languette / Sur poire, / S'apprête, / Baguette, / Et foire"

21 "You shall have a bit. / Do you like chocolate? Let it melt in your mouth / Mummy, there is a bone in it. / No, my love, it is an almond. / The little boy wants to eat the whole box. / My, he is greedy! / His mummy gently tells him not to: he must not make himself sick. / How dreadful! He is stamping with rage" (Satie 22). See also Satie's piece "Eating his Bread and Butter" which plays on the superstitious fears associated with the sin of gluttony: "Get used to seeing bread and butter without feeling the need to pinch it. / It could make your head swell up if you touch a friend's bread and butter" (22).

22 These are merely adumbrated by the opening scene of the film, where the thief, after pissing on the man who owes him money, threatens next time to make him eat his own shit.

23 Moreau's novel, a supreme example of the author's "visceral arts" (the title is a pun on "Jesus" and "jejunum", the middle part of the intestine), purports to offer a double auto-portrait of the artist as both madman and "madman's carrion" ("charogne de fou") (240).

24 Zappa's own explorations of the folly of palindromes is apparent in the "inverted" lyrics of "Ya Hozna" and "Won Ton On," which reverse the lyrics of "Sofa" and "No Not Now", respectively.

25 In a 1973 interview, Van Vliet claimed that he chose the carp because it was the only fish "to be able to thrive in polluted waters, and I'm waving to tell people that no one else thrives in polluted waters" (Barnes 108). Van Vliet's ecological concerns echo Zappa's own preoccupation with industrial pollution in such pieces as "Ship Arriving Too Late . . .," "Nine Types of Industrial Pollution," "Food gathering in Postindurstrial America" and "Outrage at Valdez," an instrumental piece originally written for a Jacques Cousteau documentary about the Exxon oil spill in Alaska. Conceptual continuity addicts will no doubt be reminded of Bruce Fowler's apocryphal tale of an "intellectual placoderm-type of a fish" persecuted by religious fanatic sharks on the *Make a Jazz Noise Here* version of "King Kong." If further proof was needed of Zappa's fascination with aquatic life, one would mention the song "The Mud Shark", from the *Fillmore East* album, and "Goblin Girl," which describes the effects of the green light shining down on "the black

guys in the band," making their skin look like fish skin.

26 Or cultural exploitation, if we think of Don Van Vliet's favourite aphorism: "we're all coloured otherwise we would be invisible."

Chapter Three

1 On the albums *Lost Episodes* and *Mystery Disc*.

2 Bill Harkleroad tells strange, contradictory anecdotes about Van Vliet's relationship with Muddy Waters, and his own rather fraught encounter with Charles Mingus (see Harkleroad 27 and Barnes 149), while the oppositional image of the "real" black bluesman haunts Zappa's œuvre through the fugitive but ubiquitous figure of Johnny "Guitar" Watson.

3 A baffling awkwardness of absence-in-presence, as Flaubert noted in *L'Education Sentimentale*: "Il y a un moment, dans les séparations, où la personne aimée n'est déjà plus avec nous." ("There is a moment in all separations when the loved one has gone already.") (524)

4 In this sense it is close to John Cage's 4'33o which paradoxically uses the social noise of behaviour in order to step beyond representation and gesture towards the silence of being.

5 Van Vliet's interviews are riddled with references to the hated heartbeat. The following is a representative example taken from an interview with Dave DiMartino conducted in 1981: "I don't do BUM-BUM-BUM—you know, mama heartbeat drums. I can't imagine anyone wanting to put that much emphasis on a heartbeat, because a heartbeat . . . well, I don't want my heart to attack me so I don't do that. I won't." (unpag.)

6 An exception to this rule is "China Pig" (*Trout Mask Replica*), where the speaker, caught at the crossroads between economic necessity and his love of animals, has murdered his piggybank.

7 Available on the Captain Beefheart Radar Station at: http://www.beefheart.com/walker/dog.htm

8 Chapter 3.14-15

9 This is precisely the gap which Dr Moreau tries to close in Wells's novel, in which apocalyptic science stands as a new version of the creation myth, defined by its attempt to cancel out the hierarchical distinction between creator and created. In such a world, simile would no longer be possible, and metaphor would fill the linguistic field, with everything partaking of everything else in a proliferating promiscuity.

10 Mike Barnes, for example, cites Dean Blackwood's comparison between John Fahey and Captain Beefheart: "Blackwood also sees a connection between Revenant founder John Fahey's self-description as an 'American primitive' and

Beefheart's music. 'Fahey was thinking of course of the "primitive painters", those who were not classically trained and were sometimes immune to notions of what, by all rights, they should have been doing,' he explains. 'Just so, Beefheart seems to have had no notion of any incongruity between Howlin' Wolf and Roland Kirk.'" ("The Bathroom Tapes" unpaginated).

11 If Rousseau wasn't such a naif painter we would be tempted at this point to read the title as a reference to the amorous misadventures of his namesake, the philosopher Jean-Jacques who, having shared Mme Warens with her servant until the latter's death in 1734, returned from a trip to Montpellier in March of 1738 to find his lover freely entertaining a M. de Courtilles! (*Confessions*, 311).

12 The maximalist critic would be more than tempted to ask whether Wallis painted his boat pictures in the same way as Gump rescued fallen fellow soldiers or executed a topspin drive.

13 Though the addition of Art Tripp to the Magic Band for *Lick My Decals off Baby*, *Clear Spot*, and *The Spotlight Kid* allowed the marimba to be exploited for its abjectly percussive hesitation between the rhythmic and the melodic.

14 For Joyce too in *Finnegans Wake*, the bosky cleft of the vagina becomes a jungle, as the reader hesitates before the tangle of proliferating meanings: "You is feeling like you was lost in the bush, boy? You says: It is a puling sample jungle of woods. You most shouts out: Bethicket me for a stump of a beech if I have the poultriest notions what the farest he all means." (112)

15 If "Glider" suggests one kind of horror cliché, Zappa's "Goblin Girl" (*You Are What You Is*) suggests another familiar trope: the transformation of innocent children into monsters, under cover of teenage social ritual: "she's black and green 'cos it's halloween" we are told, but is there in fact another reason?

16 Mike Barnes quotes guitarist John Fahey, who detected something of the mutant in the real life Williams, something reminiscent of those irrational horrors imagined by H.P. Lovecraft: "He was the strangest person I ever met. He was like some alien from another world who was part alligator or something." (*Captain* 93)

17 Available on the Captain Beefheart Radar Station at:
http://www.beefheart.com/walker/months.htm.

18 To experience this dialectic as abjection, place a mirror on the floor and stand over it, looking down. You will have the impression of falling through space into yourself, a very special kind of nausea. See also Lucien Freud's painting "Reflection with Two Children (Self Portrait)."

19 This glimpse of the moon might alert us to the gothic undercurrents in "Moonlight on Vermont" (*Trout Mask Replica*), where a mysterious force is "doing it" for the whole community: "Moonlight on Vermont affected everybody / Even Mrs Wooten well as little Nitty / Even lifebuoy floatin' / With his li'l pistol totin' / Well that goes t' show you what a moon can do".

20 Werner Herzog followed W. S. Murnau in staging the voluntary, though still rather dubious, sacrifice of Mina in his 1979 version of *Nosferatu*. The sexual logic

of this is that the only way to destroy a monster is to somehow reduce its excessive desire to a point of satiation, thus turning it back into something that may be signified, a *subject of* desire.

21 From an interview published in the *Washington Post* of Sunday January 24th 1971; available online at http://www.members.aol.com/tedalvy/cbq.htm.

22 This might suggest a reflection on the psycho-sexual scene of free improvisation. To the extent that a free improviser is both player and audience, the sado-masochistic dynamic plays itself out within his or her single psyche. He or she is simultaneously dominant and submissive, victimiser and victim. The public audience, which is logically superfluous, witnesses a particular form of psychodrama: a subject attempting to take power over itself by incorporating the other into its repertoire of musical acts. This is the musical equivalent of self-mutilation, and raises the possibility that a musician like Derek Bailey should be considered alongside body artists such as Vito Acconci, Bob Flanagan and Ron Athey. For another take on the connection between music and self-mutilation see *The Piano Teacher* by Elfriede Jelinek, filmed as *La Pianiste* by Michael Haneke in 2000.

23 Which is one way of conceptualising the blues apotheosis of Martin Luther King in the Civil Rights movement.

24 From an interview given on Coast FM in April 1971; available online at http://www.members.aol.com/tedalvy/cbq.htm.

Chapter Four

1 From "Bill's Corpse" (*Trout Mask Replica*)

2 Atom Egoyan's 1994 erotic classic "Exotica" is structured around just such a moment.

3 Peter Greenaway exploited the edgy poetry of the animated object in his 1982 film "The Draughtsman's Contract", where a statue comes to life and wrecks the ordered atmosphere of the Renaissance garden. This violation of the edge between subject and object echoes the motif of sexual abuse in the film, which itself is a violation of the body's personal space and the subject's illusion of autonomy. As the object comes to life, the subject is stripped of its insulating layers of clothing. A similar effect is achieved in L.P. Hartley's *The Go-Between*, where the secret contact of the lovers' bodies is finally unveiled, and the multiple transgressions of the moment are condensed into an image of an animated object: " . . . it was then that we saw them, together on the ground, the Virgin and the Water-Carrier, two bodies moving like one. I think I was more mystified than horrified; it was Mrs Maudsley's repeated screams that frightened me, and a shadow on the wall that opened and closed like an umbrella." (263)

4 The definitive piece would be "Corps Etranger" in which the viewer enters a private booth to watch the film of Hatoum's insides. The peep-show atmospherics invoke the desiring gaze which travels over the surface of the body it would like

to enter, while Hatoum inverts the dynamic by channelling the gaze through the insides of her body, challenging it to discover a point of exit rather than a point of entry. The soundtrack of the work consists of a whistling tone made by the body's breathing which changes according to where the pulse has been taken. This revelation of the body's soundscape explodes the myth of absolute silence, equating it with the non-noise of our own death, something we will never hear, as John Cage discovered: "I entered one [a sound-proof chamber] at Harvard University, several years ago and heard two sounds, one high and one low. When I described them to the engineer in charge he informed me that the high one was my nervous system in operation and the low one was my blood in circulation. Until I die there will be sounds. And they will continue following my death. One need not fear for the future of music." (quoted in Warr 200)

5 See Warr 104.

6 The term began appearing in 1947 in Greene's correspondance with his lover Catherine Walston. See Sherry 261
http://www.smithsonianmag.si.edu/smithsonian/issueso2/juno2/presence.html.

7 One is reminded here of Shakespeare's Richard Duke of Gloucester who "will not dine" until he has seen Hasting's head separated from its body (Act II scene iv 78–79).

8 A work which explores the dangers of slum-fucking, or the clandestine sharing of bodies across the frontiers of social class; an activity which cuts across another kind of edge, and the pleasures and risks of which Wilde knew all about.

9 W.H. Auden recognised this tendency of Wilde's dialogues to exceed the speaking characters: "Wilde created a verbal universe in which the characters are determined by the things they say, and the plot is nothing but a succession of opportunities to say them." (136)

10 See Butler 42.

11 Zappa's defence of information in the context of sex education is also a protest against the use of euphemistic rhetoric in political discourse. As Wilde and Carroll seem to show, the euphemism is liable to degenerate into pure nonsense, and this should alert us to the potential dangers for representative democracy of a tendency to say "bathroom" instead of "toilet", "pisser" or "shithouse". The use of such rhetoric has perhaps contributed to the rise of social democracy which stands as a grand obfuscation of old ideological distinctions between left and right, and which suppresses debate (and so reduces the ammount of information available) by collapsing the distinctions between government and opposition. In this way a centre-leftist party may find itself adopting reactionary policies in order to limit the appeal of the extreme right. By turning itself over to the euphemistic practices of American political culture, Tony Blair's New Labour maximalised its appeal not just through its absorption of older class-based sympathies, but through its capacity to absorb contradictions—to be any number of ill-defined things at the same time, a raven and a writing desk for example. New Labour is almost apolitical in its abandonment of the traditional party-based approach to policy-making and the illusion it gives of administering policies that

are self-evidently a matter of consensus; its so-called "third way" is a classic euphemism along the lines of "number twos", bringing together the most convenient traits previously grouped under those discredited and now almost dirty words "socialism" and "conservatism". Tony Blair has sacrificed any erotic appeal he may have had as an axe-wielding rocker during his university days to his obscurantist belief that power thrives best in an information vacuum.

12 From "Muffin Man" (*Bongo Fury*).

13 A thid term was added to this series by the 1968 film "Carry on Up the Khyber", where a colonial official (played by that incarnation of the innuendo, Syd James) looks forward to his afternoon "tiffin" with the wife of a colleague: "Time for tiffin", he remarks, with an unparalled lewdness.

14 From "Bobby Brown" (*Sheik Yerbouti*).

15 While Breughel's over-encumbered butcher bears more than a passing resemblance to Tweedledee and Tweedledum as they appear armed for battle in Tenniel's original illustration (Carroll 171).

16 In "Powers of Horror" Julia Kristeva refers to the process of identification as a permanent transfer between inside and outside, a double occupation, or interface (*Portable* 237), and once again the human body provides us with a perfect metaphor for the psychic condition it supports, as it absorbs and voids, hesitating between objective incorporation and subjective expression, between meaningless materialist process (or duality) and entelechy (or dialectic).

17 Read alongside the Joycean imperative "Transname me loveliness, now and here me for all times!" (*Finnegans* 145), the insistent "I am here and you are my ... " seems to express the passage from demiurge to dictator, as the authority of eternal presence begins to apply itself to the practical exercise of power. Perhaps Zappa was exploring the darker Orwellian implications of his notion of the spherical constant; and this lyric should be set alongside the totalitarian implications of the Central Scrutinizer from *Joe's Garage*, which we will address in our final chapter.

18 A phrase derived from the title of Harold Rosenberg's 1966 account of New York School abstraction.

19 Reviewing the history of western painting, one might argue that the first stirrings of style began in the seventeenth century with that loosening of the artist's grasp on his objects detectable in the work of El Greco and Tintoretto. Ironically, these proto-moderns are often termed "mannerist" in standard accounts of the evolution from religious painting to something which might be loosely labelled "expressionism". Such accounts seize on signs of subjectivity while failing to theorise the subject.

20 From "The Thousandth and Tenth Day of the Human Totem Pole" (*Ice Cream for Crow*).

Chapter Five

1   In his attempts to push understanding of human psychology beyond the pleasure principle, Freud lamented the lack of a workable philosophical account of pleasure (43-44); while Deleuze reminds us of the venerable history of Freud's problematic, evoking the frustrations of David Hume: "Le philosophe Hume remarquait déjà: il y a des plaisirs dans la vie psychique, comme il y a des douleurs; mais on aura beau retourner sous toutes leurs faces les idées de plaisir, et de douleur, jamais on n'en tirera la forme d'un *principe* d'après lequel nous cherchons le plaisir et fuyons la douleur." (*Présentation* 97) ("The philosopher Hume saw the problem: in the life of the psyche there are pleasures just as there are pains; but we could examine the ideas of pleasure and pain from every possible angle without ever managing to isolate a *principle* according to which we could seek pleasure and save ourselves from pain.")

While erotic literature has grappled for centuries with the difficulty of representing pleasure, a passage from a sex manual for children offers us, perhaps, as good an approximation of the sensation of orgasm as we ever likely to read: "C'est une sensation difficile à expliquer, mais, si tu peux imaginer une chatouille qui te gratouille, qui prend naissance dans le ventre et se répand, tu auras une petite idée de ce que c'est." (Mayle *et al* unpaginated) (It's a difficult feeling to describe, but, if you can imagine a tickle which itches, which begins in the belly and spreads outwards, you will have some idea of what it's like.)

2   Entitled "Réquichot and his Body" and reprinted in *The Responsibility of Forms*.

3   Like its famous cousin, the rhizome (a seemingly endless series of nodes and intersections, figured in contradiction to the tree which has a main trunk from which the branches and roots crop out), Deleuze's baroque has no actual or conceptual center.

4   Peter Greenaway, another maximalist artist examined in this study, has also been described by critics such as Omar Calabrese as a neo-baroque artist. On the relationship between cinema and the baroque, see Tweedie 104–126.

5   We are grateful to Karen Mac Cormack for drawing our attention to Conde's writings.

6   See also Barthes's definition of the baroque as "Une contradiction progressive entre l'unité et la totalité, un art dans lequel l'étendue n'est pas sommative, mais multiplicative, bref l'épaisseur d'une accélération" (*Essais* 108). ("A progressive contradiction between the unit and the whole, an art in which the extension is not added but multiplied, in short, the width of an acceleration")

7   *A Chance Operation—The John Cage Tribute* (Various artists, 2CD, KOCH International, 1993).

8   These turbulences also evoke—at a microlinguistic level—the cut-up plicative techniques of Brian Gysin and William Burroughs.

9   The word refers to Lucretius' description of the *clinamen atomorum*, or atomic swerve, in *De rerum natura*. The clinamen is "the minimal swerve of an atom from

a laminar flow" (17) and generally refers to the random, unpredictable onset of turbulence in fluids.

10 McCaffery describes the clinamen as "a singular interaction between virtual force and actual form that creates by modifying its place in a pre-existent structure", a notion which can be compared to Bataille's definition of man as "a particle inserted in unstable and tangled groups" (xviii).

11 In the sleeve notes to the album, cellist and arranger Olli Virtaperko claims that, while rehearsing the material, they "soon learned that in a large Baroque basso continuo group the liberties and rules of accompanying the melody rhythmically and harmonically are pretty much the same as with the rhythm section of a rock group." The Ensemble apparently used the basso continuo as the equivalent of a jazz or rock lead sheet and concluded that "it made it possible . . . to arrange Zappa's music for a non-amplified ensemble, and still retain the rhythmicality and metric pulse."

12 Opposed to the (negative) Lacanian dialectic of lack and desire, Deleuze and Guattari's *Anti-Oedipus* proposes a theory of "desiring-production," which they define as a "pure multiplicity, that is to say, an affirmation that is irreducible to any sort of unity" (46).

13 From "Auguries of Innocence" (Blake 585).

14 The opening lines of Captain Beefheart's "The Blimp" (*Trout Mask Replica*) seem to endorse Barthes' observation with reference to its own perceptual exigencies: "Master master/ This is recorded thru uh fly's ear/ 'n you have t'have a fly's eye to see it".

15 Something of this effect is achieved on the inside cover of *Broadway the Hard Way*, where a section of the main photograph of Zappa at his President's desk is blown up and used for the left hand panel. The winking pencil jug holds our attention in a world of diagonals where everything is sliding off into the bottom left hand corner. Looking at the main picture we understand the perspective, in the cropped version something is very wrong; so why the wink?

The technique of close miking is a sonic equivalent to magnification. Henri Chopin's thrusting of the microphone into the mouth or throat creates a maximalist concentration on the body as the vocal's point of origin (just as Sonny Boy Williams II got closer to his instrument by chewing it). If we imagine the microphone (or the harmonica) being thrust into another of the body's orifices we arrive at a perfect conjunction of the microscopic and the endoscopic.

16 Although to speak of *one* substance is slightly misleading since God cannot be counted; number belongs to our finite understanding of a substance not its essence.

17 A comment which might be compared to Miles Davis's observation that John Lee Hooker sounds as if he is playing while buried up to his neck in mud (see http://www.epinions.com/musc-review-7665-16FB1DD3-388A1E05-prod3)

18 Douglas Gordon has attempted something similar in video with his slow-motion

projection of classic films. His "24 Hour Psycho" challenged its audience to endure a marathon viewing, while offering them the chance to see the fairies in every frame.

19 Van Vliet certainly used endurance as a technique for training his musicians. Morris Tepper reports being locked in the bathroom for three hours and forced to listen to "Red Cross Store" by Mississippi John Hurt. His release was conditional upon him "hearing" the music, and the declared aim of the exercise was to expunge the note C that he was carrying around in his head (for "conventional", "conservative"?) after over-exposing himself to the Beatles (Barnes *Captain* 236). One wonders whether Tepper would have been released sooner from the Beefheart bog if he had been forced to listen to "Love, Love Me Do"!

Further evidence that C is the key of endurance is provided by Terry Riley's seminal minimalist work of 1964 *In "c"*, during which an ensemble works its way through 53 modules to the constant pulse of two high Cs played on the piano. Did Riley resort to C for his minimalist effects precisely because it had come to be stigmatised as the key of conventionality (of "citsch" even)? William Duckworth confirms the transgressive nature of Riley's gesture: "in the late sixties no one could remember the last experimental composer who had used a key signature, much less written anything in C major" (quoted in Potter 148).

20 That Van Vliet was conversant with at least some American minimalist music is evident from his quotation of Steve Reich's "Come Out" in "Moonlight on Vermont": "Come out to show them". (Barnes *Captain* 94–95)

21 For more extensive quotation from this piece see Watson 216–217.

22 From "Teenage Wind" (*You Are What You Is*).

23 Zappa presiding over performances of his music with his all-hearing ears might also be considered as an incarnation of the myhthical Central Scrutinizer, the composer-conductor as Old Testament God.

24 "Kreisler grew in importance: he had been a shadowy and unimportant nobody. Of this he had shown no consciousness. Rather dazed and machine-like, Bertha had treated him as she had found him: suddenly, without any direct articulateness, he had revenged himself as a machine might do, in a nightmare of violent action." (Lewis 197).

25 As the "Girl on the Bus" reminds us on *Joe's Garage*.

26 An objection which draws support from Plato's distinction between real and illusory pleasures in *Republic* Book IX, where the latter are those predicated on a prior displeasure.

27 Part of the preamble to "Pena" (*Trout Mask Replica*).

28 From an interview in the BBC documentary "The Artist Formerly Known as Captain Beefheart", first broadcast in August 1997.

29 Matt Groening's account of his first encounter with *Trout Mask Replica* stands as a perfect example of how the "investment aesthetic" is supposed to work: "It was a

double record set, it cost seven dollars, it's too much, but . . . ah . . . Frank Zappa's name was on it, so I bought it. I took it home, I put it on, it's the worst dreck I'd ever heard in my life. I said 'They're not even trying! They're just playing randomly'. And then I thought 'Frank Zappa produced it; maybe, maybe, if I give it another play' So I played it again and I thought 'It sounds horrible, but they mean it to sound this way.' And about the third or fourth time it started to grow on me. And the fifth or sixth time I loved it. And the seventh or eighth time I thought it was the greatest album ever made and I still do." (From "The Artist Formerly Known as Captain Beefheart").

30 Zappa confirmed his interest in prosthetic extensions of sexuality at the end of the interview he gave for the BBC's Late Show, when he produced a magazine cover showing a couple equipped with virtual sex apparatuses. His laughing comment was "There's got to be an album in there somewhere".

31 The phrase is Ezra Pound's and appears in a letter to Joyce from 15th November 1926 in which Pound formulates his response to an early section of "Work in Progress": " . . . nothing short of divine vision or a new cure for the clapp can possibly be worth all the circumambient peripherization." (*Pound/Joyce* 228).

32 Preamble to "Penguin in Bondage" (*Roxy and Elsewhere*).

33 From "Penguin in Bondage" (*Roxy and Elsewhere*).

34 "Head like a potato . . . lips like a duck . . . big ol' hands, puffin' up [. . . .] re-LIJ-mus costumery all over yo' body!" (from "Prologue" (*Thing Fish*)).

35 For more information on this phenomenon, see Loïc Wacquant's *Les Prisons de la Misère*.

36 "Space Age couple, why don't you flex your magic muscle" From Captain Beefheart's "Space Age Couple" (*Lick My Decals Off Baby*).

37 Mathew Barney similarly presents pointless labour as a form of therapeutic play in his "Cremaster" films. See particularly "Cremaster 3" for the long sequence in which Barney mixes a sludge of cement in a lift cabin. Interestingly, Barney's *flânerie* often takes place on the vertical axis, as climbing is substituted for walking.

38 In sculptural terms, this maximalist desire to cover everything is perhaps best represented by the work of Christo, where maximalism emerges more clearly as phenomenological repossession, an intention to wrap up the world.

39 "The attitudes, gestures and movement of the human body are funny to the precise extent to which the body makes us think of a basic mechanism" (our translation).

40 The term was suggested by Julia Kristeva's "symptôme de la pensée". *Les Nouvelles maladies de L'âme*, 65.

Bibliography

Adorno, Theodor, and Max Horkheimer. *The Dialectic of the Enlightenment*. New York: Continuum Press, 1999.

Arato, Andrew, and Eike Gebhardt. *The Essential Frankfurt School Reader*. New York: The Continuum Publishing Company, 1982.

Auden, W.H. "An Improbable Life". *Oscar Wilde: A Collection of Critical Essays*. Ed. Richard Ellmann. Englewood Cliffs, New Jersey: Prentice Hall, 1969.

Baker, Jr., Houston A. *Blues, Ideology, and Afro-American Literature: A Vernacular Theory*. Chicago: University Press of Chicago, 1984.

Bakhtin, Mikhail. *Rabelais and His World*. Bloomington: Indiana University Press, 1984.

Ballard, J.G. *Crash*. London: Vintage, 1995.

Bamberger, William C. *Riding Some Kind of Unusual Skull Sleigh: On the Arts of Don Van Vliet*. Lint, Michigan. Bamberger Books, 1999.

Barnes, Mike. "The Bathroom Tapes". *The Wire* April 1999, available at http://www.beefheart.com/datharp/bathroom.htm

——— . *Captain Beefheart*. London: Quartet Books, 2000.

Barth, John. "A Few Words About Minimalism." *New York Times Book Review*. Dec. 28, 1986.

Barthes, Roland. *Essais critiques*. Paris: Seuil, 1964.

——— . *L'obvie et l'obtus: Essais critiques III*. Paris: Seuil, 1982.

——— . "The Death of the Author". Trans. Geoff Bennington. *Modern Criticism and Theory: A Reader*. Ed. David Lodge. Harlow, Essex: Longman, 1988.

——— . *The Responsibility of Forms*. Trans. Richard Howard. Berkeley: University of California Press, 1991.

Bataille, Georges. *Erotism: Death and Sensuality*. Trans. Mary Dalwood. San Francisco: City Lights, 1986.

Beckett, Samuel. "Dante . . . Bruno.Vico..Joyce.". *Our Exagmination Round his Factifcation for Incamination of* "Work in Progress". London: Faber and Faber, 1929.

———. *Murphy*. New York: Grove Press, 1938.

———. *Watt*. London: John Calder, 1976.

———. *The Complete Dramatic Works*. London: Faber and Faber, 1986.

Bergson, Henri. *Le Rire*. Paris: Quadrige, 1991.

Blake, William. *Collected Poems*. New York: Longman, 1971.

Broodthaers, Marcel. *Writings, Interviews, Photographs*. Trans. Paul Schmidt. Cambridge: MIT Press, 1988.

Brusatin, Manlio, and Jean Clair, eds. *Identity and Alterity: Figures of the Body 1895–1995*. Venice: Marsilio Editori, 1995.

Brown, Norman O. *Love's Body*. New York: Random House 1966.

Budgen, Frank. *James Joyce and the Making of "Ulysses"*. London: Oxford University Press, 1972.

Burroughs, William. *Naked Lunch*. New York: Grove Press, 1959.

Butler, Samuel. *The Way of All Flesh*. London: Jonathan Cape, 1932.

Carroll, Lewis. *Alice's Adventures in Wonderland and Through the Looking-Glass*. London: Oxford University Press, 1971.

Conde, Yago. *Architecture of the Indeterminacy*. Barcelona: Actar, 2000.

Conrad, Joseph. *Heart of Darkness*. London: Penguin, 1973.

Dalí, Salvador. *The Secret Life of Salvador Dalí*. Dial Press, New York, 1942.

———. *La Vie secrète de Salvador Dalí*. Paris: La Table Ronde, 1952.

———. "The Object as Revealed in Surrealist Experiment". *Surrealists on Art*. Ed. Lucy Lippard. Englewood Cliffs, New Jersey: Prentice Hall, 1970.

———. *Journal d'un génie*. Paris: Gallimard, 1994.

Dalí, Salvador, and Philippe Halsman. *Dalí's Mustache*. New York: Abbeville Press, 1994.

Deleuze, Gilles. *Présentation de Sacher-Masoch*. Paris: Les Editions de Minuit, 1967.

———. *The Fold: Leibniz and the Baroque*. Minneapolis: University of Minnesota Press, 1992.

Deleuze, Gilles, and Félix Guattari. *Anti-Odepius: Capitalism and Schizophrenia*. Minneapolis: University of Minnesota Press, 1985.

DiMartino, Dave. "Don't Sit on that Porcupine Fence: Beefheart's Grown the Best Batch Yet". *Creem*. March 1981, vol. 12 no. 10. Available at http://www.beefheart.com/datharp/porc.htm

Dorn, Ed. *Gunslinger*. Durham: Duke University Press, 1989.

Ehrenpreis, Irvin. *Swift: The Man, His Works, and the Age*. Volume 3: Dean Swift. Cambridge: Harvard University Press, 1983.

Feher, Michel, et al., eds. *Fragments for a History of the Human Body—Part 1*. Cambridge: MIT Press, 1989.

———. *Fragments for a History of the Human Body—Part 3*. Cambridge: MIT Press, 1989.

Flaubert, Gustave. *L'Education Sentimentale*. Paris: Livres de Poche, 2002.

Frascina, Francis, and Jonathan Harris, eds. *Art in Modern Culture: An Anthology of Critical Texts*. New York: Phaidon Press, 1996.

Freud, Sigmund. "Au-Delà du principe de plaisir". *Essais de Psychanalyse*. Trans. Jean Laplanche and J.B. Pontalis. Paris. Petit Bibliothèque Payot, 1981.

Gelder, Ken. *Reading the Vampire*. London: Routledge, 1994.

Grier, James. "The Mothers of Invention and *Uncle Meat*: Alienation, Anachronism and a Double Variation". Unpublished ms.

Gray, Michael. *Mother! Is the Story of Frank Zappa*. London: Proteus Books, 1985.

Harkleroad, Bill. *Lunar Notes. Zoot Horn Rollo's Captain Beefheart Experience*. London: SAF Publishing Ltd., 1998.

Harris, William. *The Poetry and Poetics of Amiri Baraka—The Jazz Aesthetic*. Columbia: University of Missouri Press, 1985.

Ishiwari, Takayoshi. "The Body That Speaks: Donald Barthelme's *The Dead Father* as Installation". Unpublished Master's thesis. Osaka University, 1996. Available at: http://www.asahi-net.or.jp/~KP7T-ISWR/

Jaffe, David. "Orchestrating the Chimera—Musical Hybrids, Technology, and the Development of a "Maximalist" Musical Style". *Leonardo Music Journal*. Vol. 5, 1995.

Jameson, Fredric. *Postmodernism, or, The Cultural Logic of Late Capitalism*. London: Verso, 1991.

Jelinek, Elfriede. *The Piano Teacher*. Trans. Joachim Neugroschel. London: Serpent's Tail, 2001.

Joyce, James. *Finnegans Wake* London: Faber and Faber, 1975.

———. *Ulysses*. London: Penguin, 2000.

Kirshenblatt-Gimblett, Barbara. "Playing to the Senses: Food as a Performance Medium". *Performance Research*, Vol. IV, No 1, 1999: 1–30.

Kostelanetz, Richard, ed. *The Frank Zappa Companion*. London: Omnibus Press, 1997.

Kristeva, Julia. *Les Nouvelles maladies de l'âme*. Paris: Fayard, 1993.

———. "Powers of Horror". *The Portable Kristeva*. Ed. Oliver Kelly. New York, Columbia University Press, 1997.

Kundera, Milan. *The Unbearable Lightness of Being*. London: Faber, 1985.

———. *Identity*. London: Faber, 1986.

Lewis, Wyndham. *Tarr*. London: Penguin, 1982.

Mann, Thomas. *The Magic Mountain*. Trans. H. T. Lowe-Porter. London: Penguin, 1960.

Marinetti, Filippo T. *The Futurist Cookbook*. San Francisco: Bedford Arts, 1989.

Marshall, Bob. "Frank Zappa Interview". October 22, 1988. Available at http://www.science.uva.nl/~robbert/zappa/interviews/Bob_Marshall/

Maugham, Robin. *The Servant*. London: W.H. Allen, 1973.

Mayle, Peter et al. *Et moi, d'où je viens?* Trans. Dominique Kaszemacher. Paris: Bernard Neyrolles, 1980.

McCaffery, Steve. *Prior to Meaning: The Protosemantic and Poetics*. Evanston: Northwestern University Press, 2001.

Menn, Don, ed. *Zappa!* Special, unnumbered issue of *Guitar Player*. 1992.

Meshberger, Frank. "An interpretation of Michelangelo's Creation of Adam Based on Neuroanatomy". *Journal of the American Medical Association* 264 (1990): 1837–1841.

Michalski, Sergiusz. *Neue Sachlichkeit: Malerei, Graphik und Photographie in Deutschland 1919–1933*. Cologne: Benedikt Taschen Verlag, 1992.

Miklitsch, Robert. *From Hegel to Madonna: Towards a General Economy of "Commodity Fetishism"*. Albany: SUNY, 1998.

Moreau, Marcel. *La vie de Jéju*. Arles: Actes Sud, 1998.

Orwell, George. *1984*. London: Penguin, 2000.

Ovid. *Metamorphoses*. Trans. John Dryden et al. Ware, Herts.: Wordsworth, 1998.

Partridge, Eric. *Dictionary of Historical Slang*. London: Penguin, 1972.

Pauwels, Louis. *Dalí m'a dit*. Paris: Carrère, 1989.

Penelhum, Terence. "The Logic of Pleasure". *Essays in Philosophical Psychology*. Ed. Donald F. Gustafson. London: Macmillan, 1964.

Phelan, Peggy. *Unmarked*. London: Routledge, 1993.

Potter, Keith. *Four Musical Minimalists: La Monte Young, Terry Riley, Steve Reich, Philip Glass*. Cambridge: Cambridge University Press, 2002.

Pound, Ezra. *Personae, Collected Shorter Poems of Ezra Pound*. London: Faber and Faber, 1952.

———. *Pound/Joyce*. Ed. Forrest Read. London: Faber and Faber, 1967.

Punter, David, ed. *A Companion to the Gothic*. London: Blackwell, 2001.

Reich, Wilhelm. *The Mass Psychology of Fascism*. London: Penguin, 1970.

Rey, Anne. *Erik Satie*. Paris: Seuil, 1974.

Rimbaud, Arthur. *Album zutique: suivi de pièces diverses*. Paris: Éd. Mille et Une Nuits, 2000.

Rosenberg, Harold. *The Anxious Object*. Chicago: University of Chicago Press, 1998.

Satie, Erik. *A Mammal's Notebook: Collected Writings of Erik Satie*. London: Serpent's Tail, 1997.

Sherry, Norman. *The Life of Graham Greene*. Vol. 2. New York: Viking, 1994.

Smith, Gavin. "Food for Thought." *Film Comment*, Vol. 26, No 3, 1990: 54–61.

Spinoza. *Ethics*. Trans. Andrew Boyle. London: Everyman, 1910.

Spinrad, Paul. *The RE/Search Guide to Bodily Fluids*. San Francisco: Juno Books, 1999.

Stein, Gertrude. *Look at Me Now and Here I Am: Writings and Lectures 1909–45*. London: Penguin, 1971.

——. *Writings 1903–1932*. New York: The Library of America, 1998.

Thomson, Philip. *The Grotesque*. London: Methuen, 1972.

Tweedie, James. "Caliban's Books: The Hybrid Text in Peter Greenaway's Prospero's Books". *Cinema Journal*, 40 (2000): 104–26.

Tzara, Tristan. *Seven Dada Manifestos and Lampisteries*. Trans. Barbara Wright. New York: Riverrun Press, 1988.

Van Vliet, Don. "Three Months in the Mirror". Unpublished poem available at http://www.beefheart.com/walker/months.htm

Wacquant, Loïc. *Les Prisons de la misère*. Paris: Editions Raisons d'Agir, 1999.

Wald, Eliot. "Conversation With Captain Beefheart". *Oui* July 1973, available at http://www.beefheart.com/datharp/oui.htm

Walley, David. *No Commercial Potential: The Saga of Frank Zappa*. New York: Da Capo Press: 1996.

Warr, Tracey and Jones, Amelia (eds.). *The Artist's Body*. London: Phaidon Press, 2000.

Watson, Ben. *The Negative Dialectics of Poodle Play*. London: Quartet Books, 1994.

Wells, H.G.. *The Island of Dr Moreau*. London: Everyman, 1993.

Wilde, Oscar. *The Importance of Being Earnest and Other Plays*. London: Penguin, 2003.

Zappa, Frank. *Them or Us (The Book)*. Los Angeles: Barfko Swill, 1984.

——. with Peter Occhiogrosso. *The Real Frank Zappa Book*. London: Picador: 1990.

——. "Air Sculpture". BBC Radio 1 interview, broadcast on 20 Nov 1994. Interview date unknown.

Frank Zappa Discography
—official releases—

Freak Out! (The Mothers of Invention) 1966
Absolutely Free (FZ/The Mothers of Invention) 1967
Lumpy Gravy (FZ/Abnuceals Emuukha Electric Symphony Orchestra & Chorus) 1967
We're Only In It For The Money (FZ/The Mothers of Invention) 1968
Cruising With Ruben & The Jets (FZ/The Mothers of Invention) 1968
Uncle Meat (FZ/The Mothers of Invention) 1969
Hot Rats (FZ) 1969
Burnt Weeny Sandwich (FZ/The Mothers of Invention) 1970
Weasels Ripped My Flesh (FZ/The Mothers of Invention) 1970
Chunga's Revenge (FZ) 1970
Filmore East—June 1971 (FZ/The Mothers) 1971
200 Motels (FZ) 1971
Just Another Band From L.A. (FZ/The Mothers) 1972
Waka/Jawaka (FZ) 1972
The Grand Wazoo (FZ/The Mothers) 1972
Over-Nite Sensation (FZ/The Mothers) 1973
Apostrophe (') (FZ) 1974
Roxy & Elsewhere (FZ/The Mothers) 1974
One Size Fits All (FZ/The Mothers of Invention) 1975
Bongo Fury (FZ/Beefheart) 1975
Zoot Allures (FZ) 1976
Zappa In New York (FZ) 1978
Studio Tan (FZ) 1978
Sleep Dirt (FZ) 1979
Sheik Yerbouti (FZ) 1979
Orchestral Favorites (FZ) 1979
Joe's Garage Acts I, II & III (FZ) 1979
Tinseltown Rebellion (FZ) 1981
Shut Up 'N Play Yer Guitar (FZ) 1981

You Are What You Is (FZ) 1981
Ship Arriving Too Late To Save A Drowning Witch (FZ) 1982
The Man From Utopia (FZ) 1983
Baby Snakes (FZ) 1983
London Symphony Orchestra Vol. I & II (FZ) 1987
The Perfect Stranger (Pierre Boulez/FZ) 1984
Them Or Us (FZ) 1984
Thing-Fish (FZ) 1984
Francesco Zappa (FZ) 1984
FZ Meets The Mothers Of Prevention (FZ) 1985
Does Humor Belong In Music? (FZ) 1986
Jazz from Hell (FZ) 1986
Guitar (FZ) 1988
You Can't Do That On Stage Anymore Vol. 1 (FZ) 1988
Broadway The Hard Way (FZ) 1988
You Can't Do That On Stage Anymore Vol. 2 (FZ) 1988
You Can't Do That On Stage Anymore Vol. 3 (FZ) 1989
The Best Band You Never Heard In Your Life (FZ) 1991
Make A Jazz Noise Here (FZ) 1991
You Can't Do That On Stage Anymore Vol. 4 (FZ) 1991
You Can't Do That On Stage Anymore Vol. 5 (FZ) 1992
You Can't Do That On Stage Anymore Vol. 6 (FZ) 1992
Playground Psychotics (FZ/The Mothers) 1992
Ahead Of Their Time (FZ/The Mothers of Invention) 1993
The Yellow Shark (FZ/Ensemble Modern) 1993
Civilization, Phaze III (FZ) 1994
The Lost Episodes (FZ) 1996
Läther (FZ) 1996
Frank Zappa Plays The Music Of Frank Zappa (FZ) 1996
Mystery Disc (FZ/The Mothers of Invention) 1998
Everything Is Healing Nicely (FZ/Ensemble Modern) 1999
Live in Australia (FZ) 2002

Captain Beefheart and The Magic Band Dicography
—official releases—

Safe as Milk (1967)
Strictly Personal (1968)

Trout Mask Replica (1969)
Dropout Boogie (1970)
Lick My Decals Off, Baby (1970)
Mirror Man (1971)
The Spotlight Kid (1972)
Clear Spot (1972)
Unconditionally Guaranteed (1974)
Bluejeans and Moonbeams (1974)
Bongo Fury (Frank Zappa/Beefheart/Mothers) (1975)
Shiny Beast (1978)
Doc at the Radar Station (1980)
Ice Cream for Crow (1982)
Grow Fins (1999)

Index

Printed in the United States
69449LVS00013B/11